Ralph Reed is an articulate advocate for faith and freedom, and this book makes a compelling case for why, even though they are under attack, liberty and belief in God will not only survive but prosper. If you want to understand why Ralph has played such an important role in American politics, then read this book. It will encourage and challenge you.

– Senator Rand Paul

America's greatness is rooted in faith, hard work, freedom, personal responsibility, and family. Ralph Reed captures the importance of these values, how they drew my parents and the forebears of other Americans to these shores, and why they are worth preserving.

– Senator Marco Rubio

This book shows why Ralph Reed is one of the most effective and respected impact players in American politics. He demonstrates that what looked like a secular liberal renaissance may in fact be the prelude to a spiritual awakening and a conservative resurgence. I think he's right, and I highly recommend this book.

– Sean Hannity

AWAKENING

HOW AMERICA CAN TURN FROM ECONOMIC AND MORAL DESTRUCTION BACK TO GREATNESS

RALPH REED

BEST-SELLING AUTHOR AND FOUNDER OF FAITH & FREEDOM COALITION

WORTHY PUBLISHING

Published by Worthy Publishing, a division of Worthy Media, Inc., 134 Franklin Road, Suite 200, Brentwood, Tennessee 37027

HELPING PEOPLE EXPERIENCE THE HEART OF GOD
eBook available wherever digital books are sold

Library of Congress Control Number 2014930323

Published in association with Rick Christian, Alive Communications, alivecommunications.com

For foreign and subsidiary rights, contact rights@worthypublishing.com

ISBN: 978-1-61795-287-6

Cover design: Christopher Tobias | tobiasdesign.com
Cover photo: Maxim Khytra | Shutterstock
Interior Design and Typesetting: Christopher D. Hudson & Associates, Inc.

Printed in the United States of America

14 15 16 17 18 QUAD 8 7 6 5 4 3 2 1

Contents

To Nicole

Acknowledgments

Many people helped bring this book to fruition from the first breakfast meeting I had with Byron Williamson and Ted Squires in Atlanta to discuss whether I had something to say about the role of faith in America. Special thanks go to my literary agent Rick Christian for his vision, friendship, and counsel.

The entire team at Worthy Publishing has been terrific, starting with my very capable editors, Anita Palmer and Jennifer Stair, who helped translate my academic prose into accessible English. I also want to thank Byron, Dennis Disney, Sherrie Slopianka, and Morgan Canclini for their passion for this book and its message that with faith in God and a repentant heart there is still hope for wayward individuals and societies, including our own.

Ashley Samelson McGuire and Celine Villongco were indispensable to this book becoming a reality under a tight deadline with their dedication and hard work in digging up relevant research, suggestions, facts, and sources. Their enthusiasm for the subject was infectious and I am grateful for their contribution. My assistant Linda Ingram kept the trains running on time, as she has for sixteen years. I also wish to thank my colleagues at Century Strategies and Faith & Freedom Coalition for their support and friendship. Deal Hudson read every chapter and proved a good friend can also be an unflinching editor.

Many people talked to me about the rise of the religious conservative movement and what some have termed the Fourth Great Awakening, including Pat Robertson, James Robison, Paul Pressler, Richard Land, Cal Thomas, and John Conlan. Others talked to me about the early days of the pro-family movement but did not wish to do so for attribution, and I have respected their wishes.

My wife Jo Anne and I got married as I began work on my doctoral dissertation and she has endured the perpetual intrusion of multiple books since then with a rare patience, otherworldly grace, and immeasurable support. Our children sacrificed so their father could write at night, on the weekends, and on a family vacation. They are the joy of my life and I am grateful for their support and love.

Foreword by Mike Huckabee

Ever since I was a teenager in Hope, Arkansas, I have believed that the United States is a great nation because it's a special nation. And I believe the United States is a special nation because it was founded by people who were first on their knees before they were on their feet.

We are a nation rooted in our faith.

The progressives, libertarians, or libertines may not like me saying that, but I don't care. After two decades of a successful political career, I care more about my country's future than about being accepted by the liberal elite.

I know Ralph Reed feels the same, and that's why he's written this intelligent and perceptive book. *Awakening* is an urgently needed critique of a culture that is fast abandoning its guiding principles, which are rooted in the Holy Bible and written into its U.S. Constitution.

There is no doubt in my mind that the United States needs political change—and fast. But there also is no doubt in my mind that there is something more crucial than civic engagement or policy change.

Our politics will only reflect truth if and when we get back on our knees and experience a spiritual awakening. The ultimate answer to what ails America isn't found in politics but in repentance and moral renewal.

That's what *Awakening* is calling us to.

I've known Ralph since the 1990s when, as the prodigy executive director of the Christian Coalition, he built one of the most effective public policy organizations in recent political history. Not even his detractors can question his gifts as a political strategist. Ralph has helped elect U.S. senators, members of Congress, governors, and presidents.

As one who has traveled the sawdust trail myself, I recognize political wisdom when I see it.

But Ralph did not write this book because he thinks we need another grassroots primer for activism. Yes, Christians should and must be involved in politics. Jesus called us to be salt and light in every area of life, and that includes government. If we refuse that calling, then we should not be surprised if our culture does a one-eighty and abandons our founding principles. We won't be able to blame liberals or cable news networks or President Obama. We'll have only ourselves to blame.

But I don't think that's going to happen. Why? Because of God's mercy as seen in the spiritual cycle Ralph writes about in *Awakening*.

With his brilliant perspective as both an academically trained historian and an experienced political operative, Ralph shows us the pattern of obedience, affluence, rebellion, moral decline, and then spiritual revival that has occurred in our magnificent country repeatedly since its founding.

And God, in His mercy, has always blessed a recommitment to our first principles of life, liberty, and the pursuit of happiness.

I believe He will again.

Remember the promise of 2 Chronicles 7:14? It says, "If my people, which are called by my name, shall humble themselves, and pray, and seek my face, and turn from their wicked ways; then will I hear from heaven, and will forgive their sin, and will heal their land" (KJV).

I invite you to dig deep into *Awakening* and then spread its message. Let's humble ourselves, pray, seek God's face, and turn from our wicked ways.

Our future demands it.

Preface

I wrote much of this book while on a working vacation in Europe with my wife, Jo Anne, and our daughters, Brittany and Nicole. Each morning I rose at dawn and worked until the early afternoon, spurred by the urgency of its message. The rest of the day I played tourist with my family, even as I sometimes wrote in the car or at a roadside café, inspired by my setting.

In Italy we visited the ruins of Roman civilization, walking through remains of ancient cities, amphitheaters, citadels, and waterworks that were the pride of an empire. Nations rise and fall, and Rome was certainly no exception. As I reflected on its demise, I wondered, *Is the United States experiencing its own decline and fall?*

On a side trip to Amsterdam, we were only a short train ride from Leiden, where four hundred years earlier members of a Puritan congregation departed for America aboard the *Mayflower*. John Adams spent time in Amsterdam during the American Revolution, pleading with Dutch bankers for aid to the United States. The Dutch Republic was once the leading maritime and trading power in the world, while Amsterdam was the busiest port and the wealthiest city on earth. Today it is more famous for its red-light district, where prostitutes display themselves in shop windows alongside hash bars and sex shops. Like Rome, Holland's majesty slipped away—the victim of pride, immorality, and corruption.

America is not immune to this cycle. In our time the U.S. is experiencing economic and moral decay that some believe foreshadows a descent to the status of a second-rate power. More than $16 trillion in U.S. wealth evaporated during the Great Recession. The economy has recovered at the sluggish rate of only around 1 percent a year since, due almost entirely to the "stimulus" of a $1 trillion federal deficit and the Federal Reserve inflating the money supply. When not paralyzed by partisanship and dysfunction, Washington is taking over the health-care system, with disastrous results. Our culture is fraying at the seams, with four out of every ten children in the U.S. born out of wedlock, an epidemic of crime and drugs fueling the highest incarceration rate in the world, and the redefinition of marriage threatening the most important and enduring social institution in the history of civilization.

Nevertheless, this book is not a doomsday warning to a dying nation. In spite of what ails us, I believe America's best days are still ahead. Why? First, because I hope in God. And God, throughout history, has heard the prayers of the faithful and intervened in human affairs to stop this downward spiral by sparking a spiritual and moral awakening among His people.

Second, I believe America's best days are ahead because our nation has in its DNA a bright and enduring strand of faith; we have been blessed by God because we believed in God. The United States has experienced untold abundance, leading to pride and self-sufficiency, with consequences that have forced the faithful to their knees asking for God's forgiveness. Throughout history this repentance has sparked spiritual awakenings and spawned social and political movements that reformed society, leading to greater obedience to God's laws, defending the poor and the downtrodden, and thereby creating a more perfect union. In this spiritual cycle, the circle of inclusion has always grown wider, embracing the marginalized and improving the American experiment.

Such an awakening can happen today. Some might think that in our postmodern world, this notion is quaint and old-fashioned. Sociologists point to the rise of the "nones," people who profess no religious affiliation at all and now make up almost one out of five Americans. But even many of the "nones" profess faith in God and say they pray regularly. They are turned off by organized religion, not by the things of God, and they remain spiritually hungry.

In any case, this spiritual awakening will not require a majority vote. It only requires men and women of faith to repent, pray, and act with moral courage, as well as leaders to inspire and mobilize the faithful. And it will occur only if the Holy Spirit covers our efforts with blessing, protection, and humility.

I have written this book to encourage those of us who are concerned about our country and worry that it has lost its way. It is my prayer that *Awakening* provides a road map we can follow to restore our nation from moral, economic, and political destruction back to God's blessing.

Jesus warned us not to be like the man invited to a wedding feast who showed up without the proper clothes and was thrown out (Matthew 22:11–13). When the awakening comes and shakes America to its foundations, we must be prepared and equipped. I trust these pages will prepare us for these challenging and exciting times.

—Ralph Reed
Atlanta, Georgia
October 29, 2013

Part 1

In Motion

CHAPTER 1

The Spiritual Cycle

Are we watching our nation commit suicide?

The United States of America was founded on the principles of limited government, individual liberty, and personal responsibility based on faith in God. Yet it seems we have abandoned those principles to such an extent that it may be too late for this beacon of faith and freedom to turn around.

Is America, like a crumbling modern-day Roman Empire, doomed to inevitable decline and demise?

This is the central question of our time. While things aren't always as they appear (more on that later), the trends are not encouraging.

"If the Foundations Are Destroyed . . ."

Edward Gibbon argued in *The History of the Decline and Fall of the Roman Empire* that Rome fell not because of military foes but because of its own corruption. Similarly in America, the most lethal threat to freedom today comes not from a foreign military opponent. It comes from within.

Consider the following facts that define our time:

- A United States president passed government-run health care that includes taxpayer-funded abortion and regulations that force Christian charities to pay for services that violate their religious beliefs. He also is the first major-party presidential candidate to support same-sex marriage. Yet despite taking these extreme positions, Barack Obama was easily reelected.
- Twelve years after the United States declared war on terrorism, the Middle East is in flames and the forces of terror are on the offensive. The sole priority of U.S. foreign policy since 2009 has been the withdrawal of American troops from Iraq and

Afghanistan. Israel is surrounded by hostile nations. Egypt fell to radical Islam, then descended into chaos and bloodshed. Terrorists murdered a U.S. ambassador in Libya as our own government stood by helplessly. Iran, the leading state sponsor of terrorism in the world, stands on the threshold of a nuclear weapon. America now leads from behind, an oxymoron for any global power.

- The longest economic slowdown since the Great Depression has left many countries in the European Union on the verge of default, threatening the global economy.[1] The U.S. suffers from high unemployment, a low labor participation rate, ballooning public debt, anemic growth, and swelling welfare rolls.
- In 1960, the federal budget was $92 billion, and the federal government ran a *surplus* of $300 million. In 2013, the federal budget skyrocketed to $3.8 trillion, and the federal government ran a *deficit* of $900 billion. The national debt stood at $17 trillion, 37 percent of which had been run up since 2009.[2]

Historian Niall Ferguson argues that the U.S. and Western Europe are suffering because of a "Great Degeneration." Throughout history, the West's contributions to humanity have been representative government, free markets, the rule of law, and a vibrant civil society. As these four civilizational institutions have withered and decayed, Ferguson contends, Western economies have stagnated and the culture that made prosperity possible has lost its way.[3]

The Bible puts it this way: "If the foundations are destroyed, what can the righteous do?" (Psalm 11:3). Is there anything we, as concerned citizens who love our country, can do to slow or reverse this trend and restore America to moral greatness before it's too late? I believe there is, and the foundations of a society—including our own—can be rebuilt.

Alarming Social Trends

Leading U.S. cultural indicators also flash urgent warning signs.

Opinion elites treat abortion-on-demand as the civil rights issue of our time, ignoring the unborn child's competing claim to life. Cecile

Richards, president of Planned Parenthood, took a leave of absence from the pro-abortion group in 2012 to promote Barack Obama's reelection. Obama showed his gratitude in 2013 when he became the first sitting president to address Planned Parenthood, proclaiming to cheers, "No matter how great the challenge, no matter how fierce the opposition, if there's one thing the past few years have shown, it's that Planned Parenthood is not going anywhere."[4] The not-so-subtle message is that people who advocate abortion-on-demand are considered acceptable, while those who take the opposite view are labeled intolerant or misogynist.[5]

Marriage defined as the union between a man and a woman has been supported by presidential hopefuls of both parties throughout U.S. history and as recently as 2008. Barack Obama changed his position in 2012 to energize his base and, according to blogger Andrew Sullivan, to raise more campaign funds from the gay community.[6] The *New York Times* celebrated Obama's flip-flop as the dawn of a new era of tolerance.[7] Nor was the *Times* alone in its liberal bias. When the Supreme Court took up the California Proposition 8 marriage case in 2013, one study found that media coverage favored the pro-same-sex marriage argument by a factor of five to one.[8] Little wonder that the first public statement Hillary Clinton made after stepping down as secretary of state was in support of same-sex marriage.

Signs of America's cultural decline extend far beyond the push for abortion and same-sex marriage. Consider these alarming social trends:

- In 2010 the out-of-wedlock birthrate reached 40 percent of all births, 50 percent of all Hispanic births, and 70 percent of all African-American babies born in the United States.[9]
- After declining during the administration of George W. Bush, drug use is back on the rise. Fully 25 percent of all eighteen- to twenty-four-year-old Americans are categorized as regular users of marijuana or other illegal substances. After Colorado and Washington State legalized marijuana at the ballot box in 2012 and in direct violation of federal law, the Justice Department declined to enforce the law, announcing it would not prosecute those who grew or distributed pot.[10]

- Pornography is a $97-billion-a-year industry; its U.S. revenues rival the film industry's annual box-office take. Forty million Americans regularly visit porn websites, and 10 percent of the U.S. adult population is addicted to pornography. Though treated by our society as a benign source of entertainment, pornography wrecks marriages and encourages the sexual exploitation of children.[11]
- Human trafficking generates an estimated $9.5 billion a year in the United States, and the FBI estimates that up to three hundred thousand children annually are at risk of commercial sexual exploitation. Many are forced into prostitution between the ages of thirteen and fourteen years. Cybersex slavery thrives on the Internet, which has surpassed brothels and strip joints as a marketing tool for pimps and organized crime.[12]
- Legalized gambling is a national epidemic, boasting $93 billion in annual revenues. Today forty-eight states have some form of legal gambling, and eighty-two casinos have opened in the past decade. There are an estimated six million compulsive gamblers in the U.S.[13]
- Violence, foul language, and sexually explicit material that once shocked sensibilities and sparked societal resistance no longer even raise eyebrows. Popular late-night comics like Comedy Central's Jon Stewart have their profanity bleeped with a knowing wink to younger viewers in case parents are watching. Others, like Bill Maher, refuse to make even that concession to decency. At the Video Music Awards in 2013, Miley Cyrus stripped to latex underwear and began "twerking," a fad best described as dance simulating sex. Previous performances on the same show by Lady Gaga and Britney Spears were no less explicit.

Not Hearing or Understanding

We are living in a time of moral, social, and economic decline. But people of faith have always lived among the sinful and rebellious. That is nothing new. Still, God does not abandon the faithful. Throughout the Bible, God promises men and women of faith that we will be granted insight into the mysteries of His kingdom, and thus we can know and understand our times in ways that elude others.

In ancient Judea, when asked by His followers why He spoke in parables, Jesus replied, "To you it has been granted to know the mysteries of the kingdom of heaven, but to them it has not been granted. . . . Therefore I speak to them in parables; because while seeing they do not see, and while hearing they do not hear, nor do they understand" (Matthew 13:11, 13).

While seeing they do not see, and while hearing they do not hear, nor do they understand. This is an extraordinary statement. Jesus told His disciples He used parables to obscure the truth from those whose hearts God had hardened so they would not grasp that the kingdom of God was at hand. Conversely, to those of faith God had granted the right to know the "mysteries of the kingdom" so they could be effective and faithful followers themselves.

As believers, then, it is possible for us to know the mysteries of an unseen world, the truths of a kingdom that is both here now and is yet to come—but we must seek and understand this knowledge. As we learn the things of God's kingdom, we will see the realities of our world more clearly and understand what we must do as believers and citizens to ignite a moral renewal that will restore our nation to its founding faith.

City of God, City of Man

As Augustine put it in *City of God*, his stirring defense of Christianity after Rome's decline, there are two worlds: one visible and the other invisible. The visible world is of the flesh, while the invisible world is of the Spirit.

This Augustine classic was one of the most influential books in history, shaping Western thought for millennia. In it Augustine calls the unseen world the City of God. He calls the seen world the City of Man. To Augustine, the City of Man is just a temporary way station on the path to eternal life where believers are to work for the creation of a just and virtuous society.

As he defends Christianity against the critics who blamed it for Rome's decline, Augustine builds a larger argument that the counsel of God governs the affairs of nations and that the celestial kingdom of God makes superior claims on us. The Roman state's pagan gods had failed it, he pointedly observed, while the heavenly City of God remained safe and secure because "it is preserved (or rather purchased) by faith" of believers.[14]

This distinction between the temporal and the eternal has special relevance today as we begin to examine our own nation—and our world. As people of faith, we desire to be effective as citizens of both the City of God and the City of Man. We may experience setbacks and defeats in our political and social efforts here on earth, but the kingdom of God is eternal and transcendent. This is our hope, and we must never give up.

The Spiritual Cycle

Taking a historical view, we notice that political systems—for example, fascism, Soviet communism, and modern liberalism—seem to collapse at the peak of their influence and power. Why is that?

The answer is the spiritual cycle: the tendency of human societies to move from faith to prosperity to pride to destruction, and then regeneration.

This was true of ancient Israel, and it has been the case in the United States, which may be thought of as a kind of New Jerusalem whose history imitates that of Israel.[15] (The concept will be fleshed out in chapter 2.)

The spiritual cycle moves through a series of six stages:

- Faith leading to obedience to God's laws
- Obedience creating abundance
- Abundance leading to pride
- Pride leading to apostasy
- Apostasy leading to defeat and judgment
- Repentance leading back to faith

Unlike Marxism's view of the stages of history, though, the spiritual cycle is not set in stone. Free will, leadership, and individual choices still affect human events. We are not mere cogs trapped in a fatalistic machine. We can affect our destiny through our own choices. If we, as men and women of faith, repent and call out to God, we can see America return to faith and obedience, bringing her back to the fullness of His blessing and protection.

Good and Evil

What causes the spiritual cycle? Ultimately the Fall, which introduced evil into the world. Sin and evil have produced conflict, brokenness and violence in human affairs since the Garden of Eden.

Consider the parable of the wheat and tares, which can be seen as Jesus' view of history. Jesus taught that evil would always exist but would not ultimately triumph:

> The kingdom of heaven may be compared to a man who sowed good seed in his field. But while his men were sleeping, his enemy came and sowed tares among the wheat, and went away. But when the wheat sprouted and bore grain, then the tares became evident also. . . . And [the landowner] said to [the slaves], "An enemy has done this!" The slaves said to him, "Do you want us, then, to go and gather them up?" But he said, "No; for while you are gathering up the tares, you may uproot the wheat with them. Allow both to grow together until the harvest; and in the time of the harvest I will say to the reapers, 'First gather up the tares and bind them in bundles to burn them up; but gather the wheat into my barn.'" (Matthew 13:24–30)

In Christ's parable, the landowner is our heavenly Father, the enemy is Satan, the wheat is the saints, and the tares are the sinners. Jesus makes it clear that God has allowed the wheat and the tares to grow together according to His sovereign will and in order to fulfill His purpose. Until the final ingathering, neither good nor evil will completely triumph.

The French Catholic philosopher Jacques Maritain cited this parable to argue that "good is not divided from evil in history—they grow together."[16] The saints follow Jesus, engage in works of charity and goodwill, and are bound for heaven. The sinners follow the enemy, engage in evil, and are headed for hell. Both engage in the conflict inherent in their earthly journeys. People of faith will experience triumph and defeat—incremental advances followed by crushing and perplexing setbacks—but they are not to lose heart or quit, for their compass points ultimately to heaven.

Until we get to heaven, good and evil will coexist in this world. We will see miraculous medical breakthroughs occurring side by side with acts of genocide; millions coming to faith in Christ even as dictators oppress their people and persecute Christians and Jews; amazing technological advances coexisting with the threat of nuclear annihilation. Here on earth we are to contend with evil, seek justice, advance virtue, and trust God in the process.

Ronald Reagan underscored this idea in his 1983 address to the National Association of Evangelicals, in which he called believers to resist evil and tyranny and trust God for the outcome. "There is sin and evil in the world, and we're enjoined by Scripture and the Lord Jesus to oppose it with all our might," Reagan said. Critics denounced him as a simpleton for holding to this view. Nevertheless he urged evangelicals to resist the temptation to label each side in the Cold War equally at fault "and thereby remove yourself from the struggle between right and wrong and good and evil." In that struggle, Reagan asserted:

> Communism is another sad, bizarre chapter in human history whose last pages even now are being written. I believe this because the source of our strength in the quest for human freedom is not material, but spiritual. And because it knows *no limitation*, it must terrify and *ultimately triumph* over those who would enslave their fellow man.[17]

How Evil Empires Perish

Reagan was right. The spiritual cycle turned, and he and a resurgent West helped bring about the downfall of the "evil empire." How were communism's last pages written?

Throughout the Cold War the Soviet Union aggressively expanded, tightened its grip on eastern and central Europe, gained satellite nations in Latin America and the Middle East, and built a formidable nuclear arsenal. The West, checkered by self-doubt and plagued by weak political leadership, was in retreat. After suffering defeat in Vietnam, the U.S. slashed its military spending, delayed or terminated critical weapons systems, and, through a combination of cooperation and appeasement, failed to rise to the Soviet challenge.

The Soviets, meanwhile, pursued a strategy of small wars, training and arming guerrilla forces, and seeing country after country fall to communism in the 1960s and 1970s. Motivated by a Marxist-Leninist ideology of global domination, the Soviets deployed missiles in Europe, engaged in covert disinformation campaigns, and toppled pro-Western governments across the globe.

Yet just when the Soviets appeared to be at the pinnacle of their power, in the blink of an eye, communism came crashing down. The Berlin Wall fell, the Warsaw Pact disbanded, the Soviet Union disintegrated, former Soviet republics declared their independence, and the liberation of Eastern Europe lifted 250 million people out from beneath the iron boot of Soviet oppression.

As the American novelist John Dos Passos, a convert from communism to Christianity, observed, "Often things you think are just beginning are coming to an end."[18] The Soviet dissolution was the most stunning and sudden collapse of a state in history, and few saw it coming.

One of the most influential books in the early 1980s among conservatives was Jean-François Revel's *How Democracies Perish*, which reached the chilling conclusion that Western democracies were incapable of defeating communism. Revel believed the very things that made Western democracies so virtuous—pluralism, openness, tolerance, basic freedom of speech and association—made them vulnerable. "Clearly, a civilization that feels guilty for everything it is and does and thinks will lack the energy and conviction to defend itself when its existence is threatened," Revel concluded.[19]

But this theory failed to account for the willingness of free people to defend their freedom, for free will and the counsel of God, or for the difference leaders make. Those leaders included Ronald Reagan, Margaret Thatcher, Pope John Paul II, Lech Walesa in Poland, Vaclav Havel in Czechoslovakia, and dissidents like Alexander Solzhenitsyn and Andrei Sakharov, who changed the course of history and won the Cold War.

The lesson of the Cold War is that political and economic systems that deny God's law contain the seeds of their own destruction. At the threshold of realizing their goals, they collapse under their own weight, especially when pushed by the prayers and deeds of the faithful and courageous. Once the spiritual cycle turned in the U.S. and the West, the Soviets faced a formidable adversary and lost one of the most consequential struggles in human history. These leaders made a difference in their time, and so can we. With God, all things are possible. With faith and moral courage, we can spark an awakening in our time and see the spiritual cycle turn until America is once again restored to greatness.

Destined to Decay—or Ready for Awakening?

So how does this lesson from the Cold War relate to our question of whether America is like a modern-day Rome? Some contend the United States is just another civilization like all the rest, destined to decay and perish. But such an analysis ignores how different America is from ancient Rome and previous civilizations.

Unlike America, Rome had no Constitution or Bill of Rights, no right to freedom of the press and speech and religion, and no right to keep and bear arms to resist tyranny. Also, whereas Christianity in the United States is a mass movement, with more than fifty million Bible-believing evangelicals and faithful Roman Catholics, Christianity in the Roman Empire was an underground movement of a small band of believers combined with a top-down movement of elites. The pagan gods that Romans worshipped prevented a true embrace of Christianity; Jews were systematically persecuted. The moral rot, political corruption, military repression and brutality, and overextended empire that brought Rome to its knees had no faith-based constituency to reverse its decline.

However, there is no denying that the United States, like Rome, is experiencing the downward spiral of the spiritual cycle today. As Americans have sought pleasure and comfort, they have rejected God and His law and substituted the twin idols of self-gratification and government.

A society oriented in this direction cannot long endure, but it need not perish. We can reverse this decay, renew our country, and see God heal our land.

There have been times in U.S. history when immorality was followed by repentance and social renewal. The spiritual cycle turned. There is reason to hope that the current state of social decay in America will lead to an awakening that sparks spiritual searching, revival, and a rediscovery of the principles found in the Bible, the Declaration of Independence, and the U.S. Constitution. As long as there is a faithful remnant who repents and seeks forgiveness, and as long as God's character remains constant in granting forgiveness to those who seek it (and it will), societies can and do regenerate. Like the dry bones prophesied over by Ezekiel, we can see this sleeping giant—our nation—rise again.

In the spiritual cycle, like the weather pattern or the business cycle, the momentum in one direction can produce a turn in the opposite direction. So we must keep the faith, for spiritual darkness does not necessarily portend hopelessness; it can be a prelude to a new dawn and a spiritual awakening.

Throughout our history America has frequently moved through these cycles of national apostasy, chastening, repentance, and restoration. There is nothing especially unique about the current sad state of affairs. The victories of the secular liberal agenda, like the City of Man, are temporary, while the City of God transcends all human systems and will ultimately triumph.

Some saw in the reelection of Barack Obama the final and irreversible victory of the radical, secular progressive agenda, signified by bigger and more intrusive government. But as Obamacare has creaked under its own weight, and as the multiplying failures of his agenda become clear, the opposite is occurring. Instead of signaling its triumph, Obama's second term is beginning to look more like a disaster for secular progressivism.

So take courage! America will not perish as long as faithful men and women repent and humble themselves before God, call the nation back to its founding principles, and fight to restore the moral foundations of our society.

But as we move forward in faith to spark an awakening in our nation, we must be "shrewd as serpents" as well as "innocent as doves" (Matthew 10:16). In other words, our spiritually wise response must be based on a full knowledge of the reality we face—starting with understanding the present from the vantage point of the past.

Action Points

1. Read Matthew 13:24–30. What does this parable say about our call to resist evil in our own time?
2. What are the six stages of the spiritual cycle? At what stage do you think the United States finds itself today? Why did you choose that stage?
3. Read Ronald Reagan's 1983 remarks to the National Association of Evangelicals, often called the "evil empire" speech.[20] In what ways do Reagan's themes apply to us today? Be specific.

CHAPTER 2

Launching a New Jerusalem

At a G-20 summit in April 2009, a reporter asked President Obama if America is an exceptional nation with a unique role in the world. Obama replied, "I believe in American exceptionalism, just as I suspect the Brits believe in British exceptionalism and the Greeks believe in Greek exceptionalism."

Obama went on to say that America's contributions do not "lessen my interest in recognizing the value and wonderful qualities of other countries." He also acknowledged "that we're not always going to be right, or that other people may have good ideas, or that in order for us to work collectively, all parties have to compromise and that includes us."[1]

Obama's backhanded slap at his own country sought to obscure with empty flattery (*other countries are special too!*) and a dodge (*we must all work together and get along!*) his sentiment that America is not really that special.

The founders of America would disagree.

As we will see in this chapter, the spiritual cycle identified in chapter 1 is ingrained in our character because we, as Americans, see ourselves as a people set apart. This idea is in our DNA, forged—alongside our commitment to personal liberty, our passion for the right to bear arms, and our rugged individualism—in the early Americans' encounter with the New World.

Most importantly, the founders saw America as a "New Jerusalem," a society signaling a glorious new beginning for the human race; a civilization birthed and blessed by God; an experiment in self-government, human rights, and righteousness so compelling that other nations would emulate it. This notion molded America's character, and more than anything else explains why the spiritual cycle—from prosperity to pride to downfall to repentance—has repeated itself in the American story.

Errand in the Wilderness

Upon arriving in America, the Pilgrims saw themselves as sojourners in a strange land, building a holy society. Contrary to popular belief, the Separatists who boarded the *Mayflower* in 1620 for the New World were not fleeing religious persecution; they had done that when they fled to Holland in 1608 and established a congregation in the town of Leiden. Of the roughly four hundred members of their tight-knit congregation, only about fifty of them made the journey across the Atlantic. Their purpose was to build, in John Winthrop's phrase, "a city upon a hill."[2] Historian Perry Miller called this sentiment an "errand in the wilderness," in which God sent the first Americans to build a society that would be a model for the rest of the world.[3]

This noble errand drove the Pilgrims deep into an untamed wilderness to bring something back to the civilized world—namely, a renewed England. Their hope was not to break from England but rather to save it through the power of their example. William Bradford, who led the Pilgrims' journey to the New World, equated their trek to "Moses and the Israelites when they went out of Egypt. . . . Our fathers were Englishmen which came over this great ocean, and [like the Israelites] were ready to perish in the wilderness, but they cried unto the Lord, and he heard their voice."[4]

The Pilgrims sought to build a society that reflected biblical precepts. Separated from the Anglican Church and its bishops by a vast ocean, they ordered church and civic life according to Puritan theology. Historian Nathaniel Philbrick labeled Puritan society a "virtual laboratory experiment" of how to organize a congregation of believers and enforce discipline against sin, slothfulness, and heresy. As Bradford put it, "as one small candle may light a thousand, so the light here kindled hath shone unto many, yea in some part to our whole nation; let the glorious name of Jehovah have all the praise."[5]

But it was not to be. By the second generation of Puritans, it became painfully clear that few in England were paying much attention to the society being built an ocean away, much less emulating it. The British government saw the colonies as an outpost of its empire and a market for obtaining raw materials (cotton, tobacco) and selling finished English goods, nothing more. This response by the British created a crisis of identity for the Christians who settled America, and they gradually began to see America as a distinct and separate society that would play a redemptive role in the future of human civilization.

This conviction became an article of faith during the First Great Awakening (1740–1760), led by the famous evangelists George Whitefield and Jonathan Edwards, whose stirring sermon "Sinners in the Hands of an Angry God" left crowds rapturous. Revivalism sent some into paroxysms of shouting, hymn singing, and rolling around in the grass, and the sermons enjoyed a huge popular following. During 1739–41, over half of all the books published by Benjamin Franklin were by or about George Whitefield.[6] The preachers they inspired constituted a "black regiment" that planted the seeds of rebellion in the minds of colonists while adherents of revivalism became the grassroots support for rebellion.

By the time the conflict with Great Britain began, the colonists had reached the reluctant conclusion that Europe was a lost cause. Boston minister Jonathan Mayhew saw it sinking into "luxury, debauchery, venality, intestine quarrels, or other vices."[7] They saw Europe going the way of the Roman Empire, plagued by corruption and moral depravity, the church having lost its soul, incapable of leading a spiritual renewal. In a letter to Alexander Hamilton, Samuel Seabury wondered whether England had become "an old, wrinkled, withered, worn-out hag."[8] All this led John Adams to hope that America, by "design in providence," would become God's instrument "for the illumination of the ignorant and the emancipation of the slavish part of mankind all over the earth."[9]

"All Things New"

This concept of America as the New Jerusalem shaped the thinking of the colonists. When Thomas Paine published *Common Sense* in 1776, he cast American colonists as the spiritual heirs to the ancient Israelites who had asked God for a king and blamed Satan for introducing a monarchy to the world.

"Government by kings was first introduced into the world by the heathens, from whom the children of Israel copied the custom," argued Paine. "It was the most prosperous invention the Devil ever set on foot for the promotion of idolatry." Though Paine would later become a religious skeptic, he used stark religious language to appeal to the colonists: "But where say some is the King of America? I'll tell you, Friend, he reigns above."[10] Paine compared England's King George III to the Bible's King Saul and other failed kings. During the rebellion many church pulpits thundered with the demand, "No king but King Jesus!"

Paine was not alone in seeing the colonists as Israelites fleeing a contemporary Egypt. Presbyterian minister George Duffield preached that the new nation was the "American Zion," a land of promise in which George Washington was Joshua and King Louis XVI of France was Cyrus, the Persian ruler who permitted the Israelite exiles to return to Jerusalem from Babylon.[11]

The colonists saw themselves as a chosen people and a holy nation. And why not? How else to explain the stunning defeat of the greatest military power on earth by a ragtag band of farmers, artisans, and merchants?

To the colonists, America was not only a New Jerusalem in the sense of exile, liberation, and return, but also in a millennial sense, the place where God would establish His kingdom on earth. The United States would become "the foundation of a great and mighty empire, the largest the world ever saw to be founded on such principles of liberty and freedom, both civil and religious . . . [and] which shall be the principal seat of that glorious kingdom which Christ shall erect in the latter days."[12]

This was not an uncommon theme. Historian Paul Johnson has observed that the key text of the American Revolution was the promise of a coming kingdom in Revelation 21:5 ("Behold, I make all things new" [KJV]), which he described as "the text for the American experience as a whole."[13]

Whether this view was rooted in reality is less important than the hold it had over the American mind. It is impossible to separate this religious enthusiasm from the revolutionary impulse. The colonists broke from Great Britain fitfully, reluctantly, but irrevocably, believing the Crown had violated their God-given rights. "We claim them from a higher source," asserted Pennsylvania lawyer John Dickinson, "from the King of kings and Lord of all the earth. They are not annexed to us by parchments or seals. They are created in us by the decrees of Providence, which establish the laws of nature."[14]

God-Given Liberty

At a time when the civilized world still believed in the divine right of kings, claiming God-given rights was a radical idea, one that would find its penultimate expression in the Declaration of Independence. The colonists believed their God-given rights trumped any kings, including the king of England. Once this idea gained acceptance, the logic of rebellion was irresistible. As one Baptist preacher put it, the colonists had "as just a right, before God and man, to oppose King, ministry, Lords, and Commons of England when they violate their rights as Americans as they have to oppose any foreign enemy . . . now present invading the land."[15]

This radical belief in God-given liberty provided the raw material for resistance to British rule. The Bible became the handbook of many patriots. As the Stamp Act controversy raged, Jonathan Mayhew preached from Galatians 5:12–13: "I would they were even cut off which trouble you. For, brethren, ye have been called unto liberty" (KJV). Equally popular during the American Revolution was Galatians 5:1: "Stand fast therefore in the liberty wherewith Christ hath made us free, and be not entangled again with the yoke of bondage" (KJV).

Royal governors, Loyalists, Tories, and more than a few British ministers blamed the rebellion on preachers who whipped their flocks into frenzied opposition to the Crown. Others saw God's chastening in the conflict with Great Britain. John Hancock urged "this people to humble themselves before God on account of their sins, for He hath been pleased in his righteous judgment to suffer a great calamity to befall us, as the present controversy between Great Britain and the colonies."[16]

But God's deliverance did not come without bloodshed. Once the battle had been joined, there was no turning back. "Resistance to tyranny becomes the Christian and social duty of each individual," declared the Massachusetts Provincial Congress in 1775. "Continue steadfast, and with proper sense of your dependence upon God, nobly defend those rights which heaven gave, and no man ought take from us."[17]

A Miraculous Constitution

Another aspect of the New Jerusalem was the colonists' belief in God's hand in the affairs of America, guiding it from independence to the Constitution and Bill of Rights. George Washington wrote to Lafayette that the Constitution was a "miracle."[18]

James Madison, the primary author of the Constitution, agreed. "It is impossible for the man of pious reflection not to perceive in [the Constitution] a finger of that Almighty hand which has been so frequently and signally extended to our relief in the critical stages of the revolution," he declared in Federalist No. 37. At a particularly tense moment at the Constitutional Convention when all hope of compromise appeared lost, Ben Franklin urged the delegates to pray. Franklin's motion for daily prayer was replaced by a July 4 sermon preached to the delegates, at which solemn prayers for their deliberations were offered. This episode, which came after five weeks of fruitless debate, marked a turning point, and the founders considered it a reminder that God's hand had guided America from rebellion to revolution, to independence, and finally to victory over Great Britain.[19]

John Adams, who was not present at the convention but supported the Constitution, claimed it embodied the double helix of civil liberty and self-restraint, with the appetite of the people chained by religion and morality. "Our constitution was made only for a moral and religious people," observed Adams. "It is wholly inadequate to the government of any other."[20]

A government that was limited to specific powers, had no standing army or police force, was prohibited by the Bill of Rights from passing any law infringing the people's liberties, and was without the power to levy a direct tax—this was a system that required what the founders called a "virtuous citizenry," a people animated by an internalized moral code of conduct.

The necessity of virtue and morality to the success of the American experiment was an obsession to the founders. "Only a virtuous people are capable of freedom," remarked Franklin, a statement intended as much as a warning as a compliment. Or, as Washington put it in his farewell address, "Of all the dispositions and habits which lead to political prosperity, religion and morality are indispensable supports."[21]

Disestablishment of the Church

Foremost among the defining characteristics of American democracy was freedom of religion. Long before the First Amendment was ratified along with the rest of the Bill of Rights in 1791, disestablishment of the church had become the colonists' practice. America simply did not offer fertile soil for transplanting the established European church.

During the Great Awakening, Baptists in Virginia protested and some refused to pay taxes to maintain Anglican meeting houses and support Episcopal priests, petitioning the Virginia House of Burgesses for relief. Separation of church and state was an idea designed to protect believers from being forced to fund the efforts of a religious doctrine they abhorred. Its purpose was to protect the church from the state, not the other way around.

Thus America evolved into a society where religion held unrivaled sway. Alexis de Tocqueville remarked in *Democracy in America* that, upon arriving in the United States, "it was the religious aspect that first struck my eyes." Whereas in Europe "the spirit of religion and the spirit of liberty march almost always in opposite directions," in America they were "intimately joined the one to the other; they reigned together over the same country." Indeed, liberty "considers religion as the safeguard of morality, and morality as the best security of law and the surest pledge of the duration of freedom." The reason was due "principally to the complete separation of Church and State."[22]

Priests and pastors largely operated in the spiritual sphere, not in public office, keeping government and church separate while guaranteeing freedom of religion. This did not in any way diminish religion's influence over society and the government—it enhanced it. Tocqueville noted:

> Religion in America takes no direct part in the government of society, but it must be regarded as the first of their political institutions; for if it does not impart a taste for freedom, it facilitates the use of it. Indeed, it is in this same point of view that the inhabitants of the United States themselves look upon religious belief. I do not know whether all Americans have a sincere faith in their religion—for who can search the human heart?—but I am certain that they hold it to be indispensable to the maintenance of republican institutions. This opinion is not peculiar to a class of citizens or to a party, but it belongs to the whole nation and to every rank of society.[23]

Tocqueville added, "Despotism may be govern without faith, but liberty cannot." To those who argued otherwise, he asked the pointed question of "what can be done with a people who are their own masters if they are not submissive to the Deity?"[24] This uniquely American belief—that faith and freedom were inextricably linked—explains the persistence of religious fervor in shaping the political debate in the U.S. over issues of public morality, from slavery and temperance in the nineteenth century to segregation and abortion to the present day.

Civilizing a Wilderness

Another aspect of the New Jerusalem was the wilderness that early Americans confronted, a frontier that needed to be cultivated, conquered, and tamed.

The wilderness became a character in the drama. Frederick Jackson Turner argued that the frontier shaped American democracy by presenting continual danger and continual opportunity.[25] Far removed from theoretical expositions on liberty by Enlightenment thinkers or ancient philosophers, Americans built a democratic society with three practical tools: an ax, a plow, and a gun. The result was the emergence of a culture that stressed self-reliance, violence, a rejection of authority, a class-based society, and religious schism.[26]

Life in early America was dangerous. Smallpox, scurvy, and tuberculosis threatened to wipe out entire villages. Of the first five hundred English settlers who arrived in Jamestown, Virginia, in 1607, all but sixty were dead within three years.[27] Roughly half of the 150 passengers and crew aboard the *Mayflower* died their first winter in the New World. Armed conflict with Native Americans raged intermittently for the better part of two centuries, destroying communities, disrupting trade and economic life, and killing tens of thousands.

The frontier also shaped Americans' conception of themselves, not merely in the cultural icons of the cowboy, the rodeo, and the wagon train, but in a larger sense: they saw themselves as a special people chosen to overcome great challenges and subdue the land. California offered rich soil, gold, and freedom from the hierarchical social structure of the East. The Homestead Act of 1862 offered free 160-acre tracts of land to anyone who could lay claim and cultivate them, fueling the settlement of the frontier.

This impulse had a religious aspect as well. The rural idealism and social isolation of the frontier gave rise to revivalism, camp meetings, and, by necessity, the Methodist practice of itinerant preachers. Religious schisms, meanwhile, fueled western expansion as much as the thirst for freedom and wealth did. When the Second Great Awakening, a spiritual revival during the early 1800s, spawned unorthodox religious sects that were subjected to social ostracism, persecution, and occasional violence, their adherents sought refuge in the frontier. The Mormons left a trail of blood and tears from New York to Illinois and Missouri before finally settling on the banks of the Salt Lake in Utah.

Each successive wave of revivalism, religious schism, and sect could thrive in the New Jerusalem, renewing Americans' view of themselves as a holy people set apart by God. That view took many forms, some controversial, others heretical—but in America the good and bad theology grew together, keeping the notion of America as a holy land fresh and alive. This helps explain why the spiritual cycle continues to turn, and why four centuries after the first Europeans landed on this continent, America remains persistently and deeply religious.

Firearms and the Frontier

Another aspect of the frontier was violence. Beginning with King Philip's War in 1675–1676, armed conflict between Native Americans and colonists raged. An estimated one out of every ten male settlers of military service age lost their lives.[28] Ongoing military conflict made self-protection an imperative and put a premium on skilled military leaders such as George Washington, who first rose to prominence during the French and Indian War.

Because they had no standing army, the colonists relied on militias for their defense. Militia service was mandatory for all men, and they were required to own their own firearms. Some of the early flash points in the revolution were over attempts to restrict or confiscate colonial gunpowder supplies that might be used against British soldiers. Thus Americans came to view the possession of firearms as necessary to the defense of liberty, a right eventually codified in the Second Amendment.

On the frontier, firearms were a means not only of defending personal freedom but of sheer survival. The men and women who braved the unknown to seek a better life relied on weapons to protect themselves against wild animals, Indians, and thieves. Also, living far from general stores or trade routes, these pioneers hunted with firearms to keep themselves from starving. It is no exaggeration to say that the musket and rifle settled the North American continent.

Stephen Ambrose records that during the Lewis and Clark expedition the Native American warriors were most impressed by their "hand held cannons."[29] The association of firearms with masculinity, virility, and power became suffused with American manhood, of which James Fenimore Cooper's frontiersman was the archetype.

With the rise of the film industry in the twentieth century, this character found its iconic fulfillment in John Wayne, who personified the heroic ideal for generations of American moviegoers. Ronald Reagan's penchant for wearing cowboy boots and a cowboy hat while riding his horse at his California ranch captured the same spirit. The modern-day action hero is in some ways the urbanized descendant of the American male on the frontier: have gun, will travel. Asked to name his idea for the central character in a screenplay, Tony Gilroy, scriptwriter of *The Bourne Identity* and its sequels, replied, "A man between 30 and 50 years of age, with a gun."[30]

Regardless of the politics of gun control, the right to own guns for personal defense and as insurance against tyranny is as thoroughly embedded in the American DNA as the Puritan notion of America as a city upon a hill.

Under the Influence

Another aspect of early America that had far-reaching and unforeseen consequences was that it was awash in alcohol. The *Mayflower* carried more beer than water on its way to the New World. The Pilgrims drank beer from the large stores aboard the vessel while the crew and non-Pilgrims drank even more, leading to numerous conflicts during the voyage.

It was not uncommon for ships making the Atlantic passage to carry enough alcohol to provide each crew member and passenger with two pints of beer per day. This pattern continued when the settlers landed. A traveler who kept a record of his journey through the Delaware Valley in 1753 reported on forty-eight different beverages he encountered along the way, all but three of which contained alcohol.[31] Taverns in colonial America were often located next to churches and meeting houses, becoming a locus for politics, community affairs, and, eventually, resistance to Great Britain.

Thomas Jefferson wrote the first draft of the Declaration of Independence at a tavern near Independence Hall. Samuel Adams, second cousin of John Adams and organizer of the Boston Tea Party, was a partner in his father's malt house. After he retired from the White House, George Washington set up a whiskey distillery at Mount Vernon and became one of the most successful liquor distributors in the country. So steeped in alcohol was America that historian Daniel

Okrent concludes, "Drinking was as intimately woven into the social fabric as family or church."[32]

It was not by accident that the first uprising against the new U.S. government was the Whiskey Rebellion of 1794, in which largely rural farmers who had distilled liquor in their own stills for decades objected to paying the federal tax on their whiskey. Washington called out state militias to put down the farmers' revolt in Pennsylvania and Massachusetts, and the federal government survived an early test of its power. But subsequent attempts to rein in the nation's drinking culture during the Second Great Awakening and Prohibition would meet with checkered results. America may have been a religious culture, but it was also one that liked its alcohol.

On the Backs of Slaves

A final factor shaping the colonial experience in the New Jerusalem was slavery. Even as they resisted what they saw as a British conspiracy to reduce them to slaves, the colonists built their society on the foundation of slavery. The first slaves arrived in America in 1619, and from that day on their presence—and the fact that their enslavement completely contradicted America's claim as land of the free—would haunt the republic until the Civil War . . . and long after.

As historian Edmund Morgan has argued, American freedom was built on the back of slaves.[33] The slave system not only contradicted the nation's stated ideals of liberty and independence, but it advanced those ideals by using the blood and sweat of slaves.

The contradiction tortured the founders' consciences and twisted the charters of American freedom. The Constitution ended the slave trade in 1808, but the increase in the slave population in America ended any prospect that slavery would die a natural death. The Northwest Ordinance of 1787 prohibited slavery in the western territories, imposing another check on its spread. But the founders could not arrive at a solution for limiting slavery, and with the South's increasing dependence upon the crops of cotton and tobacco, the slave labor of millions of fellow human beings became even more intertwined in the American economy.

From the Dred Scott decision to *Plessy v. Ferguson* to *Brown v. Board of Education* and its progeny, the Supreme Court wrestled with how to right the wrong of racism. Even as recently as the 2013 session of the highest court, which decided cases involving affirmative action in law school admissions and enforcement of the Voting Rights Act of 1965, race remains among the most controversial and difficult issues for the nation to resolve (more on this in chapter 9).

Living Up to the Ideal

Americans have always thought of themselves as a chosen people destined for liberty, called to build a righteous society that respected human rights and to spread freedom to others yearning to be free around the world. George W. Bush encapsulated this idea when he said, "The liberty we prize is not America's gift to the world; it is God's gift to humanity."[34]

Because the idea of America as the New Jerusalem is so powerful and abiding, it became a yardstick for measuring whether America lived up to the ideals of the Declaration of Independence and the Constitution. As we have seen, the colonists fell short of the mark quite early, discovering that establishing a just society is an enormously complicated enterprise, even in a wilderness far removed from Europe.

Successive generations of Americans have likewise confronted their shortcomings in living out these ideals, which turns the spiritual cycle from decay to rebirth, and from pride to spiritual awakening. These awakenings, occurring intermittently and even cyclically throughout history, have renewed the American experiment and the spirit of liberty. And as we will see in the next chapter, they give us hope that we, too, can bring about an awakening that will renew America and make it a more perfect union.

Action Points

1. Read the U.S. Constitution and the Bill of Rights. Keep a copy handy and refer to it frequently.
2. Read the Declaration of Independence. Where do the grievances against the king apply to our rights today as Americans?
3. Do you believe America is an exceptional nation? If so, in what specific ways and why?

CHAPTER 3

Early Awakenings

In the classic 1946 film *It's a Wonderful Life*, an angel shows small-town hero George Bailey what Bedford Falls would have become had he never been born. The storefronts and ice cream shops of his youth have been replaced by saloons where workers drink away their paychecks. Brothels and gambling joints take the place of bakeries and toy shops. George Bailey, played by Jimmy Stewart, realizes that capitalism without a virtuous citizenry can become ugly and dehumanizing.

The film captured the optimism of Americans after World War II, a metaphor for the victory of "Christian civilization" (Franklin Roosevelt's famous phrase) over fascism and spiritual darkness.

Bailey's fictional story is in some ways the narrative of the spiritual cycle that turned in America from its founding until well into the twentieth century. Throughout U.S. history, men and women of faith combated evil and advanced the common good as they saw it, battling many social ills, including slavery, dueling, alcohol, and poverty.

Starting with the early nineteenth century, in this chapter we will trace how the hopes of the spiritual heirs of the first Americans we met in chapter 2 confronted sin and debauchery in the young republic. As we look at the experiences of the Puritans, we will be inspired by their example and gain a greater understanding of how we can confront evil and injustice in America today.

The Age of Infidelity

The New Jerusalem the Puritans envisioned did not materialize. Instead, America became a swashbuckling, violent frontier society drenched in alcohol, filled with the vices of dancing, drinking, dueling, cockfighting, Sabbath breaking, and gambling. Against this backdrop, men and women of faith viewed the nineteenth century as the Age of Infidelity.

During this time, greed and avarice sapped the American economy, bitter partisanship paralyzed its politics, and sin and indifference tainted the church, rendering it compromised and dull. In their struggle against evil, believers saw themselves as a people within a people, a society within a society. One Methodist clergyman warned that "over society at large degeneracy has gone like a wave of ruin." A Virginia Baptist concluded in 1847, "The signs of the time are truly ominous. The vast kingdoms of dark and light are contending for victory."[1]

Chief among the social evils was alcohol. As mentioned in chapter 2, for most of American history, alcohol was a staple of the typical diet. George Washington plied soldiers with rum and whiskey at Valley Forge, John Adams fortified himself each morning with hard cider, and Thomas Jefferson filled Monticello's cellars with fine French wines, yearning for the day when American vineyards could rival them. At Andrew Jackson's inauguration in 1828, the drunken crowd became so unruly that it had to be moved out of the White House to save the furniture. In some towns, saloons and taverns were more common than churches.

The church saw a nation beset by public drunkenness, brawling, theft, gambling, bankruptcy, the abandonment of wives and families, and a host of other social problems. All this led a New York grand jury to conclude in 1829 that heavy drinking was "the cause of almost all the crime and almost all the misery that flesh is heir to."[2]

Taverns, hard cider houses, tippling joints, and beer and whiskey stores proliferated in early America. By 1830 the average American adult consumed seven gallons of pure alcohol per year. To people of faith, demon liquor was a cancer spawning a host of social evils. Even prior to the temperance movement, towns with evangelical populations banned liquor shops within a five-mile radius of town limits, prohibited card shops and gambling houses, and passed blue laws outlawing the conduct of business on Sunday. They saw no distinction between personal holiness and public morality.[3]

Another sign of immorality run amok was dueling. The practice was imported from Europe and became a permanent feature of American life among lower classes as well as elites. Pulpits flamed with righteous indignation toward the bloody ritual. The Rev. Mason Weems, the Anglican pastor best known for the story of George Washington and the cherry tree, condemned the practice in *God's Revenge Against Dueling*. Benjamin Franklin called duels "a murderous practice" that "decide nothing," and Washington praised one of his officers for declining a duel during the Revolutionary War.[4] Alexander Hamilton's death in a duel with Aaron Burr in 1804 elicited national revulsion, leading Pastor Eliphalet Nott of Albany, New York, to decry dueling as an assault on biblical morality.[5]

Dueling, though, remained a part of American culture. Andrew Jackson killed a man in a duel in 1806 after he accused him of cheating in a horse race and questioned his wife's honor, an episode that haunted him the rest of his life.[6] Abraham Lincoln narrowly averted a duel by apologizing to an Illinois rival he had insulted.[7]

The Second Great Awakening

Men and women of faith responded to the Age of Infidelity with revivalism. The Second Great Awakening broke out with the Great Revival of Kentucky in 1800 and spread eastward across the continent, reaching its apex in 1831, when Charles Finney preached a series of revivals in western New York.

Finney and other preachers acted like modern-day prophets, calling God's people to repent and turn from their wicked ways or face God's judgment. Finney preached uproarious revivals, as nightly revival services swept up entire towns into religious enthusiasm for months. The resulting spiritual outpouring mended marriages, sobered drunks, shuttered taverns, and relieved labor tension as employers joined workers during their lunch hour for prayer and Bible study. Women went door to door to pray for the salvation of neighbors, while men previously engaged in the liquor trade poured whiskey into the street to the cheers of believers who pledged to abstain. So far-reaching were the effects that one convert marveled, "You could not go upon the streets and hear any conversation, except upon religion."[8]

Finney, an attorney who converted to Christianity, was a genuine innovator and social entrepreneur. He introduced many of the modern conventions of revivalism, such as musical instruments, choirs, an "inquirer's room," and the altar call. The Second Great Awakening turned conversion into a collective experience, with broad social and political implications.

Just as the First Great Awakening in the eighteenth century had prepared the American mind for revolution and independence, the Second Awakening equipped believers to begin a social crusade against evil in their nation.

Chief among these evils was slavery. As early as 1784 the Methodist Church passed a code of discipline requiring members to free their slaves within two years or face excommunication. An earlier Methodist conference condemned slavery as "contrary to the laws of God, man, and nature, and hurtful to society, contrary to the dictates of conscience and pure religion." The resulting controversy nearly destroyed Methodism in the United States, forcing the church to adopt a strategy of moral suasion.[9]

The Second Great Awakening took the long-simmering evangelical sentiment against slavery and set it ablaze. William Lloyd Garrison's *The Liberator* began publication in 1831, and two years later the American Anti-Slavery Society was founded. Outside the South, evangelicals equated slavery with sin. Some saw abolition as a precursor to the Second Coming, leading one denomination to proclaim that "the abolition cause . . . must prevail before the halcyon day of millennial glory can dawn upon the world."[10]

As tensions grew between the North and South, many feared this combustible mix of religion with politics would divide the nation and lead to bloodshed. But pleas for compromise fell on deaf ears among the church's abolitionists, who were inspired by the example of William Wilberforce, the politician and social reformer who led the fight to end the slave trade. Following his Christian conversion in 1789, Wilberforce joined Thomas Clarkson, the Quakers, and former slave Olaudah Equiano in opposing the British slave trade. To Wilberforce, "the slave trade was a sin for which Britain had to repent or be damned." Pricking the conscience of the nation, he asked why any man would contradict "the principles of justice, the laws of religion, and of God."[11]

The Anti-Slavery Movement

The U.S. anti-slavery movement merged religious enthusiasm with political action. Spiritual awakenings have sparked political and social reform throughout America's journey, including in our own time. Why? Because the same Holy Spirit that causes us to examine ourselves and align our hearts and conduct with God's Word also leads us to examine society and how it falls short of God's standards of holiness and justice. This applies to our own time as surely as it did to our spiritual forebears.

During the nineteenth century, the controversy over slavery and whether it violated God's law tore through churches and denominations, each side hurling at the other accusations of heresy, blasphemy, and false doctrine. By 1845 both the Methodists and the Baptists had split into northern and southern branches. The Presbyterians had already gone their separate ways in 1838.

Meanwhile, the political repercussions of evangelicalism rippled through the electorate. One study of voting patterns in the 1840s found that support for anti-slavery candidates was highest in areas boasting the largest number of evangelical churches.[12] Eventually the Republican Party benefited from the upheaval, welcoming the anti-slavery evangelicals who poured into its ranks (more on this in chapter 13).

People of faith affected America's culture as well as its politics and religion. Among the most influential was Harriet Beecher Stowe, who taught at a women's Christian school in Connecticut. Stowe was repulsed by the Fugitive Slave Act, which required federal marshals to forcibly return blacks who had escaped from slavery. Stowe serialized a fictional account of a former slave, based on the true story of a freedman named Josiah Henson, in a Northern anti-slavery periodical. The response from readers was so great her editor suggested she compile the articles into a book.

The resulting work, *Uncle Tom's Cabin*, published in 1852, depicted slavery as a brutal and dehumanizing institution while offering hope that Christian love could overcome evil.[13] The book became an instant sensation, selling three hundred thousand copies in its first year in print. This portrait of slavery, so stark in its moral power and so simple in its presentation, captured the imagination of the American public. A decade later Lincoln welcomed Stowe to the White House, greeting her with the words, "So you're the little lady who made this big war."[14]

For those involved in the anti-slavery cause, victory was anything but assured, especially after the Supreme Court ruled 7–2 in the Dred Scott decision in 1857 that blacks had no rights of citizenship even in free states and territories. After a quarter century of political agitation, they were no closer to abolition than at the beginning of their movement.

What to do when decades of anti-slavery political engagement came to naught? Some, led by William Lloyd Garrison, withdrew from politics entirely. Others concluded America could never become a color-blind society and turned to colonization projects for freedmen in Africa, a vision Lincoln supported. But most Christians reacted as they always do to disappointment: they turned to God.

The Third Great Awakening

The Third Great Awakening broke out in New York City in September 1857, with a prayer meeting at North Dutch Reformed Church led by Jeremiah Lanphier, a forty-eight-year-old businessman.[15] Within weeks, entire neighborhoods were swept up in revivalist fervor, with churches packed every night for preaching, teaching, and intercessory prayer.

Believers saw God's hand in the gathering war storm and interpreted the bloody harvest as His judgment on the nation for its sins. For them the war took on the flavor of a religious crusade. Frederick Douglass, a former slave who became a leader in the abolitionist movement, claimed that lynchings, floggings, and other "devilish outrages" committed under slavery could only be expunged "by suffering, by sacrifice, and if need be, by our lives and the lives of others."[16] In Union encampments, soldiers built chapels for prayer, campfires resounded with hymns, and revival services were commonplace. They marched to the cadence of "The Battle Hymn of the Republic."

Temperance and Suffrage

Like the anti-slavery movement, the temperance movement began with prayer. A December 1873 lecture by a well-known doctor and temperance advocate in Hillsboro, Ohio, fired up the Christian women of the community. Eliza Jane Trimble Thompson—a devoted Methodist, daughter of an Ohio governor, wife of a prominent judge, and mother of eight—led a group singing through the streets. For ten days the women descended on saloons, hotels, and drugstores in six-hour shifts, kneeling in prayer for the souls of the proprietors and customers.

The effects were dramatic. Of thirteen establishments selling alcohol in Hillsboro, nine ceased doing so. After reports of the spiritual upheaval appeared in the press, the movement sprouted branches in New York and New England and then beyond.[17]

Alcohol consumption, however, rose dramatically in the U.S. in the late nineteenth century, fueled by immigration and technology. Two-thirds of the 7.5 million immigrants who arrived in America between 1820 and 1870 came from Germany and Ireland, countries with strong drinking cultures. Pasteurization, advances in refrigeration, and the construction of railways also made it easier for breweries to transport their product.

The result was skyrocketing beer consumption, which quadrupled from 1870 to 1900. Beer distributors also invested heavily in saloons, providing cash, underwriting mortgages, and paying local liquor license fees if a saloon agreed to sell only their brand of beer. This led to a proliferation of places to drink, especially in poor, immigrant neighborhoods. The number of saloons tripled from around 100,000 in 1870 to almost 300,000 in 1900, or approximately one saloon for every 150 to 200 adults. The progressive journalist Jacob Riis counted 4,065 saloons to only 111 churches in one section of Manhattan in 1890. Saloons in turn facilitated card games, gambling, and prostitution, taking a cut of the action and arranging police protection.[18] Alcohol rose to become the fifth-largest industry in the country.

Religious folk reacted with horror. "The liquor traffic with the accompanying saloon [is] allied with political corruption, crime, gambling, and prostitution," trumpeted the Federal Council of Churches, leaving in its wake "the wreckage of men and the degradation of families," evidence "social workers and ministers saw constantly in their daily work." Through absenteeism and an inebriated labor force, alcohol "produced needless inefficiency in industry."[19]

Women who suffered economic deprivation or worse as a result of their husbands' drinking had little recourse. Legally they were the property of their husbands, and politically they had no right to vote.

The temperance and suffragist movements thus became inextricably linked, each dependent on the other for grassroots support and moral fervor. Women needed the vote to restrict the saloon, and suffragists found in demon alcohol an issue that drove women to the polls in a crusade to protect home and hearth.

These activists were overwhelmingly Christians, pro-life, and defenders of the traditional family. They were anything but forebears of modern, secular feminism. Susan B. Anthony, for example, gave her first public speech at a temperance meeting in 1849. Prayer vigils, leaflets, petition campaigns, singing hymns outside of saloons, and peaceful but boisterous public demonstrations gave the movement a decidedly grassroots flavor.

The Women's Christian Temperance Union, led by Frances Willard, was the leading temperance organization in the country and a strong supporter of women's suffrage. When the Republican Party, fearing a backlash from Irish and German voters, declined to make temperance a litmus test for candidates, Willard bolted the GOP and founded the Prohibition Party. (Her failure is a reminder that social reform rarely occurs outside the two-party system, for all its flaws.) Leadership in the temperance movement passed to the Anti-Saloon League, led by brilliant political organizer Wayne B. Wheeler. The League adopted a bold strategy of passing prohibition measures in the states. Wheeler assembled an all-star cast of speakers, including politician William Jennings Bryan, boxing champion John L. Sullivan, J. H. Kellogg of cornflakes fame, and evangelist Billy Sunday, who said of the liquor lobby, "I will fight them till hell freezes over, then I'll buy a pair of skates and fight 'em on the ice."[20]

By 1914, fourteen states had passed prohibition laws; three years later, two-thirds of the states had. As a result, three-quarters of the country's population lived in dry states or counties. In 1916 Wheeler and the ASL gained a majority in Congress. The Eighteenth Amendment passed in 1917, and the sale and distribution of alcoholic beverages became illegal in January 1920, a remarkable achievement in a country steeped in alcohol for three centuries.[21]

Prohibition proved a failure, though, hobbled by the overly stringent Volstead Act, a law so strict it outlawed near-beer and some nonalcoholic beers. It was the equivalent of a thirty-mile-an-hour speed limit on an interstate highway. Because Congress had relied on local law enforcement to carry out the federal law, states that had never passed a prohibition statute were asked to enforce a law they had never adopted. In big cities like Chicago and New York, such enforcement ranged from lax to nonexistent, undermining respect for the law.

Prohibition's failure offers a cautionary note for men and women of faith today who desire to stir an awakening in our nation: passing laws without changing hearts and minds will not change our culture. Still, efforts by eighteenth-century Christian reformers did have a positive effect on society: per capita alcohol consumption in the U.S. fell by 70 percent of its pre–Eighteenth Amendment level. In that narrow respect Prohibition succeeded in achieving a key objective.

Cycles of Change

These awakenings and the social reform movements they sparked demonstrate that cultural decline can be reversed, and even endemic social pathologies can be redressed by a combination of prayer, a revival of faith, and civic action.

What was true in previous American awakenings can be true in our own time. If men and women of faith bring biblical principles to bear on the larger polity, they can change history—and America's destiny. Most of the causes detailed in this chapter looked hopeless for most of the struggle, many even on the eve of their triumph. Because evil and good grow together, we cannot fully know the future or God's plan.

But for those who persevere, holding on to hope when there seems little tangible reason for it, walking by faith and not by sight, social change will come.

Nor is this just the stuff of history, a past populated by George Whitefield, John Wesley, Charles G. Finney, Frederick Douglass, William Lloyd Garrison, and Billy Sunday. It has happened in our own time in what some historians have called the Fourth Great Awakening, and it is to that spiritual outpouring that we now turn.

Action Points

1. Pray and ask God to bring a spiritual awakening to our nation, beginning with us. Encourage others in your church, Bible study, or Sunday school class to pray as well.
2. Learn more about William Wilberforce and how he led the fight against the slave trade in Great Britain and inspired abolitionists in America.
3. What lessons can believers today learn from the failure of Prohibition?

CHAPTER 4

Turn! Turn! Turn!

What some have called the Fourth Great Awakening began in the 1970s with an evangelical backlash against the sexual revolution, sparking a massive shift in membership from so-called mainline denominations to fundamentalist and evangelical churches. It was preceded by decades of evangelical isolation from politics. The collapse of Prohibition ended three generations of social reform that had flowed out of America's churches. For more than eighty years, abolitionism, civil rights, temperance, women's suffrage, and the settlement house movement had shaped American politics, mobilizing millions of evangelicals and holding politicians accountable.

But Prohibition made a mockery of these hopes, giving rise to the speakeasy, bathtub gin, the cocktail party, organized crime, police corruption, and Al Capone. The Jazz Age flaunted evangelical proscriptions against dancing and drinking, drawing flappers and rebellious youth to nightclubs and speakeasies. Enforcement of Prohibition was nonexistent, especially in the big cities. Alarmed, evangelical women's groups formed the Women's National Committee for Law Enforcement, which claimed over twelve million members and lobbied for stricter enforcement.[1] Congress ignored their pleas. In New York, Chicago, and Boston, turf battles between rival mob gangs for control of the liquor trade grew increasingly violent, culminating in the Valentine's Day Massacre of 1929.

Evangelicals suffered another embarrassing defeat in the Scopes trial of 1925. John T. Scopes was a high school teacher who had violated a Tennessee law that prohibited teaching evolution in public schools. The media descended on Dayton, Tennessee, for the "Monkey Trial," featuring William Jennings Bryan and famed liberal attorney Clarence Darrow.

The first trial ever broadcast live on national radio, it drew a huge audience. *Baltimore Sun* columnist H. L. Mencken used his daily dispatches to skewer fundamentalists. The sixty-five-year-old Bryan, who was in poor health and died just five days after the trial ended, was called by Darrow as a witness to defend a literal reading of the Bible, and his listless, halting performance was a sad footnote to an otherwise brilliant career. The jury convicted Scopes but fined him only one hundred dollars. His conviction was later overturned on appeal, but the crude caricature of evangelicals endured.

Thus began a half century of retreat from politics by religious conservatives, a self-imposed exile in which they largely withdrew from civic life and focused on their churches, schools and colleges, evangelism, and foreign missions. As they saw it, politics offered few returns while holding them out for ridicule and humiliation.[2]

What would awaken religious conservatives from their slumber and bring them back into the civic arena? Ironically, it was a pill.

Tough Pill to Swallow

The oral contraceptive or birth control pill—soon known by the shorthand "the Pill"—helped transform American society, fueled the rise of feminism, and, at least in appearance, contributed to the sexual revolution. By giving women greater control over when they became pregnant, the Pill shifted the balance of power between men and women and seemed to promise, at least initially, an era of sexual freedom.

Developed as a treatment for infertility for married couples, the Pill quickly spread to the single population. In 1961, its first full year on the market, an estimated four hundred thousand women took the Pill; by 1965, that number had increased tenfold to nearly four million.

Legislators in some states passed laws that restricted or banned contraception, sparking court challenges. The Supreme Court ruled in *Griswold v. Connecticut* (1965) that a state law banning contraception violated a woman's constitutional right to privacy, which included the right to control her own reproductive system. The same legal argument would reappear eight years later as the central argument in the majority opinion written by Justice Harry Blackmun in *Roe v. Wade*. In this respect, contraception was an early skirmish in the abortion wars.

As the sexual revolution unfolded, evangelicals and faithful Catholics were in a defensive position. In the papal encyclical *Humanae Vitae*, Pope Paul VI argued contraception reduced human beings to sexual instruments and severed the procreative potential—the most profound and mysterious aspect of human sexuality—from the sex act. The encyclical also argued that bearing children fulfilled the biblical mandate to "be fruitful and multiply" (Genesis 1:28), not only populating the earth but making disciples who would populate heaven.[3]

Protestant leaders had no theological objection to contraception but were nonetheless alarmed by the sexual promiscuity it abetted. Methodist bishop Gerald Kennedy of Los Angeles bemoaned, "There is more promiscuity, and it is taken as a matter of course by people. In my day, they did it, but they knew it was wrong."[4] Nor were these concerns confined to popes and preachers. A 1966 cover story in *U.S. News & World Report* that detailed shocking increases in sexual activity among teens and wife-swapping in Long Island asked, "Can [the Pill's] availability to all women of childbearing age lead to sexual anarchy?"[5]

Most of these trends occurred coincidentally with the advent of the Pill; they were not caused by it. Sexual permissiveness did not begin in 1961. Sex had become untethered from marriage beginning in the early twentieth century, a trend that accelerated after World War II. The Beat Generation of the 1950s celebrated drug use and sexual adventurism, popularized by the writings of Jack Kerouac and the radical poet Allen Ginsberg. The first issue of *Playboy* had appeared in 1953. What seemed new was the blur of social change, the rise of the counterculture, and a lack of shame bordering on exhibitionism. When Helen Gurley Brown published *Sex and the Single Girl* in 1962, a literary forerunner to the television series *Sex in the City*, she portrayed the sexually active single woman as a symbol of female empowerment, advocating that women have sex with many male partners, single and married, in order to advance their careers as well as for personal pleasure.[6]

Hollywood also loosened its standards. Movie studios discarded the Motion Picture Production Code, which forbade sexually explicit material, for a movie rating system in 1968. Soon films like *Bob and Carol and Ted and Alice* (1969) depicted "free love" and wife-swapping; *Carnal Knowledge* (1971) delved into sexual addiction (leading to the arrest of a movie theater manager in Albany, Georgia, on obscenity charges); and *Easy Rider* (1969) was an ode to the counterculture that explored recreational drug use. *Midnight Cowboy*, a film about a male hustler in New York City starring Jon Voigt and Dustin Hoffman, won Best Picture for 1969, becoming the first X-rated film to receive an Academy Award.

The publishing industry joined in this revolution. After an American publisher released an uncensored edition of D. H. Lawrence's *Lady Chatterley's Lover* in 1959, the U.S. Post Office seized copies sent through the mail. A federal appeals court struck down the action as violating the First Amendment, and this act of judicial fiat effectively opened the floodgates for pornography. Bob Guccione's *Penthouse* magazine, which displayed women in graphic poses that left nothing to the imagination, forced the more staid *Playboy* to keep up. Hugh Hefner followed suit, pushing circulation of *Playboy* to seven million copies. The pornographic film industry also exploded, aided in part by advances in technology, as movies shot on film gave way to the less costly video. And while pornography had existed for centuries, this flood of sexually explicit material had no precedent in American history.

"Judgment Is Coming"

Evangelicals reacted with shock and horror at what they saw as a new age of hedonism that threatened to overwhelm society and bring about its ruin. Billy Graham published *World Aflame* in 1965, a stark warning that if the West did not repent, it would suffer God's judgment. "The world is on the moral binge such as was not known even in the days of Rome," Graham wrote. "We have at our fingertips every pleasure that man is capable of enjoying, including sex, until he no longer finds joy and satisfaction in them." Deploring "immoral acts of such depravity that they cannot be recounted here," Graham saw "human nature, without God, expressing itself. And it is a sign of the end." In vivid language, he warned:

> The sins of the West are now so great that judgment is inevitable, unless there is national repentance. . . . America and Western Europe are on a moneymaking, pleasure-mad spree unparalleled in the history of the world. God is generally ignored or ridiculed. Church members in many cases are only halfhearted Christians. Judgment is coming.[7]

Graham said a mark of decaying civilizations was an obsession with sex, suggested God might be using the Soviet Union to bring judgment on the U.S. for its wicked and wayward ways, and cited a historian who had asserted, "The moral deterioration in the West will destroy us by the year 2000 A.D. even if the Communists don't!"[8]

Echoing these fears, Norman Vincent Peale decried promiscuity and illegitimacy as symptoms of a culture run amok. Like Graham, he pointed to history, including the fall of Rome and Greece, as evidence that America's immorality would lead to its death. Peale cited Cambridge historian J. D. Unwin, who had studied "eighty civilizations over a period of four-thousand years" finding that "a society either chooses sexual promiscuity and decline, or sexual discipline and creative energy," but it cannot do both and survive "for more than one generation."[9]

The Fourth Great Awakening?

But instead of perishing, America experienced the opposite: a spiritual and moral awakening. This awakening occurred because believers repented, prayed, brought moral renewal to their own lives, and got involved in good works—both charitable and civic—that reformed society.

Historian Robert W. Fogel has argued that the U.S. experienced a Fourth Great Awakening during this period, roughly from 1970 until 2000, signified by a renewed emphasis on personal holiness, theological orthodoxy, and increased civic engagement. He points out that beginning in the mid-1960s, the membership of evangelical churches more than doubled.

Whether or not this increased religiosity merits description as a "Great Awakening," I have no doubt that God was in its midst, responding to the prayers and actions of faithful men and women. This awakening primarily involved three movements that changed America's direction: a conservative reformation within the Southern Baptist denomination; the charismatic renewal; and a return to orthodoxy in the Roman Catholic Church. As in earlier spiritual awakenings, this outpouring of faith impacted politics, particularly in the rise of an effective faith-based mass political movement for the first time in decades.[10]

The Southern Baptists

In the 1970s Southern Baptists began rejecting theological liberalism over the flashpoint of the inerrancy of Scripture as the infallible, literal Word of God. Throughout the fundamentalist-modernist controversy of the 1920s and its aftermath, Southern Baptists held fast to their belief that the Bible was without error and should be read by believers literally.[11]

Beginning in the 1960s, many Southern Baptist seminaries abandoned the doctrine of biblical inerrancy. Seminary student Clayton Sullivan described his experience: "I was more certain of what I *didn't* believe than I was of what I *did* believe. Southern Seminary had destroyed my biblical fundamentalism, but it had not given me anything viable to take its place."[12]

The move began among the laity. Paul Pressler—former justice of the Texas Court of Appeals, a pillar of Houston society, and a friend of George H. W. Bush—had taught a Sunday school class at Second Baptist Church for years. One of his former students, a freshman at Baylor University, came home one weekend and shared the disturbing news that his professors had questioned Baptist beliefs. Pressler decided he needed to take action to ensure that Southern Baptist colleges and seminaries did not drift further from orthodoxy.

Pressler joined forces with Paige Patterson, president of Criswell College and protégé of W. A. Criswell, the influential, fundamentalist pastor of First Baptist Church of Dallas. With Criswell's active support, Pressler and Patterson devised a grassroots strategy of electing the next president of the Southern Baptist Convention, thereby gaining control of the boards of the church's seminaries and agencies. The two men burned the phone lines and crisscrossed the country, meeting with pastors and lay leaders to encourage them to send conservatives to the next convention. The convention's president was elected at two-year intervals at the denomination's annual meeting, with each church sending a certain number of delegates, or "messengers," based on the size of their membership and ministry.[13]

After coming up short at the annual meeting in Kansas City in 1977, the Patterson-Pressler coalition elected Memphis pastor Adrian Rogers as the first conservative president of the Southern Baptist Convention in June 1979, signaling the beginning of a reformation of the denomination, a move to the right theologically with major political repercussions.

Liberals and moderates denounced the move as a fundamentalist "takeover" driven by partisan politics. The liberal faction tried to counter the Pressler-Patterson coalition by recruiting candidates for convention president more palatable to the conservatives in the pews. The conservatives solidified their control by electing Bailey Smith in 1980, Texas pastor Jimmy Draper in 1982, First Baptist of Atlanta pastor Charles Stanley in 1984, and Adrian Rogers again in 1986. By the early 1990s liberals threw in the towel and announced grandiose plans to form a rival Baptist denomination, but their effort fizzled.

Historians have long presumed that religious enthusiasm evolves from fundamentalism to secularism. But Southern Baptists had reversed the liberal drift of their denomination. For that reason, the Baptists' shift from theological liberalism to conservative orthodoxy was one of the most significant cultural developments in post–World War II America. Conservatives gained control of the six seminaries, publications, and the domestic and foreign missionary agencies of one of the largest Protestant denominations in the Western world.

Their triumph also signified an increase in religious conservatives' influence. Gerald Ford became the first sitting U.S. president to address the Southern Baptist Convention in 1976, praising Baptists for "rich contributions of religious liberty, democratic principles, social equality, evangelistic fervor, and moral strength [that] have reserved for your people an honored place in American society."[14] Since that time, the convention has been addressed by presidents Ronald Reagan and George H. W. Bush as well as Secretary of State Condoleezza Rice, among other dignitaries. Led by the conservative Richard Land, the denomination's public policy arm, the Ethics and Religious Liberty Commission, became highly influential on Capitol Hill and in the Reagan White House after 1981.

The Moral Majority

As the Southern Baptist reformation unfolded in 1979, three New Right political organizers made the trek from Washington, D.C., to Lynchburg, Virginia, to meet with Jerry Falwell. The group included Paul Weyrich, a former Capitol Hill staffer and president of the Free Congress Foundation, direct-mail wizard Richard Viguerie, and Howard Phillips, chairman of the Conservative Caucus.[15] Weyrich and Viguerie were Catholic and Phillips was Jewish, but their mission was to recruit perhaps the most influential fundamentalist preacher in the country.

Falwell, then forty-six, came from rough-hewn origins that hardly prefigured his career as a pastor and national political figure. His father was a bootlegger, a heavy drinker, and an agnostic haunted by the memory of shooting his own brother to death. His grandfather, who blamed God for the death of his wife, was a committed atheist.

At age eighteen Falwell experienced a dramatic Christian conversion and attended a small Bible college in Missouri where he heard the call to preach the gospel. In 1956, when he was twenty-two, he founded Thomas Road Baptist Church, and in 1971 he founded Liberty Christian Academy (later Liberty University). His weekly *Old-Time Gospel Hour* broadcasts were carried on hundreds of television stations, reaching twelve million homes. As a fundamentalist and independent Baptist, Falwell believed in a separationist doctrine that called for withdrawal from the world and was therefore an unlikely candidate to head a national political organization. He initially demurred, saying he was not sure he was the right one to lead such a movement, given his many other responsibilities.[16]

"Jerry," urged Weyrich, "there is in America a moral majority that agrees about the basic issues. But they aren't organized."

Falwell perked up. "That sounds like the great name of an organization," he replied.

Thus was born the Moral Majority, marking the reentry of religious conservatives into direct political engagement after generations of retreat. Falwell pictured an organization that would unite fundamentalists, evangelicals, Catholics, and Jews in advancing patriotism, a strong national defense, a rebirth of traditional morality, and support for Israel.

"I was convinced," Falwell recalled later, "that there was a 'moral majority' out there . . . sufficient in number to turn back the flood tide of moral permissiveness, family breakdown and general capitulation to evil and to foreign policies such as Marxism-Leninism."[17]

Against the backdrop of disappointment with Jimmy Carter and the liberal drift, the Moral Majority exploded in membership. In 1980 it grew to over three million members and spent $10 million on literature distributed in churches, direct mail, and television and radio ads to turn out the Christian vote. Though it made missteps along the way, the Moral Majority ended evangelicals' withdrawal from the political arena, signaling an awakening that led to their return to the mainstream of American civic life. This was a remarkable historic achievement.

The Charismatic Movement

The charismatic renewal represented a second religious movement that crossed denominational lines. Charismatics emphasized the power of the Holy Spirit and argued that the spiritual gifts of the early apostles—speaking in tongues, healing the sick, prophecy, and casting out demons—were available to modern believers.

The charismatic renewal began in 1967 at a Catholic prayer meeting at Duquesne University in Pittsburgh with students studying the book of Acts and the best-selling *The Cross and the Switchblade* by David Wilkerson. The charismatic renewal soon spread to evangelicals, influencing the parallel Jesus Movement spearheaded by Pastor Chuck Smith and his Calvary Chapel in California, contributing to the proliferation of nondenominational megachurches, and swelling the ranks of Pentecostal denominations. At its peak in the mid-1980s, the movement claimed as many as one out of every four evangelicals and faithful Catholics, and the Assemblies of God became the fastest-growing denomination in the United States.[18]

Largely ignored by the dominant media, the charismatic renewal transformed American Protestantism, integrating churches and bringing together African-Americans, Hispanics, and whites in congregations—in many cases for the first time, especially in urban areas. Some criticized the theology of charismatic preachers, especially those who advanced the "prosperity gospel," which taught that believers could experience wealth through generosity. There were also tensions with fundamentalists, who considered Pentecostal theology heretical. But the spiritual impact of charismatic revivalism was significant. It reached its peak in 1995 when the Brownsville Revival broke out at an independent charismatic church in Florida, a revival that lasted nearly two years and drew an estimated three million people to nightly revival services.[19]

Just as Falwell smoothed out the rough edges of fundamentalism, Pat Robertson did the same for the charismatic renewal. The son of a U.S. senator from Virginia, a graduate of Yale Law, and an ordained Southern Baptist minister, Robertson became one of the most important figures in the religious world. In 1960, he founded the Christian Broadcasting Network with a single low-power UHF station in Portsmouth, Virginia, and he built it into a global ministry with $137 million in revenues that helped fund a cable channel, television and radio stations, charitable endeavors like Operation Blessing, and Regent University, a graduate university and law school.

Though raised as a Democrat whose father served in Congress and chaired the powerful Senate Banking Committee, Robertson held strongly conservative political views, which he increasingly voiced on his daily television program, *The 700 Club*. A pivotal moment in his political journey was Washington for Jesus, a prayer rally in April 1980 attended by an estimated five hundred thousand people, which called the nation back to God. Robertson sat on the steering committee, actively recruited evangelical leaders to participate, and heavily publicized it on his television network. Over time, he became increasingly engaged in politics. In 1985 Robertson founded the Freedom Council to register and mobilize evangelical voters, sought the Republican nomination for president in 1988, and founded the Christian Coalition in 1989.[20]

Robertson also played a central role in the rise of the electronic church. In 1960, the same year he founded CBN, the Federal Communications Commission ruled that local TV stations could fulfill their obligation to public interest programming with paid as well as free time. This created on opportunity for religious broadcasters with national audiences to purchase more local airtime, displacing the broadcasts of local church services on Sunday morning television. Oral Roberts, Rex Humbard, Pat Robertson, Jerry Falwell, Jimmy Swaggart, and Paul Crouch built huge audiences as a result.[21]

The viewing audience and donor base of these television ministries provided the foundation for the religious right's growing influence. Weekly viewership for religious broadcasting soared from five million in the late 1960s to nearly twenty-five million by 1985.[22] Technology played a vital role. In 1977 Robertson leased a satellite transponder to enable him to beam his *700 Club* program to cable systems nationwide. He then founded the Family Channel, which became the tenth-largest cable outlet in the U.S., reaching ninety million homes.

The final legacy of the charismatic renewal was bridging the gulf separating evangelicals and Roman Catholics. The two communities had been divided since the Reformation, and in the U.S., evangelicals had long viewed Catholicism as a foreign religion, suffused with popery and dual loyalties with Rome. The charismatic renewal bridged and healed this breach. Within the movement, Catholic leaders like

Father Michael Scanlan (president of the University of Steubenville) cooperated with Lutherans like Harald Bredesen (a member of the board of the Christian Broadcasting Network) and Methodists like Oral Roberts in a common call for personal sanctification and social renewal.

The pro-life movement also brought Catholics and evangelicals together in a common cause, engendering mutual cooperation and respect. When Catholic pro-life legislators like Henry Hyde joined forces with Falwell, Robertson, and James Dobson of Focus on the Family, the results were historic.

Pope John Paul II

The symbiotic relationship between Catholics and evangelicals reached its apex during the papacy of Pope John Paul II. The election of Cardinal Karol Józef Wojtyła came as a surprise: his predecessor died after only thirty-three days in the papacy, and he was the first non-Italian pope in 455 years. When it was announced after a lengthy conclave that the Cardinals had chosen Wojtyła, commentators stammered in shock as the hundreds of thousands in St. Peter's Square cheered. What may have appeared an unlikely choice would soon have far-reaching consequences in the struggle against communism, the renewed confidence of the West, and the return of the Catholic Church to orthodoxy.

In retrospect, John Paul II's election made perfect sense. The Catholic Church had broken into factions over the meaning and interpretation of the Second Vatican Council. Vatican II, meant to help bring the church into modernity, had divided Catholics over custom and tradition, and many priests and nuns began to openly flout Church teachings on social issues. Pope Paul VI's *Humanae Vitae* led to open dissent. In 1972 Pope Pius VI famously warned that "from some fissure the smoke of Satan has entered the temple of God." He argued that something sinister sought to "disturb" and "suffocate the fruits of the Ecumenical Council, and to prevent the Church from breaking out in a hymn of joy for having recovered in fullness the awareness of herself."[23]

Pope John Paul II became the perfect antidote to these forces. He played an important role in the council, he helped edit *Humanae Vitae*, and his charismatic stage presence unified the hearts of Catholics and captured the moral imagination of evangelicals with a mixture of traditional teaching and populist style. His papacy was essential in quelling much of the post–Vatican II furor and helped to establish a revival of orthodoxy in the Catholic Church. He wrote fourteen encyclicals that reaffirmed Vatican II, and his 129-part series of Wednesday addresses on the topic of human sexuality were developed into an authoritative Catholic anthology known today as the *Theology of the Body*. He encouraged traditional and orthodox lay movements like Communion, Liberation, and Opus Dei, and he installed Cardinal Joseph Ratzinger, an orthodox theologian, as prefect of the Sacred Congregation for the Doctrine of the Faith, where for twenty-five years he defended Church theology. Cardinal Ratzinger, known as "God's Rottweiler," would succeed John Paul II as pope.

Pope John Paul II encouraged traditional piety and took bold positions on social issues like abortion and euthanasia. Perhaps most importantly, his papacy was the longest in six centuries, which enabled him to appoint a majority of bishops and cardinals in the United States, giving the American Catholic Church a decidedly more orthodox flavor.

Like Ronald Reagan, John Paul II was a fierce anticommunist for reasons that were as deeply personal as theological and political. Also like Reagan, he narrowly survived an assassination attempt (probably at the hands of a Soviet agent) and believed his life had been spared to fulfill a special purpose. He reasserted the Catholic Church's opposition to political movements like communism and Marxism and batted down liberation theology, a Catholic economic political movement that had roiled Central and South America. One of his hallmark encyclicals, *Centesimus Anus*, was written on the one-hundred-year anniversary of *Rerum Novarum*, Pope Leo XIII's encyclical on the topic of economics and liberty. Written at the end of the Cold War, *Centesimus Anus* was a strong rebuke of political ideologies that crush freedom in the name of economic equality and a strong defense of foundational economic liberties like property rights.[24]

John Paul II's return to his native Poland in 1983 electrified not just Roman Catholics but also evangelicals, who had historically viewed Soviet communism as an atheistic system that denied religious freedom and persecuted Christians as well as Jews. Millions attended his open masses, which functioned as not-so-subtle rebukes to the Soviet-backed regime that had crushed the Solidarity Movement. His emphasis on ecumenical cooperation and his humble forsaking of past sins of the church won him many friends in the evangelical world.

John Paul II inspired "lay theological and political initiatives" between Catholics and evangelicals who were "bound by their shared impatience with the cultural rebellion against God, both outside and inside Christendom." This emerging Catholic-evangelical cooperation "was further nurtured when Evangelical leaders spoke openly about their respect for John Paul II. Billy Graham was quoted in *Time* saying, 'Pope John Paul II will go down in history as one the greatest of our modern popes.'"[25]

A Prelude to Collective Repentance

The late-twentieth-century awakening turned the spiritual cycle back to repentance and faith. It did so when religious folk feared America was going the way of Rome, sliding from debauchery and hedonism to ruin. But as it turned out, the sexual revolution of the 1960s did not signal America's decline. Instead, it was the opening act in a larger drama that led to repentance, renewal, and a return to faith. With the increased number of religious converts, with the shift in church membership to evangelical denominations, with a rebirth of revivalism, and with the social and political impact of its adherents, this religious resurgence ranks as one of the most consequential in American history. It transformed American society and its politics, moving tens of millions of people of faith from the sidelines to the front lines of cultural renewal.

Some had feared that America's ruin was near, but a movement of God led instead to an awakening. It has happened repeatedly, one might almost say cyclically, throughout the American journey. It can happen again if men and women of faith today unite in prayer, repentance, piety, and, yes, political action.

Action Points

1. If your church does not already have one, talk to your pastor about starting a Civic Concerns Ministry in your church to address moral and civic issues in your community.
2. Working with your church leadership, sponsor a voter registration drive in your church.
3. Discuss the following question with your Bible study or discipleship group or with your family over dinner: If moral decay spurred what some call a Fourth Great Awakening at the end of the twentieth century, why do you believe so many in the church today remain indifferent to moral issues and political involvement?

CHAPTER 5

The Reagan Revival

Spiritual awakenings need more than just adherents. They need leadership to fully flower, including in the political arena. By the late 1970s, the awakening among evangelicals and faithful Catholics had built ministries, churches, colleges, and broadcast outlets that enabled them to leave their mark on society. Yet they still required a gifted political leader, one who shared their biblical worldview and passion for spiritual renewal.

They found him in a former Hollywood actor affectionately known as "the Gipper."

In September 1979, Ronald Reagan walked into a Washington hotel suite for a meeting with evangelical leaders. The gathering, arranged with assistance from former Arizona congressman John Conlan, included Bill Bright of Campus Crusade for Christ, Southern Baptist Convention president Adrian Rogers, pastor Charles Stanley, evangelist James Robison, Presbyterian minister and broadcaster D. James Kennedy, and Christian author Tim LaHaye.

Reagan glided into the room wearing a crisp shirt and tailored suit that perfectly fit his barrel chest and broad shoulders and let a hint of white cuff show. Sitting at the head of the table as the leaders introduced themselves and described their ministries, he greeted each of them with a bob of the head and an infectious smile. After he made some brief remarks, Reagan fielded questions from the leaders on a range of topics. At ease and comfortable, he made eye contact and gave crisp, direct answers.

Kennedy boldly asked what reason Reagan would give God to let him into heaven. Reagan looked at the ground for what seemed like minutes. "I wouldn't give God any reason for letting me in," he finally said softly. "I'd just ask for mercy because of what Jesus did for me at Calvary."

The room fell silent as the evangelical leaders exchanged approving glances around the table. When they took a brief break, Robison pulled Reagan aside to a sitting area. He asked him if Jesus was real to him. Reagan replied that he had never really had a father because his father was an alcoholic, so the greatest influence in his life was his mother. "Jesus is more real to me than my mother," he said.[1]

To those who knew him, Reagan's answer was not a surprise. A mystical spirituality and deep Christian faith had guided him from boyhood. It had sustained Reagan through the ups and downs of a movie acting career, the death of a child and a painful divorce, his subsequent remarriage to Nancy, and his rise in politics. The spiritual cycle requires what Jesus called "workers" of "His harvest," and He instructed His disciples to pray for the "Lord of the harvest" to raise them up (Matthew 9:38). The kingdom needs workers, and it requires leaders to inspire and organize them into an effective force. Reagan was such a leader, an indispensable man in the awakening that renewed America.

Great and Good

The deification of Reagan began with the fall of the Berlin Wall and reached its zenith with his death in 2004. Its court composers were the Reaganites who served and loved him. "He was probably the sweetest, most innocent man ever to serve in the Oval Office," exuded Peggy Noonan, a speechwriter for Reagan in the White House. "'No great men are good men,' said Lord Acton, who was right, until Reagan."[2]

Eulogizing Reagan in 2004, George Will recalled that his "rhetoric lingers like a melody," reminding the American people that "at a turbulent moment in their national epic, Reagan became the great reassurer, the steadying captain of our clipper ship. He calmed the passengers—and the sea."[3]

These plaudits are richly deserved. But the apotheosis of Reagan actually makes understanding him more challenging. To unlock the keys to Reagan's success, we must first retrace the steps of his spiritual journey. The broad outline of his life is familiar: Midwestern upbringing, Hollywood, "The Speech," governor of California, election to the presidency, tax and budget cuts fueling an economic boom, "Tear down this wall!," winning the Cold War without firing a shot, the onset of Alzheimer's and the poignant fade to black, then his death in 2004, unleashing national grief and mourning.

Before his deification, Reagan was a paradox. A conviction politician, he displayed a wily pragmatism that at times left supporters perplexed and disappointed. The first divorced man to serve as president, he rarely attended church and didn't use the term *born again*, yet he ushered evangelicals into the mainstream of civic life. He signed the most liberal abortion law in the nation as governor of California, but he became the first pro-life president since *Roe v. Wade* and authored a pro-life book while in office. The patron saint of supply-side economics, he cut taxes across the board, but then he signed tax increases every year of his presidency thereafter except 1988. A dedicated anticommunist, he negotiated the most comprehensive arms agreement with the Soviet Union since détente in the 1970s. A champion of smaller government, he was unable to balance the budget and presided over deficits not exceeded as a share of the economy until Barack Obama's presidency.

In spite of these apparent contradictions, Reagan remains enormously popular among the American people, driving critics battier today than when he was alive. Those who suffered the fate of following him on the national stage found it a vexing experience. George H. W. Bush inherited Reagan's playbook but not his mantle. Bill Clinton's dreams of a liberal legacy went down to defeat with his health-care plan and the election of a Republican Congress in 1994. Even Barack Obama, running for president in 2008, aspired to emulate Reagan. "I think Ronald Reagan changed the trajectory of America in a way that, you know, Richard Nixon did not and in a way that Bill Clinton did not," said Obama.[4] Reagan's reputation will grow as future generations reflect on his presidency. Even so, we should not fall victim to a false nostalgia, mythologizing Reagan until he becomes inaccessible. Reagan was not perfect. Instead, he saw himself as an ordinary man on an extraordinary mission. We do him a disservice when we call him the Great Communicator, implying that his strength lay in his oratory.

The vital aspect of Reagan's leadership was that he reaffirmed what the American people believed. "I wasn't a great communicator, but I communicated great things," Reagan said in his farewell address in 1989. "And they didn't spring full bloom from my brow; they came from the heart of a great nation—from our experience, our wisdom, and our belief in the principles that have guided us for two centuries."[5]

As George Will has put it, Reagan understood that Americans more often need to be reminded than informed. Reagan's greatness lay in the fact that he aligned himself with God's purpose for his life and what he saw as the Lord's plan for America. Only through a clear-sighted assessment of Reagan's achievements can we appreciate his example, his adherence to conservative principles, and his faith in God.

The Young "Practical Christian"

Reagan's commonality with evangelicals sprang from his own encounter with Jesus, an experience as a young man that led Reagan to the firm conviction that God had a plan for his life. He came to this belief through the crucible of heartache and disappointment. Because of his infectious optimism, we may be tempted to think Reagan led a charmed life. But quite the opposite was true.

Reagan's father was an itinerant alcoholic and a gambler who lost multiple jobs due to his excessive drinking. He moved his family from town to town and often disappeared for days at a time. In *Where's the Rest of Me?*, a 1965 memoir written before he held public office, Reagan described trudging home in the snow at the age of eleven and stumbling upon his father passed out on the front porch. "He was drunk," Reagan recalled. "Dead to the world." Sprawled out in the snow, arms and legs akimbo, "his hair soaked with melting snow, snoring as he breathed," stinking of whiskey, his father looked "as if he were crucified, as indeed he was," laid low by the "dark demon in the bottle."[6]

Not long after, his mother, Nelle, a devout Christian and active member of the local Disciples of Christ church, gave Ronnie *That Printer of Udell's*—a 1902 Christian novel by Harold Bell Wright, a Disciples minister. The book contains a deeply spiritual message, arguing that the true measure of Christianity lay in its mysterious ability to transform lives and reform the larger society.

The plot involves a boy who escapes an unhappy home dominated by an abusive, alcoholic father. He runs away, becomes an apprentice in a printing shop owned by a committed Christian, and decides to become a "practical Christian" himself. Leading a local moralistic crusade, the young man rids the town of saloons, burlesque shows, and bordellos, replacing them with thriving businesses and churches. So impressed are the people by his leadership that they elect him to represent them in Congress, and he goes to Washington to fight for a stronger, better America.[7]

The book had a profound impact on Reagan, instilling in him "an abiding belief in the triumph of good over evil."[8] Weeks after finishing the novel, Reagan announced he wanted to be like the boy in the novel and asked to be baptized. Joining the church, he never missed a worship service, and he taught Sunday school. He became active in the YMCA and Christian Endeavor, an evangelical youth group that stressed evangelism and service to others, and ironically its creed would later inspire the founding of Alcoholics Anonymous.[9]

Throughout the rest of his life, Reagan's Christian faith informed a deep belief in his own destiny. "God has a plan and it isn't for us to understand, only to know that He has His reasons and because He is all merciful and all loving we can depend on it that there is a purpose in whatever He does and it is for our own good," he wrote to Nancy Reagan in the 1960s. "What you must understand without any question or doubt is that I believe this and trust Him and you must, too."[10]

Reagan's faith would be tested by personal trials. After graduating from Eureka College, a Disciples of Christ college in Illinois, he went to Hollywood and built a highly successful career as a movie actor. But by the late 1940s, Reagan found himself displaced by younger actors. His personal life fell apart. While Reagan's acting career flagged, his wife, Jane Wyman's soared. She was nominated four times for an Academy Award and won for Best Actress, becoming a major star. Their disparate career trajectories strained their marriage. Then, while Jane was pregnant with their second child, Reagan fell ill with pneumonia and was hospitalized for weeks, at one point nearly dying, and Jane suffered a miscarriage. The tragedy devastated the couple. Already damaged by their unequal status in Hollywood and Reagan's growing interest in politics, the marriage ended in divorce.

Face-to-Face with Communism

Grief-stricken and with his movie career on the rocks, Reagan reached bottom. He went into an emotional tailspin, drinking, partying, and serially dating, wallowing in his sorrow. For a time he slept on the couch in William Holden's home. His mother encouraged him, saying that God allowed everything to happen for a reason. This proved to be the case for Reagan. In March 1947, the top board members of the Screen Actors Guild resigned amid charges of self-dealing, and Reagan was chosen as the new president of the film actors' union. This role honed his talents for hard-nosed negotiation, advocacy, public speaking, and service to others, which—along with a well-calibrated moral compass—would send him to the White House.

As Peter Schweizer demonstrates in his book *Reagan's War*, it was during his involvement with SAG that Reagan came face-to-face with communism and dedicated himself to defeating it. Today Americans fondly remember the Reagan of the "Evil Empire" speech or standing at the Brandenburg Gate in Berlin and demanding, "Mr. Gorbachev, tear down this wall!"[11]

But thirty years earlier, Reagan had battled the communists in Hollywood, a conflict so fierce he feared for his life. It was also during this period that he met Nancy Davis, the woman who became his best friend and the partner he needed to succeed in politics. Ironically, he and Nancy first met when she reached out to him because she feared her name might have accidentally turned up on a Hollywood blacklist.

The Red Scare gripped America in the late 1940s and early 1950s, and in 1947 the House Un-American Activities Committee held extensive hearings and investigated communist infiltration of the U.S. entertainment industry. A number of actors, writers, and directors invoked their Fifth Amendment right against self-incrimination rather than testify. Reagan decided to fully cooperate, testifying before the committee and even becoming an FBI informant. In Hollywood it was a time of fear, intimidation, and the threat of the blacklist, which kept actors and directors out of work for their alleged association with communist front groups. Fighting back, communist-infiltrated actors' groups went on strike, hoping to bring the film industry to its knees.

The Screen Actors Guild declined to join the strike, and the atmosphere soon grew tense. To get to work each morning, many actors crossed picket lines in buses with guards armed with shotguns, dodging rocks and bricks hurled by protestors. Some got to work on the Warner Brothers lot by sneaking through a storm drain pipe. The communists and their supporters despised Reagan for leading the opposition to the strike. They targeted him for physical violence, threatening to throw acid in his face to ruin his good looks and ensure he could never work in films again. Fearing for his safety, Reagan began to carry a holstered .38 caliber Smith and Wesson pistol on his belt, and he slept with it on the nightstand.[12]

Reagan never achieved John Wayne–like stardom, but at SAG he found his calling. He became involved in the Crusade for Freedom, a leading anticommunist organization that rallied the public during the Cold War. For the remainder of his life—as a television personality and corporate spokesman, governor, public speaker, radio commentator, and president—Reagan condemned communism as the focus of evil in the world and asserted America's role as the defender of freedom, not just for its own citizens, but for those yearning to be free in every dark corner of the globe.

In a commencement address at William Woods College in Fulton, Missouri, in 1952, Reagan echoed John Winthrop's idea of America as a city upon a hill, placed there by God for a special mission and purpose. America, Reagan asserted, "was set aside as a promised land. . . . I believe that God shedding his grace on this country has always in this divine scheme of things kept an eye on our land and guided it as a promised land."[13]

One can see in this early speech by Reagan a foreshadowing of the role he would later play in the coming awakening and of his profound understanding of America's spiritual cycle from the time the Puritans settled this land.

An Evangelical Ally

From the beginning of the evangelicals' political reengagement, Reagan expressed common cause with them. In August 1978, for instance, the IRS announced it would deny or revoke the tax-exempt status of Christian schools unless they could prove they were not segregated. The proposed regulations, which included a thinly veiled minority quota system, required Christian schools to act "in good faith on a racially non-discriminatory basis." Reagan denounced the IRS edict, saying, "Chief Justice John Marshall once declared, 'The power to tax is the power to destroy.' The I.R.S. threatens the destruction of religious freedom itself with this action." He called for a public outcry, urging that the IRS "Commissioner and your Congressman should be hearing from you right now."[14]

The evangelical community exploded in protest, raining down an estimated 125,000 letters on the IRS alone. Members of Congress, deluged with complaints from constituents, vowed to fight the regulations. Congressman Robert K. Dornan of California thundered that the American people "are sick and tired of unelected bureaucrats engaging in social engineering at the expense of our cherished liberties."[15] Bowing to political pressure, the IRS withdrew the regulations. But the damage was done; the controversy helped irrevocably turn evangelicals against Jimmy Carter.

From this experience, evangelicals learned that withdrawal from politics was no longer an option because eventually the government would discriminate against them, their churches, and their schools. The IRS edict sparked the emergence and awakening of the religious conservative movement, and evangelicals found an ally in Reagan.[16]

The same was true of the pro-life movement. Earlier, in 1967, Governor Reagan signed the Therapeutic Abortion Act, legalizing abortion to protect the physical and mental health of the mother, and the law had the unintended effect of permitting abortion-on-demand. The impetus for the legislation was public outcry over the prosecution of two doctors in San Francisco who performed abortions on eight women with German measles, which had a history of causing birth defects. Reagan had been governor less than six months when the bill landed on his desk, and by all accounts he was unprepared to deal with the controversial issue.

Reagan found the bill's provision allowing abortion in cases of "substantial risk" of deformity of the fetus morally objectionable, fearing it would lead to selective abortions of handicapped children in the womb, which he said was "not different than what Hitler would do."[17] Reagan biographer Lou Cannon recounts that when Reagan held a news conference as the legislature debated the bill he made confusing statements suggesting he would sign the bill if the offending provision were removed. The bill's Democratic sponsor quickly dropped the fetal deformity section, backing Reagan into a corner. Republicans in the California Assembly simply wanted the issue to go away. With his staff divided, Reagan sought counsel from his father-in-law, a practicing physician (who encouraged him to sign it) and Cardinal James Francis McIntyre (who urged him to veto it).[18] "I did more study and soul-searching than on anything that was to face me as governor," Reagan recalled.[19]

In the end Reagan signed the bill, with disastrous results. In 1967, there were 518 legal abortions in the state of California. After the Therapeutic Abortion Act became law, California averaged one hundred thousand abortions per year for the remainder of his two terms in office, more than in any other state in the country prior to *Roe v. Wade*. In the next six years, twenty states liberalized their abortion laws, most of them using California's statute as their model. Biographer Edmund Morris said Reagan was tortured by an "undefinable sense of guilt" as he watched abortion-on-demand sweep the country.[20] William Clark, a devout Catholic who served as counsel in the governor's office and opposed the measure, later said that signing the California abortion law was "perhaps Reagan's greatest disappointment in public life."[21]

Over time Reagan adopted a strong and consistent pro-life position. He allowed for exceptions in the case of rape, incest, or endangerment of the mother's life, a view he held throughout his public life. And while the Republican Party platform called for a Human Life Amendment to the Constitution, Reagan argued unborn children were already protected under the Fourteenth Amendment's due process clause. Because they were "persons" under the law, he believed amending the constitution should not be necessary.

As he argued in a presidential debate in 1984, "With me, abortion is not a problem of religion; it's a problem of the Constitution. I believe that until and unless someone can establish that the unborn child is not a living human being, then that child is already protected by the Constitution, which guarantees life, liberty, and the pursuit of happiness to all of us."[22]

In the spring of 1983, Reagan wrote an unsolicited piece for the *Human Life Review*. Commenting on the ten-year anniversary of *Roe*, Reagan remarked on the "15 million lives snuffed out by legalized abortions . . . over ten times the number of Americans lost in all our nation's wars." As he did in 1967, he condemned the use of abortion to take the lives of babies with disabilities such as Down syndrome, and he drew parallels between the legal reasoning in *Roe* and the Dred Scott decision, which had denied black citizens their right to equal protection under the Fourteenth Amendment.

This argument was deeply revealing of Reagan's view of America: always hopeful and optimistic, simply in need of being reminded of its founding principles.

"A Hunger in This Land"

On August 21, 1980, fifteen thousand cheering men and women of faith filled Reunion Arena in Dallas for the National Affairs Briefing of the Religious Roundtable. They were to receive the formal laying on of hands from Ronald Reagan, who had accepted the Republican nomination for president. As the first stop of Reagan's general election campaign, his presence dramatized Jimmy Carter's collapsing support among religious conservatives and signaled their movement into the Republican Party.

When the Reagan entourage arrived at the arena, a disagreement ensued over whether Reagan would sit onstage prior to his own remarks. James Robison, who had organized the event, insisted Reagan needed to be onstage so believers would see him applauding and approving the messages from the evangelical leaders. Mike Deaver, the unofficial keeper of Reagan's image, feared Reagan would be blamed for the rhetorical flourishes of Robison and others who filled the undercard. Reagan overruled Deaver and agreed to go onstage.

Robison, youthful and handsome, grasped the podium with both hands and jabbed his finger in the air to punctuate his points. "If the righteous, the pro-family, the moral, the biblical, the godly, the hardworking, and the decent individuals in this country stay out of politics," Robison thundered, "who on earth does that leave to make the policies under which you and I live and struggle to survive?" The answer was obvious. "I'm sick and tired of hearing about all the radicals, and the perverts, and the liberals, and the leftists, and the communists coming out of the closets. It's time for God's people to come out of the closet, out of the churches and change America! We must do it!"[23]

Reagan's words were fewer but no less important: "I know that you can't endorse me. I only brought that up because I want you to know that I endorse you and what you're doing."[24] The arena erupted in a standing ovation.

When Reagan addressed the Religious Roundtable, he was doing more than seeking votes—he was sparking an awakening. He believed that even more than needing a new president, America needed a moral and spiritual revival. In an interview with *Christianity Today* in 1976, he bemoaned "a wave of humanism and hedonism in the land" but said he remained optimistic because "I think there is a hunger in this land for a spiritual revival, a return to a belief in moral absolutes—the same morals upon which the nation was founded."[25] As president, he went even further, telling an interviewer, "What I have felt for a long time is that the people in this country were hungry for what you might call a spiritual revival. . . . I decided that if it was possible for me to help in that revival, I wanted to do that."[26]

The Presidency

In the spiritual cycle, Reagan's election as president marked a turning point. In 1979, the year of conservative resurgence, Margaret Thatcher became the first woman prime minister of Great Britain, Pope John Paul II became the first Polish pope, conservatives gained control of the Southern Baptist Convention, Jerry Falwell formed the Moral Majority, and Reagan announced his candidacy for the presidency.

Jimmy Carter, the most explicitly evangelical president since Woodrow Wilson, presided over an administration adrift, buffeted by foreign policy crises abroad and a weak economy at home. Interest rates rose to their highest level since the Civil War, the top income tax rate was 70 percent,[27] inflation was at 13 percent,[28] long lines snaked out of gas stations, Soviet troops occupied Afghanistan, and American hostages languished in Iran. Carter was outmatched by events. He imposed a grain embargo against the Soviet Union that hurt U.S. farmers more than it did the despots in Moscow, announced the U.S. would boycott the 1980 Olympics in Moscow, and ordered Desert One, a failed and belated attempt to rescue the hostages that resulted in a helicopter crash and eight dead servicemen.

On Election Day evangelical voters who had given two-thirds of their votes to Carter in 1976 broke for Reagan with an astonishing 64 percent of the vote. That single constituency swung more dramatically than any other voter group between 1976 and 1980. Viewers of religious television programming—more than one out of every four voters—voted 62 percent for Reagan. Meanwhile, a Harris poll found that white Baptists voted for Reagan by 56 to 34 percent.[29]

At his inaugural, Reagan moved the ceremony to the west front of the Capitol so he could look toward the Washington, Jefferson, and Lincoln Memorials, placing his hand on a page of his mother's Bible turned to 2 Chronicles 7:13–14: "If . . . My people who are called by My name humble themselves and pray and seek My face and turn from their wicked ways, then I will hear from heaven, will forgive their sin and will heal their land." In the margin, his mother had written, "A most wonderful verse for the healing of the nation."

Reagan had no doubt he had been placed in office to play an important role in history. This view was reinforced when he survived an assassination attempt in March 1981. He told visitors in the Oval Office that whatever time he had left on earth, he owed to God. In June 1982, he met with John Paul II for the first time, and the men retired to the Vatican library and talked alone for fifty minutes. The focus of their conversation was the ongoing crisis in Poland. Soviet tanks and troops had rolled into Warsaw the previous December, crushing the Solidarity Movement, rounding up and arresting Solidarity leaders like Lech Walesa. The two men shared a yearning for a free Poland and an Eastern Europe no longer dominated by the Soviet Union.

During the meeting, Reagan and John Paul II agreed to undertake a joint operation between the U.S. and the Vatican to provide material and financial support to Solidarity in the hopes of liberating Poland and thereby beginning the process of the disintegration of the Soviet Empire. Over the next seven years, huge sums of money and vital supplies for maintaining the Polish labor movement were funneled to the Solidarity underground through a clandestine network of U.S. intelligence agents and Roman Catholic priests. As Reagan's national security adviser later remarked, "This was one of the great secret alliances of all time."[30]

Reagan believed that God had called him to bring liberty to those behind the Iron Curtain. After the U.S.-U.S.S.R. standoff at Reykjavik, when Reagan walked away empty-handed rather than give up the Strategic Defense Initiative, the American president reached a sweeping arms agreement with the Soviets that eliminated all intermediate-range missiles in Europe. Reagan's emotional bond with Gorbachev strengthened the Soviet leader's hand in reforming Russian society and displacing the old Soviet guard. When the Berlin Wall crumbled and the Soviet Union disintegrated, the Cold War ended, and central and Eastern Europe were liberated from communism.

Emulating Reagan

Reagan proved that ordinary individuals can do extraordinary things and that common people can perform uncommon deeds. His moral courage and clarity during the Cold War make clear that leadership matters in spiritual awakenings and that prayer affects human affairs. The moral, spiritual, and economic decline that plagued the West in the post–World War II period did not mean its demise, and it need not mean its end today.

If we emulate Reagan's example and live for Christ and others, seeking to carry out God's plan for us and for our nation, we can witness another awakening that will shake our country to its foundations and return her to founding principles. This awakening also requires believers who, like Reagan, will run for and serve in public office.

With faith and hard work, we can restore America to moral greatness. As Reagan said in his first inaugural address, "After all, why shouldn't we believe that? We are Americans."[31]

Action Points

1. Reagan believed God had a purpose for his life. Do you feel the same about your own life? Why or why not? If you believe God has a purpose for your life, what is it?
2. Write those elected officials whom you most admire for having qualities similar to Reagan and encourage them to have the courage of their convictions (U.S. Senators, U.S. Capitol, Washington, D.C., 20510; House of Representatives, U.S. Capitol, Washington, D.C., 20515).
3. Pray for God to raise up in our time more leaders like Reagan who believe they have a special mission and purpose to fulfill in their public service.

CHAPTER 6

A Coalition of Christians

Reagan's presidency gave evangelicals a vital role in politics, but it did not bring them into the promised land. For some, this proved a bitter disappointment, in part because they had invested more hope into politics than it could deliver.

When Reagan nominated Sandra Day O'Connor to the U.S. Supreme Court in July 1981, fulfilling a campaign pledge to appoint a woman to fill the first vacancy that occurred in his presidency, conservatives cried betrayal, alleging O'Connor was an unreliable moderate (complaints that would later prove accurate).

Not that Reagan didn't try to add a conservative voice to the Supreme Court. When Justice Lewis Powell announced his retirement in 1987, Reagan nominated the brilliant former Yale law professor and federal appellate court judge Robert Bork to fill the vacancy. After the radical left launched a vicious campaign and defeated Bork's nomination in the U.S. Senate, Reagan nominated federal judge Douglas Ginsburg, who withdrew after revelations that he had smoked marijuana as a faculty member at Harvard. Finally, Reagan nominated Anthony Kennedy of San Francisco, a relative centrist who was easily confirmed.

Kennedy and O'Connor became the swing votes on the court, deciding the outcome on high-profile cases involving cultural issues like abortion and gay rights. O'Connor cast the critical vote upholding *Roe v. Wade* in *Casey v. Planned Parenthood* (1992). Kennedy would do the same in *Lawrence v. Texas* (2003), which struck down the sodomy law in the Lone Star State and laid the foundation for overturning the Defense of Marriage Act in *U.S. v. Windsor* (2013), with Kennedy writing the majority opinion in both cases.

For evangelicals, having Supreme Court justices who had been appointed by conservative Republican presidents cast the deciding votes upholding abortion-on-demand and striking down traditional marriage laws suggested that their strategy of political engagement might be flawed.

Reacting to Disappointment

Religious conservatives, like anti-slavery and temperance activists before them, found that victory at the ballot box did not solve the country's problems overnight. Like the Israelites who fled Egypt only to encounter the bitter water at Meribah (Numbers 20:1–13), religious conservatives complained about suffering on the journey and criticized their leaders for their cowardice and pride, and even the American people for their spiritual sloth.

In 1999 Cal Thomas and Ed Dobson, two early staff members of the Moral Majority, published *Blinded by Might*, in which they argued that leaders of the religious right had been deceived by "the aphrodisiac of political power," pursuing a misguided strategy of political engagement that had failed in its mission to ban abortion, strengthen the family, and restore traditional values.[1]

Paul Weyrich, one of the early architects of the New Right, declared the "culture war has been lost" and urged believers to withdraw again to their own institutions—churches, schools, and seminaries—to protect themselves against the contagion of immorality infecting the larger society. "Politics has failed," Weyrich concluded. "And politics has failed because of the collapse of the culture."[2] Sometimes the critique got personal. When Reagan reached an arms control agreement with Mikhail Gorbachev, Howard Phillips, chairman of the Conservative Caucus, called him "a useful idiot for Soviet propaganda."[3]

But the setbacks of the Reagan era did not mean the pro-family cause was lost or even that political engagement represented a wasted endeavor. It simply meant the successors of the founders of religious conservatism would rejoice one day at seeing what the founders saw only with the eyes of faith.

Today's evangelicals and faithful Catholics stand on the shoulders of Jerry Falwell, D. James Kennedy, Bill Bright, and others who have passed on to heaven and now surround us like "so great a cloud of witnesses" (Hebrews 12:1), urging us to finish the race they started. In His perfect timing and wisdom, God has allowed religious conservatives to go through a wilderness experience, just as he did anti-slavery and temperance advocates, so we could learn that achieving social change involves painful, incremental steps, not instant solutions. I believe He has done so to test our motives, purify our faith, and cleanse our hearts of any impure desire for power, fame, or recognition.

We want victory now, and in our way of thinking, two to three decades of social struggle ought to be sufficient. But that is not God's way, and He operates on the time clock of eternity. Moreover, except in cases of invasion or civil war, free societies can't be put in a microwave and zapped back to repentance. Social change takes decades, and the wheels of reform turn slowly.[4] America didn't get into its current mess overnight, and we won't be able to fix it overnight either. It will likely take decades of prayer, sacrifice, and civic engagement. To succeed in restoring our country, we will need perseverance and unity, praying that "the God who gives perseverance and encouragement grant you to be of the same mind with one another according to Christ Jesus" (Romans 15:5).

My Personal Awakening

The spiritual cycle or how I might play a part in the pro-family movement wasn't on my mind back on September 18, 1983, when I accepted Christ at Evangel Assembly, a church just outside Washington, D.C. I was then working at the Republican National Committee as executive director of the College Republicans, preparing to co-chair the youth effort of the Reagan-Bush reelection campaign.

I was no stranger to the claims of the gospel. I had been raised in a Christian home. My mother led our church's Methodist Youth Fellowship, and my father was chairman of the board of our church. My parents both grew up in the church, meeting at a youth group function in Miami. They married at the Methodist chapel at the University of Florida in 1958, and they named my younger brother after Methodist founder John Wesley. My best friend was my pastor's son, and I spent summers at a Methodist youth camp. But while I was around the church and experienced a heavy dose of "churchianity," I never had what I would call a personal encounter with Jesus Christ.

After graduating from high school in the small north Georgia town of Toccoa, where my family had moved when I was fifteen, I headed to the University of Georgia and immersed myself in campus politics, becoming chairman of the campus College Republican club. In general, campaigning for Reagan may have been difficult in Jimmy Carter's home state, but not among young voters. Our CR club grew to over five hundred members, making it one of the largest student organizations on campus. Reagan defeated Carter in the mock election at the University of Georgia by a landslide. It was a heady time to be a young Republican activist.

During the summer of 1981, I interned in the Washington office of newly elected U.S. Senator Mack Mattingly, the first Republican senator from Georgia since Reconstruction. Then I took the semester off and moved over to the Republican National Committee: I was a happy foot soldier in the Reagan Revolution.

As much as I enjoyed the immersion in politics and policy, there was something missing. I saw enough of the pretense of politics to know it would not satisfy my spiritual yearning. In August 1983, after an episode of drunken revelry at the RNC staff picnic, I quit drinking at the urging of a friend. A few Saturdays later, I was at dinner with friends at a Capitol Hill tavern when I suddenly felt compelled to go to church the next day. There was one minor problem: I had no idea where to go. Getting up from the table, I walked to the bank of pay phones in the hall and opened the yellow pages to "Churches—Evangelical." I found a church called Evangel Assembly and wrote down the address and phone number.

The next morning I drove to the church, walked into the sanctuary, and sat in a pew about midway back from the front. In truth, I had no real idea why I was there, and for a moment I thought of bolting for the door. I have no recollection of the sermon, the music, or the songs. When the preacher finished his message and proceeded with the altar call, I had no intention of responding. I simply wanted to dip my toe into the cool, refreshing waters of some old-time religion.

Suddenly the preacher turned to the organist and ordered him to stop playing. The sanctuary fell silent. "I don't know who you are or how you got here," said the preacher. "But whoever you are, you need to understand something: This is the day of your salvation. This is not an invitation; this is a command."

Somehow I knew the preacher was talking to me. I hadn't come to that suburban church to become one of those crazy, holy Christians. But I wondered: *If I didn't respond now, would I ever get another chance?* I raised my hand, approached the altar, and prayed with the pastor to receive Christ as my Lord and Savior.

Everything changed. Before, I had lived for the conservative cause, Reagan, and the Republican Party. Now I lived for Jesus. The first book I read after being baptized, other than the Bible, was *Born Again*, the post-Watergate memoir of Chuck Colson, founder of Prison Fellowship. Colson's spiritual journey inspired me to believe that, like him, I could make a difference for good if I relied on God to direct me.

Later, Chuck and I became friends and I benefited from his godly wisdom. When I worked at the Christian Coalition, I once asked him if he had any advice for me. "Stay on your knees," Chuck said. It was good counsel, and I have tried to follow it.

After graduating from Georgia, I spent two years on college campuses organizing for Reagan's 1984 reelection campaign. At that point I chose to pursue an academic career. In 1985, with plans to become a history professor, I enrolled in the doctoral program in history at Emory University in Atlanta. I married my wife, Jo Anne, whom I had met working on the Reagan campaign, in 1987. I thought I was done with politics. As I would soon discover, God had other plans.

Welcome Aboard!

In January 1989, I attended a youth event at the inaugural of President George H. W. Bush at which Pat Robertson was being honored. Pat and I were seated next to each other. I had admired Pat and had followed his ministry for years. Nevertheless, in part because I respected him, I shared with him what I viewed as the mistakes and miscalculations he had made during his recent presidential campaign. Whether Pat was intrigued by my precociousness or thought my points were valid, when the dinner was over, he motioned for me to follow him. We walked into the banquet kitchen as waiters and staff whisked past, carrying trays of plates and glasses.

Pat shared that Jerry Falwell was about to close down the Moral Majority and that he planned to start a new organization to mobilize evangelicals in the political arena. He asked me to come and work for the new group.

I was taken aback. I had known Pat for little more than an hour, and he was offering me a job. My mind racing, I said I was writing my dissertation and had to finish my doctorate before I could pursue other opportunities.

Pat said he understood and asked me if I would put together a memo of what the organization should look like in terms of structure and strategy.

I told him I'd be happy to write the memo. "How do I get it to you?"

Pat stepped onto an elevator. Flashing a broad smile, he said, "You know how to get hold of me." The elevator doors closed, and he was gone.

Actually, I had no clue how to reach him. But when I got back to Atlanta, I sat at my computer and banged out the memo anyway. As I composed it, I began to get excited about the untapped potential of evangelical and faithful Catholic voters to transform American politics. The more I wrote, the more convinced I became that a new faith-based organization could give Christians a greater voice in government, enact conservative public policy, and ultimately change the direction of the country.

The memo, dated February 2, 1989, suggested the opportunity before us: "There exists in American politics today a tremendous vacuum that must be filled. Estimates on the number of evangelicals range from a low of 10 million to a high of 40 million. Whatever the actual number, there is no constituency in the American electorate with greater explosive potential as a political force."

My memo recommended an ecumenical public policy organization with no theological litmus test for membership, a broad-based board of directors, state and local chapters, and a strong emphasis on grassroots training and precinct-by-precinct organizational structure. I put the document in a manila envelope with a cover letter and sent it to Pat's office in Virginia Beach—and heard nothing. I didn't know if Pat had even received it. I returned to my dissertation and started applying for college teaching jobs.

Then, more than half a year later, in September 1989, Pat called me out of the blue. He explained he had been busy restoring the Christian Broadcasting Network to sound footing following his presidential campaign, but he was now ready to launch the new political organization. He said he was having a meeting in Atlanta and invited me to attend.

About two weeks later I walked into a room at the Ritz-Carlton and found myself among Tim and Beverly LaHaye, D. James Kennedy, and other evangelical luminaries. I wasn't sure I belonged in such a distinguished group. At the end of the meeting, Pat introduced me as the first staff member of a group that as yet had no name.

Pat's announcement came as news to me. I offered a weak smile as the religious leaders looked at me. I pictured thought bubbles over their heads asking, "Who is this guy?"

When the meeting concluded, Pat walked over, his face lit up with a smile, and extended a beefy hand, chuckling. "Welcome aboard! You have no staff, no money, and no organization!"

I went home and informed my astonished wife that Pat had hired me and that we were moving to Virginia. After staying up that night talking and praying, we concluded it must be God's plan. Besides, my graduate fellowship at Emory had run out, and I needed a job. If it didn't work out, we reasoned, I could always return to teaching. Jo Anne quit her job, and we packed our meager possessions into a U-Haul, bundled up our baby daughter, and headed for Virginia. We had no idea what the future held. But we had faith in God, and we were confident we could make a difference.

Pat had solicited my ideas for a name of the group, so I put together a list of plain-vanilla names on the theory that we didn't want to unnecessarily offend with a name as triumphalist as the Moral Majority. Among those I recommended in a fax to him on September 29, 1989: "Partners for America," "Citizens for a Better America," and "Americans for Freedom." But Pat was not inclined to trim his sails.

The Christian Coalition

On vacation in Austria with his wife, Dede, Pat toyed with names while sitting at a café in Salzburg, scribbling on a napkin. Finally, he turned to Dede, saying, "We're Christians, and it's time we stopped apologizing for it. Christians are Americans, too, and the name of this organization should say so." Once Pat had *Christian*, the alliterative *Coalition* followed, and we had our name.

When Falwell closed down the Moral Majority the previous July, the media had celebrated its demise as a sign that the religious right was finished. "Rarely in modern times has a movement of such reputed magnitude and political potential self-destructed so quickly," historian Sean Wilentz wrote in the *New Republic*. The media gleefully (and prematurely, as it turned out) reported that the demise of the Moral Majority amounted to the obituary of the religious right as a political movement.[5]

We did not believe evangelicals were finished politically—far from it. Pat had a sign in his dressing room at *The 700 Club* that crisply summed up his philosophy: "Attempt something so big for God that unless He intervenes, you are destined to fail." That certainly described the Christian Coalition! At a meeting in May 1990, with our top state leaders at the Key Bridge Marriott just across the Potomac from Washington, we gathered to share ideas and plot strategy.

Pat asked me up to his suite to go over his remarks to the group. He sat at the dining room table with a legal pad, writing out our goals: ten million members, a $100 million budget, three thousand local chapters based in all fifty states, a pro-family majority in the U.S. Congress, a conservative religious president in the White House, and pro-family governors and legislatures in thirty states. I almost fell out of my chair.

Many of those goals would be achieved in the coming decade, most ahead of schedule. Pat taught me how to dream big dreams and trust God for the outcome.

Fueling the Coalition's Growth

As with the first phase of the religious conservative movement, the election of a president would fuel the rise of both the second phase and the Christian Coalition. Ironically, the person who deserves the most credit for our explosive growth is Bill Clinton.

After twelve years of Republican presidents in the White House, the American people had forgotten what it was like to have a liberal occupying the Oval Office. Clinton's decisions to raise taxes, to repeal the ban on gays in the military, and to push government-run health care had the cumulative effect of a booster rocket on our efforts. Our membership doubled from 250,000 to over 500,000 in the first year of Clinton's presidency. The phones rang off the hook, and the mail, most of it containing small contributions, came into the office by the truckload.

Not everyone was amused. When the Capitol switchboard lit up with over 250,000 phone calls opposing gays in the military, the *Washington Post* reported that Pat Robertson and his ilk had cattle-prodded their viewers to follow orders, which they were prone to do by virtue of being "poor, uneducated and easy to command."[6]

Clinton was not the only politician to inadvertently help our cause. Congressman Pat Williams, a Democrat from Montana, was incensed by our call to end federal funding of the National Endowment for the Arts after it funded exhibits that included sexually explicit photos of children and a crucifix immersed in a vat of urine, and he took to the floor to bitterly denounce the Christian Coalition. Also, after losing her seat to a Christian Coalition–backed candidate in 1992, South Carolina Congresswoman Liz Patterson held up one of our voter guides and, her voice quavering, accused us of violating the Ninth Commandment against bearing false witness.

The media reaction was borderline hysterical. One columnist referred to us as "Shiite Baptists," while *New York Times* columnist Frank Rich warned, "Make no mistake. The Christian Coalition is now a major political force that expects to dictate G.O.P. policies and have veto power over its '96 ticket in exchange for its support."[7] Not to be outdone, Barry Lynn, head of the liberal group Americans United for the Separation of Church and State, thundered, "Pat Robertson is a fundamentalist Boss Tweed, preaching morality at Americans while running one of the most venal political machines in history."[8]

Most of these attacks exaggerated the Christian Coalition's influence, often for self-serving reasons like fund-raising. Groups like People for the American Way used the bogeyman of the religious right to frighten their own supporters so they would write checks. Many of the trends of the 1990s—the emergence of state-based, reform conservatism; the GOP grassroots shifting to the right after the Reagan and Bush presidencies; people of faith running for office; a populist persuasion represented not only by the pro-family movement but also the Ross Perot phenomenon; and the election of a Republican Congress in 1994—*appeared* to be connected to the Christian Coalition, but in many cases were coincidental.

We also had our share of luck. Democrats, thinking they could win back disaffected moderates by demonizing evangelical Christians, attacked us as extremists when in fact our agenda was fairly mainstream. This strategy backfired, fueling evangelical turnout in 1994 and 1996 and increasing the influence of the Christian Coalition, while having the unintended consequence of making the Democrats appear anti-religious.

"Casting a Wider Net"

The Christian Coalition mainstreamed evangelical political involvement by broadening its agenda and incorporating taxes, spending, and welfare reform in its list of priority issues. Prior to that, social conservatives had been defined almost exclusively by issues such as abortion and school prayer.

Pro-family groups had always lobbied on other matters, but they tended to be defined by their work on abortion, gay rights, and school prayer. The Christian Coalition argued that, as important as abortion and religious freedom were, biblical principles apply to every area of life, including education, spending, welfare policy, and foreign affairs. We felt we could be more effective by advancing a broad agenda than being narrowly cast as a single-issue group. I unveiled our approach in the fall 1993 issue of *Policy Review*, a publication of the Heritage Foundation, in an article entitled "Casting a Wider Net."

It wasn't enough to just talk about a broader agenda; we needed new and compelling policy ideas. After some research, we found one such idea in a bill introduced by Congressmen Tim Hutchinson of Arkansas and Frank Wolf of Virginia that created a $500-per-child tax credit to reduce the tax burden on middle-class families. Our Capitol Hill lobbyists Heidi Scanlon and Marshall Wittman set up a meeting with Hutchinson, whom I found engaging and well informed. The Christian Coalition believed the intact family was the most successful department of health, education, and welfare in all of society, yet our government taxed it to death while at the same time subsidizing the birth of children outside wedlock through the welfare system. This was bad public policy and harmful to the family. The other aspect of the Hutchinson-Wolf child tax credit that appealed to us was the fact that it was pro-poor: because the tax credit was fully refundable, those who paid little income tax still received the benefit. In the fall of 1993, we announced that the $500-per-child tax credit was the Christian Coalition's top legislative priority.

Heads turned in the Washington policy community. No pro-family group had ever made a tax cut its top objective in Congress, and we had work to do. When I approached Newt Gingrich to ask for his support of the Hutchinson-Wolf bill, he told me I would have to persuade John Kasich, the ranking Republican on the House Budget Committee.

Kasich proved to be a hard sell. When I went to his office to make my pitch, he nearly came out of his chair. "You're just like everyone else," he said, arms waving. "All you want is goodies for your constituency."

Seeing the twinkle in his eyes, I discerned Kasich was testing my mettle. I replied that the federal tax burden now took one-fourth of the income of the average American family—ten times the tax burden in 1950. Our argument was one of efficiency: who could do a better job of spending that money—the moms and dads who earned it or bureaucrats in Washington?

Kasich said the cost was a problem. The child tax credit would reduce revenue to the federal government by about $25 billion a year, $250 billion over ten years.

"Republicans never raise the cost issue when Wall Street asks for a capital gains tax cut," I volleyed back.

Kasich, the son of a milkman, said he shared our desire to target tax cuts at the middle class. He promised to see what he could do. He also suggested setting the income threshold for tax credit eligibility at $100,000. I told him I was worried about getting into a bidding war with the Democrats for who could bash the rich. I believed all income that went to educate, shelter, clothe, and provide health care to children should be exempt from taxation, regardless of the family's income level. But Kasich wouldn't budge. I figured I had won the larger point and saw no reason to jeopardize the issue over what was, in the end, a minor difference. (The income cutoff was eventually set at $75,000 for individuals and $110,000 for couples.) The child tax credit became the centerpiece of the Republican alternative to the Clinton administration's budget.

After the GOP won control of the House and Senate in 1994, the child tax credit passed the Congress twice, only to be vetoed by Bill Clinton each time. After the budget standoff led to a government shutdown in late 1995, Gingrich and Clinton compromised, and the child tax credit finally became law. It was the deepest tax cut directed at middle-class families with children since World War II.

George W. Bush ran for president in 2000 promising to double the child tax credit to $1,000, and that provision was included in his sweeping tax package that became law the following year. The child tax credit, along with relief from the marriage tax penalty that we fought for, arguably remains the most bipartisan consensus item in the tax code. Even during the pitched budget battles between Barack Obama and the Republican House from 2011 to 2013, including the fiscal cliff (caused by the expiration of the Bush tax cuts in 2013) and the sequestration of funds, the child tax credit and marriage penalty relief remained intact.

Legislative Victories

When people say Washington is broken, what they really mean is they don't have a tool belt and aren't willing to fix it. Those of us who desire a spiritual awakening today should take note: Washington is still as responsive to change as the founders intended, which is to say slow, prodigious, and taxing.

The Christian Coalition had other legislative victories as well, which was not easy as long as Bill Clinton held the veto pen. We won passage of the Communications Decency Act, which protected children from online pornography. Although the Supreme Court later voided the law, we were able to salvage many provisions under existing federal child endangerment statutes, and George W. Bush's administration aggressively used these laws to prosecute cyberporn and child pornography. We successfully lobbied for passage of legislation creating the National Gambling Impact Commission, which documented the destructive impact the proliferation of casino gambling has on the family.

Working closely with pro-life organizations, we defeated attempts to repeal the Hyde Amendment and blocked passage of the Freedom of Choice Act, which would have codified *Roe v. Wade* in federal law. Most important, we helped pass the partial-birth abortion ban, the first federal ban on an abortion procedure. Clinton vetoed the ban, but George W. Bush signed it into law in 2003.

Our biggest and most important legislative victory, however, was working to defeat the Clinton health-care plan. This might have seemed unlikely terrain for an evangelical group, but we felt strongly that, if enacted, the plan would limit doctor choice for families, ration care, and lead to taxpayer-funded abortion.

In the fall of 1993, I met with Senator Paul Coverdell of Georgia, who warned that if Clinton's health-care plan became law, America as we knew it would be gone. Coverdell urged me to do everything we could to defeat it. I had my staff obtain a copy of the bill, took it home one weekend, and read it from beginning to end with growing alarm. The layers of bureaucracy, regional health-care exchanges, myriad taxes, and regulations looked as if they had been cooked up for a college seminar by undergraduates pulling an all-nighter.

Within weeks the Christian Coalition launched a $1 million grassroots and marketing campaign opposing the Clinton plan, including sending postcards with a preprinted message addressed to senators and congressmen to over seven hundred thousand households in key states and congressional districts. We also took out full-page newspaper ads with a Norman Rockwell–like painting of a child sitting on an examining table as a genial country doctor listened to his heartbeat through a stethoscope below the headline: "Don't Let a Government Bureaucrat in This Picture." Some Republicans on Capitol Hill toyed with the idea of offering a less offensive version of government-run health care as an alternative. But we denounced these proposals as "Clinton-lite" and pushed instead for outright defeat.

The Christian Coalition also supported the 1993 Religious Freedom Restoration Act (RFRA), bipartisan legislation passed by Congress in response to the so-called peyote case, in which the Supreme Court ruled that the government did not have to meet the highest legal standard when legislating restrictions on the practice of one's faith. The Religious Freedom Restoration Act, supported and signed into law by Clinton, was designed to prevent states and the federal government from passing laws that substantially burdened the free exercise of religion. The RFRA continues to be important because it forces the courts to put the burden of proof for any restriction on religious expression firmly on the government. Some legal strategists have speculated that it may also be the best opportunity for overturning the Obamacare mandate that religious and private employers provide health insurance that covers abortion-inducing medication and other morally objectionable services.

Giving Christians a Voice

By 1996 the Christian Coalition had grown to two million members and activists, with more than three thousand local chapters and affiliates in all fifty states and a total budget of $27 million. Our nonpartisan voter guides were distributed in more than one hundred thousand churches, reaching upwards of forty million voters each election cycle.

The Coalition was widely credited with turning out a record number of evangelical voters in 1994 and with helping to elect the first Republican House in forty years. A survey conducted by *Campaigns and Elections* magazine found the Coalition had operational control or was a significant presence in state Republican Party organizations in eighteen states. Between 1992 and 1996, our activists helped elect an estimated seventy-five new members of Congress, hundreds of state legislators, and roughly one thousand school board members, county commission members, and other local elected officials.

The Legacy of the Christian Coalition

We still lacked an American president who shared our values and would sign the pro-life, pro-family legislation we passed in Congress. But the Christian Coalition's real legacy was not just its legislative or electoral victories. In part because of our efforts, religious conservatives no longer had their noses pressed against the glass of the political system. They reasserted their historic role as agents of social reform, and they gained a place at the table and a voice in the conversation of democracy.

Those who criticized our desire to have a voice because we occasionally spoke with a raised voice—or because Jesus didn't die so we could have a place at the political table—missed the point. Some wanted to silence us; others saw our political involvement as a fool's errand unless it led to total victory. But our American citizenship does not guarantee victory; it promises the right to be heard, to exercise our constitutional rights as citizens, and to be a witness to those in power. This is our birthright as Americans, and we should claim it by acting on it.

When we began our work, many viewed the religious right as a passing phenomenon. No longer. Men and women of faith now play an enduring and vibrant role in our politics, and their participation is likely to remain as durable as labor unions, civil rights groups, the U.S. Chamber of Commerce, the AARP, or the National Rifle Association. As men and women of faith, we are unashamed of our views, we are unapologetic about our positions, and we are here to stay.

The Christian Coalition, however, made its share of mistakes, including me. I once bragged to a reporter after we won state legislative races in Virginia, unartfully employing a metaphor by saying our opponents didn't know what was happening "until you're being zipped into a body bag." Our critics quoted the line mercilessly, and I regretted the comment. I later apologized, advising our grassroots members to avoid harsh language that didn't reflect our spiritual mission or God's love.

A similar episode occurred in 1992 when we sent a letter from Pat to voters in Iowa urging them to oppose the Equal Rights Amendment. The letter included incendiary language that cited some feminist leaders who favored abortion-on-demand and overthrowing capitalism. It was a rookie mistake—and the media and our critics pounced. I had hurriedly edited the letter from a draft provided by our team in Iowa, and it hurt me to see my boss maligned. I was heartsick and apologized profusely to Pat. Ever gracious, he accepted my apology and said he was certain I had learned a valuable lesson, as indeed I had.

There were also policy differences and personal rivalries with other religious leaders that undermined unity and harmed our cause. While these were honest disagreements about strategy, I regret that those discussions were sometimes aired in public. Only when we as the body of Christ are truly of one mind—only when we leave our egos at the door—will we see our country restored. Even the early church leaders had strong differences, with Paul rebuking Peter at one point and refusing to travel with Barnabas. It is my fervent prayer that we make unity and humility a high priority in the years to come.

The Christian Coalition proved that when many predicted the demise of the pro-family movement, it can come back stronger than ever. The spiritual cycle turned in the early Clinton years, millions of people of faith woke up and got engaged, and they made a difference. The election and reelection of Barack Obama need not signal the decline of time-honored values in our nation. If men and women will put feet to their prayers and take action, we too can see an awakening in our nation that will restore America to its founding principles.

In 1997 I decided to leave the Christian Coalition, hanging my shingle as a consultant with hopes of being part of a campaign in 2000 that would put a committed Christian and conservative in the White House. It was a hard decision. Pat had been extremely supportive of me as well as Jo Anne and our young family. Pat was demanding and brilliant, with a great sense of humor and infectious enthusiasm, and working for him was a rollicking roller-coaster ride. But I couldn't play a formal role in a presidential campaign while working at the Coalition.

I didn't know who was going to be the 2000 presidential candidate who might best lead with the moral courage of our founders. But it wasn't long before the Lord put me in the path of the man I believe He had selected for the job. However, no one had any inkling of how much courage in the face of evil the job would demand.

Action Points

1. Like believers in the Reagan era, have you ever been disappointed that victory in the ballot box didn't result in immediate cultural change? Read Romans 15:5 and consider how our need for perseverance can test our motives, purify our faith, and cleanse our hearts of any impure desire for power, fame, or recognition.
2. Is your nose still pressed against the glass of the political system? Pray about some ways you could step up and play an active and vibrant role in politics.
3. Contact your local county's political party to find out the schedule of upcoming meetings. Attend a meeting by yourself, or with friends, to learn how you can become involved in current events and issues.

CHAPTER 7

A Man for the Job

One of the central truths of the spiritual cycle is the reality that evil and good prosper together in a fallen world. We believers are called to resist and combat evil with all our might. When and how that battle unfolds is not for us to know, but we are called to be faithful and ready. As are our leaders.

On September 11, 2001, President George W. Bush rose before dawn and began his day as he always did, reading the Bible and then going on a run accompanied by Secret Service agents. After jogging through the gated community where he had stayed the night before in Sarasota, Florida, Bush showered, reviewed the morning papers, ate a light breakfast, and sat down for his daily intelligence briefing. He then stepped into the presidential limousine for the short drive to Emma E. Booker Elementary School for an education event.

En route in the motorcade, White House senior adviser Karl Rove informed Bush that a small plane had flown into the north tower of the World Trade Center in New York City. Bush then took a call from Secretary of State Condi Rice, who informed him the plane that hit the tower was a commercial airliner. Stunned, he directed his staff to monitor the situation and prepare a public statement pledging the full support of the federal government to manage the emergency. Bush then walked into a second-grade classroom, where he took a seat and began reading to the assembled students from *The Pet Goat.*[1]

At 9:02 a.m., a second plane flew into the World Trade Center's South Tower, bursting apart in a flash of metal, flames, and exploding jet fuel. Chief of Staff Andy Card stepped into the classroom and whispered in Bush's ear, "A second plane hit the second tower. America is under attack."[2]

In an instant George W. Bush's presidency changed. Transformed from a peacetime president whose administration was focused on economic growth, education reform, combating poverty through compassionate conservative solutions, and creating a "culture of responsibility," Bush became a wartime president leading a global war on terror. He would leave office eight years later with the U.S. forces still in Iraq and Afghanistan, his approval ratings low, an economy in the throes of a Great Recession, and a financial system that required government intervention to save it from collapse.[3]

It was not supposed to be that way. When Bush announced his candidacy in March 1999, the Cold War had faded in the country's rearview mirror. Most Americans were oblivious to the threat of radical Islam and had never heard of al Qaeda or Osama bin Laden. The economy hummed along in spite of the Internet stock bubble bursting. A "peace dividend" had shrunk U.S. defense spending and, along with domestic cuts passed by Republicans in Congress, balanced the federal budget for the first time in forty years. The biggest domestic policy issue was how to spend the $5.7 trillion in surpluses projected over the next decade. A combination of Russian retrenchment, NATO expansion, UN cooperation, and targeted U.S. military engagement seemed to promise an era of peace and stability. There was little indication as he assumed office that Bush would soon preside over what some have termed a third world war.

Planting the Seed

George W. Bush's unlikely path to the presidency began in Midland, Texas, where he learned the importance of friends and family, risk taking, and the faith that would guide him the rest of his life. Bush had returned to Midland after graduating from Harvard Business School in 1975, and quickly dove into the oil business. With the help of investors and family friends, he founded Arbusto ("Bush" in Spanish) and began to drill wells in the oil patch of West Texas.

In a bizarre twist of fate, the Reagan administration had secretly persuaded the Saudis to increase OPEC production, flooding the market with a glut of oil and driving down its price, the objective being to choke off the Soviet Union's hard currency. This chess move squeezed the Russian economy and crippled the Soviet military buildup, but for those in the U.S. oil industry, the results were catastrophic. One of the victims was the eldest son of Reagan's own vice president. The price of West Texas crude cratered, sending the oil sector into a tailspin, and Bush was caught in the backdraft. Many wildcatters went bankrupt. Bush avoided that fate by selling Arbusto to an investment fund in 1985 and later merging it with Harken Energy, a public company. It was a challenging time in West Texas, with many at the end of their rope, searching for answers.

Among them was Bush, who had recently quit drinking, in part at the urging of his wife, Laura.[4] Bush had struggled with alcohol since early adulthood, and once he gave it up, he felt a spiritual yearning that would soon be filled with a personal relationship with Christ. He joined the Midland Community Bible Study, which taught daily prayer and modeling one's life according to Scripture, utilizing a "small group" approach that encouraged transparency and accountability, a program that was extremely popular in churches at the time. One of the men in the group who became close to Bush was Don Evans. He had also been caught in the riptide of the oil patch recession, and his life journey had brought him to a deeper Christian faith after his wife gave birth to a special-needs child. Evans would remain at Bush's side for the rest of his career as a friend and counselor, the chair of his presidential campaign, and a member of his cabinet. Encouraged by Evans and Mark Leaverton, who led the Bible study, Bush prayed to receive Jesus as his Lord in 1985.[5]

Ambassador to Evangelicals

In 1988 Bush moved with his family to Washington, D.C., to work full-time on his father's presidential campaign. Depending upon whom one talked to, Bush was Republican Party strategist Lee Atwater's wingman, his father's eyes and ears, or the enforcer. Because of his Christian faith, Bush also became his father's unofficial ambassador to the evangelical community, respected because he understood the culture and language of evangelicalism. Working with Atwater and Doug Wead, an evangelical campaign staffer, Bush advised his father on winning support in the faith community. Jerry Falwell signed on early, inviting Vice President Bush to deliver the commencement address at Liberty University. Bush also addressed the National Religious Broadcasters three years in a row and invited evangelical leaders like James Dobson and Robert Schuller to meet at the White House.

This effort paid off handsomely. In the general election, George H. W. Bush won 83 percent of the evangelical vote, the high-water line for a Republican presidential candidate in the modern era. This experience steeped the younger Bush in the dynamics, personalities, rivalries, and theological permutations of the evangelical movement, all of which would prove valuable in his own political ascent.

After his father's election, Bush wisely chose not to hang around the nation's capital as a lobbyist or straphanger. In a bold stroke, he joined a group that purchased the Texas Rangers, a team that had wallowed in the basement of the American League's eastern division for years. As general manager and part-owner, Bush soon proved to be an adept sports executive. But while Bush's business surged, his father's political fortunes flagged. Bush Sr.'s sky-high poll ratings after the Gulf War faded, the economy dipped into recession, and a budget deal that included a tax hike sparked a revolt on the right.

In February 1992, Ross Perot jumped into the race, transforming the campaign. Bush would later describe sitting in his office in Dallas, looking across the parking lot at the cars lined up outside Perot campaign headquarters, seeing them drive away with bumper stickers and yard signs, and realizing his father was in trouble.

He's Running

It was during this period that I first became aware of George W. Bush. When Pat Robertson's *700 Club* program conducted a viewer poll on the presidential race, we were stunned when Perot received 50 percent to President Bush's 47 percent. Alarmed, I sent a memo to the White House warning that Perot could siphon off evangelical support if the campaign did not direct a more robust effort at these voters. Chief of Staff John Sununu had always been our pipeline into the West Wing, but he had recently stepped down from that position, resulting in a series of staff changes. Lee Atwater's untimely death from a brain tumor had also left a vacuum on the political team, so it wasn't clear who was in charge. Hearing nothing back, I called a friend at the White House.

"Is anyone up there paying attention?" I asked.

"Don't waste your time," sighed my friend. "This place is dysfunctional."

I asked if my friend knew of anyone I could send the memo to who might have some influence with President Bush.

"Send it to Junior," said my friend. My silence indicated I had no idea who "Junior" was. "W.," he clarified. Again, I drew a blank. When he explained it was the president's son, I dutifully sent the memo to George W. Bush in Dallas, not knowing what to expect. Within a week I received a handwritten note telling me he appreciated the feedback and thanking me for my personal support of his dad. I made a mental note: this guy was sharp.

The next time our paths crossed came two years later when Bush was running for governor in Texas. The Christian Coalition had a strong grassroots organization in the Lone Star State, and our folks backed Bush early, helping him in what promised to be a bruising battle with incumbent Ann Richards. Most thought W. had bitten off more than he could chew, but we were impressed with him and thought Richards had underestimated him. We had previously helped turn out the evangelical vote in the 1993 U.S. Senate special election to fill the vacant seat of Lloyd Bentsen, who had joined the cabinet as Treasury Secretary. Kay Bailey Hutchison won by a landslide, and her victory was a telltale sign that the tectonic plates of Texas politics, dominated by the Democrats since Reconstruction, were shifting. Sure enough, Bush defeated Richards handily in the general election.

Because of the work of the Texas Christian Coalition, then under the able leadership of Dick Weinhold, I visited the state often while Bush was governor. I attended Texas Rangers games, met him at the state capitol, or shared a meal with him in Austin. A few times I spent the night at the governor's mansion. In these settings I found Bush to be far smarter and intellectually curious than his public persona suggested. He had a keen interest in public policy and razor-sharp political instincts. He was a committed Christian and a family man who loved his wife and daughters. I liked him and found he was a fun person to be around, playfully joking even as he expected excellence from those around him and always earning their loyalty. Since I had seen far too many campaigns riven by disloyalty to the candidate or competing personal agendas, the culture of Bush's world was a breath of fresh air.

As I've said, when I left the Christian Coalition in early 1997, a key reason was my desire to help elect a social conservative to the presidency. I had many friends mulling presidential bids, including Dan Quayle, John Kasich, Elizabeth Dole, and Gary Bauer. But I thought George W. had the stuff not only to win but to govern. I also believed that his Christian faith was genuine and that, if elected, he would help put the country on a higher moral plane and seek to enact sound family-friendly public policy, including lower taxes on middle-class families with children and pro-life measures. The day before I announced my departure, I was coincidentally in Austin.

While in town I had a meeting with Bush, Karl Rove, and Dick Weinhold in a hotel a few blocks from the state capitol. We talked shop and surveyed the Texas political scene. I did not volunteer that I was leaving the Christian Coalition or that I had my eye on Bush as a presidential candidate. When the meeting ended, Bush rose and we shook hands, our eyes locking. "I hope you're giving serious consideration to running for president," I said.

"I'm thinking about it," Bush replied. He leaned in closer, his face inches from mine. "I'm thinking about it *hard*."

I headed down the hall with Weinhold and got on the elevator. When the elevator door closed, I said, "I'm pretty sure he's running."

Dick burst out laughing at my understatement.

Work Out the Details

A few days after the 1998 elections, in which Bush had been reelected governor by a landslide, I was in Texas on other business and swung over to Austin to see Bush. When I arrived at the mansion, I sat down in the parlor just off the foyer, joined by Karl Rove. Bush breezed in from an event at the capitol. He surveyed the GOP field, sizing up each opponent with snippets of analysis. We discussed Al Gore, his certain general election opponent, as well as fund-raising and building the political team. Chuckling, Bush said he would have half his father's friends and all his enemies.

Turning serious, Bush said he wanted to bring new blood into the campaign, including people he had gone to Harvard Business School with or done business with over the years. The campaign would not be simply a reunion of retreads from the Reagan or the elder Bush's years, which struck me as smart. The campaign would be about the future, not a reboot of the past.

"You need two or three big issues when you run for president," Bush said, growing expansive. "I'll have an economic and tax piece, then education. The third will probably be Social Security reform."

"I get nervous about that last one," I said. Bush nodded, but he was clearly determined to tackle entitlements. When the meeting ended, we shook hands, and I said, "I'm here to sign on. If you run, I'm in."

"Glad to hear it," he said, bobbing his head in assent, not seeming in the least bit surprised. He nodded to Karl as if to say, *Work out the details.*

Tough Victory

Bush began his 2000 presidential campaign in a strong position. In early 1999 he led in the polls with about 50 percent of the Republican vote, with no one else breaking out of the teens; he raised $37 million in the first thirty-six days of the campaign, an unheard-of sum at a time when no one had raised more than roughly $25 million for the primaries.[6] During this period, I was in Austin for a meeting and asked Bush how he felt.

He replied that he felt as though he was being carried along by something greater than himself. There was something happening in the country, he said, a hunger for a culture of responsibility and an end to the idea *If it feels good, do it.* He paused. "I'm not afraid to lose. And I'm not afraid to win." He seemed to have an inner peace despite the challenges that lay ahead and the prospect that he might shortly become the leader of the free world. I knew that peace came from his faith in Jesus Christ.

The Challenge from McCain

Bush's coronation came to a halt in New Hampshire, where John McCain beat him badly. McCain, the maverick and media darling who had spent months holding town hall meetings in the Granite State, gained a head of steam.

I had earlier submitted a voter contact plan for turning out evangelical voters in South Carolina but had not received the green light from Austin. A few days after New Hampshire, I was pulling up to catch a plane at Reagan National Airport in Washington when my cell phone rang. It was Karl, and he asked if my plan would be all I needed to get the job done. When I assured him it was, he crisply told me to proceed and hung up.

I felt a surge of adrenaline. We had only two weeks to contact social conservative voters an average of five times each. Time was of the essence. Polls showed McCain had pulled even with Bush in South Carolina. A poll by John Zogby, who had accurately predicted the outcome of the 1996 election, showed Bush with 43 percent and McCain with 42 percent. We had built a voter file of about 80,000 evangelical households in the state, which translated into about 130,000 Republican primary voters. We sent out to these voters mail pieces that contrasted Bush's conservative, pro-life record with McCain's more moderate record. There was nothing stealth about what we did: one piece appeared in the *Wall Street Journal*, and another was held up by McCain in a nationally televised debate.[7]

In truth, McCain had only himself to blame for his failure to capitalize on his New Hampshire win. McCain made two major mistakes. First, in a pique he compared Bush to Bill Clinton, and in the aftermath of the Lewinsky scandal and impeachment, those were fighting words. Media consultant Mark McKinnon quickly shot an ad of Bush—he had the candidate pull off to the side of the road and walk to a wooded backdrop to record the commercial—taking McCain to task and saying it was "a low blow." The second miscue came when a reporter asked McCain if he wanted independents and Democrats to vote for him in the primary.

"Come, independents! Come, Democrats! Come, Libertarians and vegetarians! Come, all of you!" joked McCain to the laughter of the press corps. The comment offended conservative voters and caused McCain to lose altitude.

On primary night, Bush defeated McCain handily, carrying the evangelical vote (which was nearly 40 percent of the primary electorate) two to one.[8]

Post-Election-Night Victory

After his victory in South Carolina, Bush coasted to the nomination. Little did we know what awaited us in the general election—an election night in which Bush would be declared the loser and the winner within hours of each other, a recount in Florida that dragged on for thirty-six days, and the first presidential race in U.S. history decided by the Supreme Court.[9]

On election night I was in Austin when the networks initially called Florida for Al Gore at a surprisingly early hour. We were in shock, and the celebratory atmosphere at the victory party soon turned funereal. Then the news networks flip-flopped, putting Florida in the Bush column, and a group of us ran down Congress Street toward the governor's mansion expecting to hear Bush deliver a victory speech.

When Don Evans came out instead and read a brief statement saying the results were still inconclusive, we trudged back in the rain to the hotel, staying up until nearly dawn. When I stopped by the headquarters the next morning, I found Karl working the phones in his office to track results in Florida, and I walked past a conference room filled with attorneys conducting conference calls with other lawyers on the ground in the Sunshine State. Many scrambled to get to the airport to board private planes that carried them to the battle.

The next few weeks were surreal. It required a tough and battle-hardened candidate and team to prevail in the political and legal struggle that followed. Through it all, I never doubted that Bush had the character, conservative convictions, and the faith to do the job. Had he come up short in 2000, I would have been at peace that I had done the right thing by helping him. But I sure was glad (and relieved) that he won.

A Pro-Life Presidency

Once in office, Bush governed as the most pro-life president in history, helping the pro-family movement achieve many of our objectives, some of which had gathered dust through eight years of the Clinton presidency. Bush also reinstated the policy prohibiting the use of U.S. taxpayer dollars to promote or perform abortions in international family planning programs, signed a federal ban on partial-birth abortion, and vowed to build what Pope John Paul II had called a "culture of life." He appointed religious conservatives like attorney general John Ashcroft, chief speechwriter Mike Gerson, and Kay James, head of the Office of Personnel Management.

In the summer of 2001, Bush had to decide whether to use taxpayer dollars to fund embryonic stem cell research, which at the time required the destruction of a live embryo, raising ethical issues. The Clinton administration had halted the funding of the research until after the 2000 election. Millions with loved ones suffering from juvenile diabetes, Alzheimer's, and Parkinson's disease held out hope that embryonic stem cells, with their ability to reproduce rapidly, might hold the key to curing these dreaded illnesses. The pro-life community objected on the grounds that embryonic stem cell research might lead to the mass farming of embryos in order to harvest their stem cells, destroying some lives in hopes of saving others. Democrats falsely claimed that stem cell research would cure Parkinson's and cause paralysis victims like actor Christopher Reeves to "get up out of that chair and walk."[10] No matter what Bush did on this very emotional issue, he was certain to be criticized.

In a nationally televised address on August 9, 2001, Bush announced he would approve federal funding of embryonic stem cell research for cell lines that had already been developed, but he would not allow the destruction of additional embryos.[11] Bush was the first president to approve federal funding for these lines.[12] He also increased funding for adult stem cell research, which raised no ethical concerns, and appointed a commission on bioethics to advise his administration on future decisions involving medical research. Though attacked by critics who asserted he had put politics ahead of science, Bush's decision has been vindicated by medical research. Stem cell research did not provide the cures its advocates promised; the potential of embryonic stem cells was unreliable and unpredictable. In fact, adult stem cells have proven far more promising in research that might lead to cures to diseases like diabetes and Parkinson's.[13]

Nerve-Wracking Win

On Election Day 2004, I was sitting in a Wendy's along the I-4 corridor between Orlando and Tampa when the first exit polls appeared on the *Drudge Report*. They showed Bush losing decisively to Kerry in almost every battleground state, including Florida. I felt a wave of nausea, and it brought back haunting memories of similar exit polls in 2000. Soon my cell phone went off with calls from friends wanting to know if the polls were accurate. I quickly got on the phone with our political team and learned we had already exceeded our vote goal in every key county in Florida, and there were still six hours to go before the polls closed. That caused me to doubt the exit polls. I later learned from a Democratic friend that they were already celebrating at the Kerry campaign, whistling "Hail to the Chief" to Kerry, and canceling the candidate's few remaining television interviews, addressing him as "Mr. President-elect."

The remaining hours before the polls closed were nerve-wracking. At 7:45 p.m. I walked into the Hillsborough County board of elections office in Tampa, and one of our on-site attorneys monitoring the vote told me it would be a good night. He informed me Bush was already ahead by twelve thousand votes in the swing county of Hillsborough with only one-fourth of the vote counted. I got on the phone and discovered the same pattern prevailed in other parts of the state, including Miami-Dade, Jacksonville, the panhandle, and the Orlando suburbs.

A short time later I did an interview with Tom Brokaw of NBC. I told him that, based on what I had learned, Bush would carry Florida by a wide margin. I was worried that perhaps I had gotten a little too far over my skis with the bold prediction, but no one from the campaign complained. As it turned out, Bush carried Florida by 380,000 votes. Ohio was much closer, and the Kerry campaign chose not to concede, robbing Bush for the second time of an election-night victory lap. But it didn't matter. Bush won a second term by a decisive margin, and Kerry conceded with a gracious midmorning phone call the next day.

Chosen for the Moment

Bush's second term was dominated by Hurricane Katrina, sectarian violence in Iraq, the Valerie Plame controversy, the GOP loss of the House and Senate in 2006, and the financial collapse in 2008. Every president since World War II, including Obama, has seen their second term beset by trials and challenges. Eisenhower had Sputnik and a recession, Johnson had Vietnam, Nixon resigned over Watergate, Reagan had Iran-Contra, Clinton was impeached, and Bush had Iraq and a financial crisis. We will have to wait for a full assessment of his presidency by historians, but Bush was a man of devout Christian faith who brought to fruition many of the policy objectives of the social conservative movement: he upheld the sanctity of life, encouraged the delivery of social services by religious charities via his faith-based initiative, reduced the tax burden on the family by reducing the marriage penalty and doubling the child tax credit, stood firm in his support of Israel, affirmed traditional marriage, and appointed conservatives to the federal bench. I believe history will treat him kindly for protecting the homeland after the attacks of September 11 and keeping the U.S. economy strong and resilient during trying times.

If Reagan was the midwife of the pro-family movement, ushering it into the mainstream for the first time, then Bush was the groom, walking it down the aisle some years later. Whatever the verdict of future historians, George W. Bush is an important historic figure for this reason alone. The attacks of September 11, 2001, changed not only Bush's presidency but life for all Americans. Only twelve years after winning the Cold War, the nation found itself in a global conflict with an implacable foe bent on regional and global domination. The aftermath of 9/11 is a stark reminder that there is evil in the world, and we are called to combat it.

Bush's Policies

Bush's brand of compassionate conservatism is at low tide in Republican Party politics today, but his policies are not. Bush cut taxes three times—in 2001, 2003, and 2004—and never signed a tax increase. The extension of the Bush tax cuts was the central fiscal issue of Obama's presidency, and 90 percent of the Bush tax rate reductions remain in effect today. His modernization of Medicare, which included an affordable prescription drug benefit called Medicare Advantage and free-market reforms giving seniors more choices, remains the model for entitlement reform. (Much of this kind of reform was embodied in the Ryan Plan, the ten-year budget blueprint offered by House Budget Committee chairman Paul Ryan.) Bush's Social Security reform proposal to give younger workers the ability to set up personal retirement accounts, though never enacted while he was in office, still provides the best blueprint for reforming and saving that program.

Bush was not always right. He made his share of mistakes and miscalculations, as all presidents do. But he meant what he said and he acted as he promised, cutting taxes, reforming education to stress standards and close the achievement gap, modernizing Medicare, and fighting terrorism, including the state sponsors who funded the terrorists and gave them sanctuary. Even when he came up short, as he did in his efforts to fix America's broken immigration system, his consistency and clarity impressed even those who took a different view.

Bush's emergency plan to deal with the AIDS epidemic in Africa saved an estimated two million lives, bringing stability and hope to a continent too long overlooked in U.S. foreign policy. He was perhaps the most pro-Israel president in U.S. history, refusing to meet with Yasser Arafat after the Palestinian leader lied about his ties to terrorism, yet Bush also became the first president to call for the creation of a

Palestinian state. He restored honor and dignity to the Oval Office, a substantial achievement that did more for the American culture than any number of laws could have.

Finally, Bush kept America safe. Rather than waiting for terrorists to strike our shores again, he marshaled the full military and intelligence capability of the U.S. to fight terrorists in those states around the world that harbored them and funded them. While candidate Obama harshly criticized Bush's policies in fighting terrorism, as president he retained virtually all of them, expanding drone strikes, keeping the terrorist detention facility in Guantanamo Bay open, surging U.S. military forces in Afghanistan, and maintaining the NSA terrorist surveillance program.

During his presidency, Bush often found allies in unlikely places. The Bush tax cuts passed Congress in 2001 with the support of twenty-five Democrats.[14] His education reforms were supported by Ted Kennedy and Representative George Miller of California, two of the most outspoken liberals in Congress. When the U.S. went to war with Iraq, the Democratic leader in the House, Dick Gephardt, cosponsored the resolution authorizing military action, and twenty-nine out of fifty Democrats in the Senate voted for the resolution, including Hillary Clinton, John Kerry, Joe Biden, and the Democratic leader, Senator Tom Daschle of South Dakota.[15]

Bush's ability to reach across the aisle to Democrats and achieve bipartisan support for tax reduction, education reform, and the global war on terror contrasts sharply with the polarization that has characterized the tenure of his successor. Obama's economic stimulus plan passed the House without a single Republican vote, as did Obamacare.

Bush's Legacy

Some might think Bush ended up in the Oval Office by happenstance or that he was "selected, not elected," but I believe he was chosen for such a time to lead the West with moral clarity in the struggle against terrorism. Under his leadership, the federal government reformed and reoriented our armed forces, homeland security, the Justice Department, the FBI, and intelligence services to protect the homeland and maintain a forward-leaning posture in both covert and overt conflict with terrorists.

President Bush assembled the most impressive military coalition since World War II, liberated over fifty million people in Iraq and Afghanistan, and put al Qaeda on the run without the kind of grave violation of civil liberties that had characterized treatment of German-Americans or Japanese-Americans in previous world wars. Even those who disagreed with Bush's policies are likely to find that the contours and realities of the ongoing conflict with Islamic terrorism will be those established during his presidency.

Bush's presidency also reaffirms the fact that seasons of moral decay do not have to continue unabated. Many times they lead to a hunger for spiritual renewal, a desire for spiritual awakening among men and women of faith, and an earnest search for leaders who reaffirm the Judeo-Christian principles upon which America was built. Certainly that was the case with Bush after the Clinton years—and it may well be the case again among those of us who are eager to steer our nation toward a new awakening after the Obama era.

First, however, we need to think through those crucial issues that need our attention most urgently—beginning, as we will see in the next chapter, with the embattled institution of marriage.

Action Points

1. Consider this truth of the spiritual cycle: evil and good prosper together in a fallen world. What should we believers do in response to this truth? What does God require of us?
2. Read Romans 13:4. Ask God to raise up local, state, and national leaders who view their public service as that of "a minister of God to you for good."
3. Pray about whether God may be calling *you* to become a Romans 13:4 leader in your city or community.

Part 2

Off Course

CHAPTER 8

The Life of Marriage

During the 2012 presidential campaign, Barack Obama's team released an animated video titled *The Life of Julia* that chronicled the journey of a typical woman in Obama's America, aided by cradle-to-grave government assistance.[1]

The viewer follows an animated figure named Julia from age three to sixty-seven, observing how the government steps in at each stage of her life to help, with the narrator occasionally denouncing Republican attempts to make cuts in the programs. Julia goes to school and takes standardized tests. She becomes sexually active and obtains free birth control. She gets a job, starts a small business, works, and eventually retires. Along the way she benefits from Head Start, government-subsidized student loans, the federal minimum-wage law, the Lily Ledbetter Act, Obamacare, and Medicare. One thing she does not do is get married. This does not prevent her from having a child. The absent father never makes an appearance, lurking on the sidelines like an apparition, replaced by government bureaucrats—and President Obama.

In a scathing response in the *Washington Post*, Jessica Gavora criticized Obama's idealization of what she calls "the new Hubby State."[2] "Why should Julia get married?" she asks. "She doesn't need to. Like a growing number of single women with children, Julia is married to the state." Critics piled on, accusing the president of trying to win votes by glamorizing a world where women are wards of the state. Yet the strategy apparently had the desired effect: according to exit polls, Obama won 67 percent of the votes of single women, who comprised 21 percent of the electorate.[3]

Faulting the No-Fault Law

What do "Julia" and the issue of "the new Hubby state" have to do with the spiritual awakening this book is about? "Julia" is the archetype of a new generation. Her decision not to marry and to bear a child out of wedlock is now normative in the United States, a sign of the nearly complete collapse of the divinely designed institution of marriage.

The decline began decades ago with the introduction of no-fault divorce. Unilateral divorce exacerbated already dropping marriage numbers when it swept the country in the late 1960s and early 1970s. As a result, it is now easier in most states to forsake one's spouse than it is to cancel a gym membership or a cell phone contract. In California divorce boomed when the legislature passed, and then-governor Ronald Reagan signed, the 1969 Family Law Act. At the time, it was viewed as a positive reform that would reduce the animosity of divorce proceedings and assist women trapped in abusive relationships. But as Brad Wilcox points out, while it "eliminated the need for couples to fabricate spousal wrongdoing in pursuit of a divorce," it also "gutted marriage of its legal power to bind husband and wife, allowing one spouse to dissolve a marriage for any reason—or for no reason at all."[4]

Over the next twenty years nearly every state in the country copied California's no-fault law, ushering in a divorce revolution. During this period the divorce rate more than doubled. Whereas 20 percent of married couples who married in 1950 divorced, couples who married in 1970 divorced at a rate of nearly 50 percent. This had the natural effect of dramatically increasing the number of children who wound up in broken homes from around 10 percent of all children to just about half.

The California law triggered two generations of divorce on demand, leaving a toxic legacy of broken homes and poverty.[5] The Heritage Foundation noted in a 2012 report that only 6.8 percent of married, two-parent families live in poverty, compared to 37.1 percent of single-parent households.[6]

Decline in Numbers

Beginning in 1970, marriage took a beating that lasted for a generation. Only 13 percent of white adults aged thirty to forty-nine years were unmarried in 1970, but by 1990 that figure had more than doubled to 27 percent. And while the divorce rate leveled off and has since seen some decline, largely because of the Great Recession, it still remains twice what it was in 1960.[7]

Perhaps more troubling, marriage rates have plummeted by almost 50 percent in a single generation.[8] In tandem with the breakdown of the institution of marriage came the separation of marriage from childbearing. Increasingly, husbands became unnecessary, and children became optional accessories—and, with *Roe v. Wade*, disposable ones. These social trends gave rise to the phenomenon of the single mother and our modern-day Julia.

The number of American adults who are married—a number that has been in decline for decades—fell to a new low of only 51 percent in 2010. At current rates, within a few decades marriage will no longer be the norm for most U.S. adults. The main cause is young people delaying marriage. If young men even pop the question today, the answer is often not yes or no, but "not yet."

And these older brides and grooms have meant plummeting fertility rates. Nearly one in five women today will never have a child—a social phenomenon called "childlessness."[9] Of those women having children, more and more are having them outside of marriage, with nearly half of all babies born to unwed mothers.[10]

Cohabitation

Public opinion reflects these stark statistics about marriage. In a survey by the Pew Research Center in 2010, four out of ten Americans (39 percent) agreed that marriage is an obsolete institution. Who can blame them? Like Julia, they see a society where children are optional and the government meets needs once met by husbands and fathers. Most critically, our view of marriage has shifted from an institution providing economic security and social stability to a union between soul mates. Emotional satisfaction now ranks far higher than financial well-being for young people. In a 2001 survey over 80 percent of women said it was "more important to have a husband who can communicate his deepest feelings than bring home the bacon."[11]

This shift in values has positive aspects, creating more companionate, happy marriages. But it also has its downside. A society where men and women seek merely an emotional bond with a member of the opposite sex, rather than the shared sacrifice of a sacred union that brings children into the world, has misplaced priorities. There is a healthy tension between self-actualization and the demands placed on individuals by marriage and family. When men and women pursue personal satisfaction more than the shared life objectives of marriage, not only do the bonds of marriage fray, but the larger society breaks down.

In place of marriage, unwed unions of cohabiting couples are on the sharp increase, with more and more young people choosing cohabitation rather than marriage. According to the Centers for Disease Control, half of all women under the age of thirty have cohabited outside of marriage. Nearly half of the first unions in the United States are now unmarried cohabiting couples.

These unions are less stable and enduring than marriage. Their median duration is only 22 months.[12] Nearly half of cohabiting couples break up within five years.[13] These unions are not the rock-solid building blocks of an enduring society. Nor are marriages that occur after an extended period of premarital cohabitation likely to last longer or be happier than marriages without prior cohabitation. According to a study by sociologists Norval Glenn and Jeremy Ueker, "the greatest indicated likelihood of being in an intact marriage of the highest quality is among those who married at ages 22–25 years."[14]

The decay of marriage has also led to a large number of people who live alone. In 2011, 27 percent of all households were comprised of people living alone, a figure that has more than doubled since 1960.[15] *Home alone* is now the watchword for the U.S. and other Western democracies. As sociologist Robert Putnam demonstrated in *Bowling Alone*, this leads to a decline in social capital, about half of which flows from churches and other faith-based institutions.

While single life is fulfilling for a time, and certainly some people choose to be single in order to more fully serve God, all the social science demonstrates that it does not lead to the same happiness as married life.[16] "Two are better than one because they have a good return for their labor," the Bible teaches. "Furthermore, if two lie down together they keep warm, but how can one be warm alone?" (Ecclesiastes 4:9, 11).

The Marriage Gap

Those concerned about economic inequality in America should focus on the fact that marriage is now increasingly associated with advanced education and higher incomes. Marriage has made a striking comeback among the wealthy and well educated, as divorce rates have actually *declined* among the well-to-do. A woman's education level positively correlates with her odds of finding a quality spouse and directly impacts her children. Only 4 percent of children born to mothers with a college degree are born out of wedlock. But today's middle-American woman, with a high school degree or one to two years of college, has her first child on average more than two years before marriage. And 58 percent of their children are born out of wedlock.

This social phenomenon has been called the "divorce divide" or "the marriage gap." Kay Hymowitz in *Marriage and Caste in America* and Charles Murray in *Coming Apart* have demonstrated that the wealth gap in the U.S. is largely a marriage gap. As sociologist Brad Wilcox neatly summed it up, "Put simply, marriage is increasingly the preserve of the highly educated and the middle and upper classes."[17]

When Marriages End, Women Suffer

In 1991 Vice President Dan Quayle sparked a national furor when he criticized the female character in the hit television comedy *Murphy Brown* for bearing a child out of wedlock and glamorizing single motherhood as just another lifestyle choice. Nearly a quarter century later, Quayle's warning sounds puritanical to the ears of the millennial generation. But Quayle was right.

The social science on the lifestyle choice of single motherhood is clear and conclusive: single motherhood undermines women. Though the majority of single mothers in America are separated, divorced, or widowed, the number of women opting for motherhood without even taking a go at marriage is on the rise.[18] Almost half of all first births are to women who are unwed, and that number is over 80 percent for women who did not graduate from high school. By the age of thirty, two-thirds of all women will have had at least one child out of wedlock.[19]

Sadly, these women are on a path to poverty. One in four single moms has no health care, and almost 40 percent of households headed by single mothers are in poverty. Women are more likely to fall into poverty after divorce as well. The average woman sees a 73 percent reduction in her standard of living after a divorce, whereas her ex-husband typically sees a 42 percent rise in his. Perhaps this is because 40 percent of court-ordered child support is never paid, so women take on the financial brunt of raising children.[20] Somehow divorce and single motherhood came to symbolize freedom for women for the old-school feminist movement, but today there is no denying that when marriages end, women suffer.

When Marriages End, Kids Also Suffer

Marital breakdown exacts its hardest toll on children. According to a study by the Brookings Institute, if a person graduates from high school, gets married, and bears children within marriage, they have only a 2 percent chance of living in poverty. If they drop out of high school, do not get married, and bear children out of wedlock, they have a 77 percent chance of living in poverty.[21] (Rick Santorum frequently cited this study when he ran for president in 2012.)

In addition, a host of social pathologies afflict children from absent-father households. A child growing up without a father is nine times more likely to drop out of school, five times more likely to live in poverty, and twenty times more likely to end up in prison.[22] Marriage is also a safety net for the unborn, as well as those already born: in

2009, 85 percent of abortions were performed on women who became pregnant outside of wedlock.[23]

Marriage provides children with the foundation they need to build a good life and seems to prevent many social ills. Children raised by parents with a lasting marriage are far more likely to have a successful marriage themselves, bearing children within wedlock, and climbing the ladder of economic opportunity to the middle class. In this respect, it is impossible to have a middle-class agenda for America without having a marriage agenda.

Marriage and Men

Marriage is also better for men. More than thirty years ago, in his groundbreaking book *Wealth and Poverty*, George Gilder demonstrated that married men tend to work harder, earn higher incomes, accumulate wealth, obey the law, and contribute to the community more than men who are not married. Women civilize men and give emotional ballast to their lives. A wife and family impose upon men the responsibility to provide as well as give men opportunities to connect to the larger society. Whether coaching Little League, leading a Boy Scout troop, serving as ushers or elders in a church, or assisting in charitable organizations, men are more likely to play a positive role in their community if they are fathers.[24]

Untethered from marriage and family, men are more prone to antisocial behavior and violence. Sociologists have observed that 90 percent of violent crimes are committed by unmarried men.[25] The crime wave of the 1960s and '70s was due in part to the baby boom generation creating a demographic bulge of young, single men.[26]

In 2012 there were more black males in prison, on probation or parole, or otherwise in the criminal justice system than there were in slavery in 1850.[27] Nor is this phenomenon confined to the minority community, as increasing illegitimacy among whites has created a multiracial underclass. Sixty percent of those now on unemployment, almost half of those on food stamps, and 42 percent of Medicaid recipients are white.[28]

The Crisis of Fatherlessness

While running for president in 2008, Barack Obama delivered a forceful message on the crisis of fatherlessness, drawing on his own experience of being abandoned by his father and raised by his mother and grandparents. "We need fathers to realize that responsibility does not end at conception," he said. "We need them to realize that what makes you a man is not the ability to have a child—it's the courage to raise one."[29] Obama reiterated these themes in a commencement address at Morehouse College in June 2013.

As admirable as these speeches were, Obama has not aggressively pursued policies to strengthen marriage and fatherhood. Perhaps this is because he has been criticized by some African-American leaders for raising these issues.[30] But Joseph T. Jones of the Center for Urban Families argues, "The problem is so massive that we can no longer have private conversations. We need other people engaged in this conversation."[31]

What this discussion avoids is the elephant in the room: we cannot fix fatherhood without fixing marriage, and marriage won't be repaired by public policy or presidential oratory alone. It can only be solved when more men and women get married, stay married, and have children together. Illegitimacy, absent fathers, low educational attainment, child poverty, youth unemployment, delinquency, crime, and drugs—all these social pathologies flow from the breakdown of marriage.

Slighting the Sacrament of Marriage

For Christians, however, marriage is more than a social institution. It is a sacrament of their faith, a reflection of God's perfect plan for humanity, and the living embodiment of Jesus' love for the church and the church's devotion to Him. Jesus said, "For this reason a man shall leave his father and mother and be joined to his wife. . . . So they are no longer two, but one flesh. What therefore God has joined together, let no man separate" (Matthew 19:5–6).

This biblical plan for marriage has always been countercultural, and that is even more the case in today's culture of cohabitation, delayed marriage, divorce, and illegitimacy. Biblical marriage represents a complete inversion of what the world values: self-gratification, self-satisfaction, and the pursuit of one's personal desires. The world does not understand the Judeo-Christian vision of marriage, and we cannot expect it to do so. "This mystery is great," said the apostle Paul when writing about marriage (Ephesians 5:32). That is why marriage predated recognition by civil authority.

Unfortunately the Christian community in America has not lived up to this biblical standard. A 2008 study by the Barna Group found that the divorce rate for self-identified born-again Christians was virtually identical to the general population.[32] Yet research clearly shows that the vitality of one's religion increases happiness in marriage and lowers the incidence of divorce. Too many of our churches have grown cold, too many Christians are in loveless marriages, too many believers divorce, and too few churches and ministries take seriously the admonition that "what therefore God has joined together, let no man separate" (Matthew 19:6).

This is why the church has a critical role to play in strengthening marriage. My wife, Jo Anne, and I personally experienced the help our church provided us at a point in our marriage when we needed it. Too many churches today treat divorce as regrettable but inevitable, neglecting the biblical teachings about the intervention and discipline that can save marriages. Church members considering divorce should be required to undergo individual counseling as well as counseling as a couple to determine if there are biblical grounds for a divorce and whether the marriage can be saved. As believers, we must once again live as Jesus taught us, treating marriage as the most important single relationship in the human experience, one to be defended at all costs.

Courts and Same-Sex Marriage

The latest challenge to traditional marriage is the push to legalize same-sex marriage, an effort aided by activist judges who legislate from the bench. Without the courts seeking to impose by judicial fiat the most liberal marriage laws in Western civilization, same-sex marriage would not have progressed as far as it has in America. At this writing, only sixteen countries have legalized same-sex marriage.[33] In the United States, nearly two-thirds of the population live in states where marriage is defined as the union of a man and a woman.

But in 2003 the Supreme Court overturned a Texas sodomy law, finding that consensual homosexual relations between adults is protected by the right to privacy. At the time, Antonin Scalia asked in a withering dissenting opinion: If engaging in the conduct itself is a constitutional right, by what argument can gays be denied the right to marriage? Scalia's warning was prescient. In 2004 the Massachusetts high court, citing the Supreme Court's *Lawrence* decision, ordered state officials to grant marriage licenses to same-sex couples. This trend has accelerated, from California to Iowa to Washington, D.C., and New Jersey. Of the sixteen states with same-sex marriage laws, eleven have adopted them by legislation or referendum, with the remaining five states imposed by state courts.[34]

Then, in the aftermath of the Supreme Court's decision in June 2013, overturning the Defense of Marriage Act and allowing a California lower-court decision legalizing same-sex marriage to stand, the ACLU and other organizations have filed suit in Pennsylvania, attempting to use the precedent to overturn other traditional marriage laws. The gay lobby will soon hit a wall in terms of the number of states it can flip to its side in the political process, so it is using the courts to accomplish by edict what it cannot win in the marketplace of ideas or the democratic process.

Same-sex marriage has become the cause *du jour*, advanced by the media, Hollywood, and the far left. Those who object are subjected to the classic tactics of being labeled intolerant, bigots, and homophobes. Occasionally this persecution turns vicious. When California voters passed Proposition 8, the gay lobby counterattacked by picketing churches, outing donors to pro-traditional marriage groups, boycotting businesses, and threatening violence. One donor to the pro-traditional marriage committee was fired from his job at a community theater, while others unlisted or changed their phone numbers to protect themselves from harassing, threatening calls. Nor was this persecution confined to the Golden State. In violation of federal law, an IRS employee leaked the donor list of the National Organization for Marriage to gay lobbyists, subjecting its donors to personal attacks and abuse.[35]

The objective is to silence Christians. Opinion elites assert that gay marriage is the future and that its progress is unstoppable, despite the fact that nearly half of all Americans oppose gay marriage and thirty-three states have adopted laws that protect traditional marriage.

Even so, nearly three-quarters of Americans—including the majority of its opponents—believe that gay marriage is inevitable.[36] This attitude comes largely because 70 percent of millennials favor gay marriage. They have grown up with homosexuality portrayed as normative and celebrated in popular culture through films like *As Good As It Gets*, music, and hit television programs like *Will and Grace*, *Brothers and Sisters*, *Sex in the City*, and *Modern Family* with gay characters and plot lines affirmed as positively as Norman Lear's situation comedies from the 1970s glamorized feminism, single motherhood, and abortion.

Motivating the Marriage Battle

The evangelical and faithful Catholic response to the marriage debate is not motivated by animus toward gay Americans. Far from it! The issue is first about fidelity to our faith. Second, it is about protecting the essential role that marriage plays as the central procreative and socializing institution in society. Our faith teaches that "God made them male and female" (Mark 10:6), with distinct and complementary roles in their relationship and in raising children.

Cultural anthropology makes clear that mothers and fathers have very different parenting skills and styles. The social science is inconclusive about the socializing effect of gay households on children. Despite the roughly one hundred thousand gay households in the U.S., the trajectory of our culture will still be determined largely by those heterosexual couples who represent more than 90 percent of the households in America.[37]

What, then, is the role of the faith community in this age of divorce, cohabitation, illegitimacy, and gay marriage? We lost a measure of moral authority on marriage when we allowed the divorce revolution to sweep our country in the 1970s. That is why our most urgent task is to build more marriages in which husbands and wives exemplify both the sacrifice of Jesus for His church and the church's love for Him. Until we in the Christian community take bold action to save marriages by reforming unilateral divorce and upholding a higher standard among heterosexual couples, it will be more difficult for us to be effective in our efforts to preserve traditional marriage.

There have been some attempts to reform the law so that it supports keeping marriages together. In the 1990s legislatures in Louisiana and several other states passed "covenant marriage" statutes giving couples the option to choose a "covenant" union that created a higher legal bar for dissolution. Unfortunately, such laws have had little impact on the broader social trends undermining marriage. But the law can be a teacher, so no-fault divorce laws should be rewritten to make it more difficult to end a marriage unless both parties agree. Still, public policy can play only a limited role in restoring marriage. Laws can make it more difficult for men to abandon wives and children, but laws cannot force wives and husbands to love each other. If the faith community is serious about strengthening marriage, we need a comprehensive strategy that begins in our homes and churches and extends to legislatures and Congress to fix what ails traditional marriage. Sadly, we who call ourselves Christians have done more damage to this sacred institution over the past half century than the gay community.

I do, however, remain optimistic that we will rise to this challenge. One thing is certain: if we want to bring about the spiritual awakening that will restore our nation to its founding principles, it must begin in our marriages, our homes, and our families. If we truly want to see God move in our day, then let it begin with us, in our relationship with our spouses and our children.

If we do, the awakening will pour out of our homes and churches and into the larger society, with striking results. Certainly, in the realm of race relations and eradicating poverty, that is desperately needed.

Action Points

1. Get involved in a ministry dedicated to strengthening marriage. Faith and Marriage Ministries (www.faithandmarriage ministries.org) and Better Marriages (www.bettermarriages.org) are two such ministries.
2. If your church does not already have one, talk to your pastor about the need for a marriage restoration ministry in your church that will work and pray to restore marriages in need of help.
3. Invite another couple over to watch *Fireproof*, an inspiring film about marriage restoration (available on DVD at www.fireproofthemovie.com).

CHAPTER 9

Overcoming Racism and Poverty

I pointed out in chapter 2 that racism and slavery were America's original sin. Without full repentance and restitution, sin has a way of coming back to haunt future generations, so to speak, of those who sinned.

On the night of February 26, 2012, seventeen-year-old Trayvon Martin, an African-American high school student from a suburb of Miami, was shot and killed by George Zimmerman in Sanford, Florida. Martin had been raised by a single mother after his parents divorced. He had been in trouble at school, suspended for possessing drug paraphernalia and what police suspected was stolen jewelry. At the time of his death, Martin was on suspension and staying with his father. As Martin walked home from a convenience store, Zimmerman, who was on the lookout after a spate of burglaries in the neighborhood, became suspicious. He called police, stuck a pistol in his waist, and followed Martin. He claimed Martin assaulted him after a verbal altercation and that he fired his weapon in self-defense.[1]

Police questioned Zimmerman but released him. The African-American community exploded, and after six weeks of rallies and of Hollywood and sports celebrities donning "hoodies" to show solidarity with Trayvon Martin (he was wearing one at the time of his death), police charged Zimmerman with second-degree murder. After a two-week trial in July 2013, a jury acquitted Zimmerman of all charges. The Rev. Al Sharpton held protest rallies in one hundred cities; protesters in Oakland, California, burned an American flag and vandalized a police car; and in Baltimore, Maryland, a gang of youths beat a Hispanic man while chanting, "This is for Trayvon!"[2]

Conservative African-American commentator Shelby Steele denounced Sharpton and Jesse Jackson as race hustlers. "The purpose of today's civil-rights establishment is not to seek justice," contended Steele, "but to seek power for blacks in American life based on the presumption that they are still, in a thousand subtle ways, victimized by white racism."[3]

Offering a very different take, President Obama said, "Trayvon could have been me thirty-five years ago." Speaking of the pain felt in the black community, Obama added, "There are very few African-American men who haven't had the experience of being followed" or "walking across the street and hearing the locks click on the doors of cars." He pointed to "a history of racial disparities in the application of our criminal laws—everything from the death penalty to enforcement of our drug laws." On a note of optimism, he argued that race relations were improving, and "along this long, difficult journey, we're becoming a more perfect union—not a perfect union, but a more perfect union."[4]

A month before the Zimmerman verdict, the Food Network dropped celebrity chef Paula Deen from its broadcasts, and Walmart yanked her kitchen products from its shelves after she acknowledged in a deposition in a racial discrimination lawsuit that she had used the N-word years earlier. Deen also admitted that she had proposed dressing up African-American waiters as slaves for a wedding catered by her restaurant. As the controversy threatened to sink her culinary empire, she appeared on the *Today* show to tearfully apologize. Jimmy Carter, a close friend, came to her defense. But corporate sponsors canceled their relationship. Even though the lawsuit was eventually dropped, Deen had to scramble to contain the damage.[5]

Why Race Haunts Us

Why is America still haunted by the issue of race? Why does what Daniel Patrick Moynihan called the "racist virus in the American bloodstream" still afflict us?[6] One hundred and fifty years after Appomattox, racial tensions still flare with regularity. In 2007, radio personality Don Imus was fired from his syndicated radio show and dropped by MSNBC after he referred to female African-American college basketball players as "nappy-headed hos."[7] Race hangs over the criminal justice system like a specter. The O. J. Simpson trial carried heavy racial overtones, with whites and blacks viewing his acquittal differently. In 1992 the acquittal of white police officers after the beating of Rodney King sparked riots that left South Central Los Angeles in flames, fifty-three people dead, and thousands injured. King appeared before cameras and famously pleaded, "Can we get along?"

A generation later this plea still awaits an answer. And because we have never fully repented for the injustices and wrongs done during slavery and segregation, we have never experienced the healing that comes through the redemptive process of repentance and forgiveness. Until we do, we will not fully experience the spiritual awakening our nation so desperately needs.

The first slaves arrived in the New World in 1619, a year before the *Mayflower* landed. Captured in Africa and transported to America in an Atlantic passage so inhumane that many died, these slaves planted and harvested the cotton and tobacco that made whites wealthy and powerful. Yet upon arriving in America, slaves were beaten, their families divided, and their daughters and wives raped; slaves worked in the harsh conditions and were denied the opportunity to learn to read or write. Historian Edmund Morgan has pointed out that the same founders who led the American Revolution and built a new nation on the concept of freedom and liberty tolerated a system of slavery that denied freedom to millions.[8]

This evil required justice. Frederick Douglass proclaimed in 1862 that the Civil War represented God's judgment.[9] That same year Julia Ward Howe penned the "Battle Hymn of the Republic," the opening stanza of which equated the Civil War with God's wrath and the Second Coming.[10] Many of her fellow believers believed that before freedom dawned, bloodshed must purify the country.

Abraham Lincoln also saw divine judgment in the war.[11] In his second inaugural address, he cited God fourteen times. Slavery, he contended, was "one of those offenses which, in the providence of God, must needs come," but which God now willed removed. Lincoln saw a bloody symmetry between the carnage of war and the violence of slavery:

> Fondly do we hope, fervently do we pray, that this mighty scourge of war may speedily pass away. Yet, if God wills that it continue until all the wealth piled by the bondsman's two hundred and fifty years of unrequited toil shall be sunk, and until every drop of blood drawn with the lash shall be paid by another drawn with the sword, as was said three thousand years ago, so still it must be said "the judgments of the Lord are true and righteous altogether."[12]

Blacks shared Lincoln's view. "To most of the four million black folk emancipated by the civil war, God was real," noted W. E. B. DuBois. They likened themselves to the Hebrew slaves fleeing Egypt, God's hand dividing the Jordan River to clear a path for their escape, and they viewed Jesus as their Redeemer and Deliverer. Negro spirituals resounded with the promise that the day of freedom would come.[13]

Godly Civil Rights

Emancipation, however, did not bring full equality. After Reconstruction, white Democratic rule was restored. The Ku Klux Klan began a reign of terror to keep newly freed blacks in their place, while Jim Crow laws that emerged in the 1880s and 1890s consigned blacks to second-class citizenship for another century. It would take the 1960s civil rights movement to complete the unfinished work of the Civil War.

Martin Luther King's "Letter from a Birmingham Jail" echoed many of the themes of judgment and redemption found in Lincoln's second inaugural address. White preachers condemned King and other black preachers for meddling in politics. King did not back down, replying, "Injustice anywhere is a threat to justice everywhere." King often quoted the prophet Amos: "Let justice roll down like waters and righteousness like an ever-flowing stream" (Amos 5:24), an implicit criticism of America for its mistreatment of minorities and the poor.[14]

By 1967, when he began also to criticize the Vietnam War, King was more direct, warning that "our failure to deal positively and forthrightly with the triple evils of racism, economic exploitation, and militarism" would "lead to national disaster." A nation whose "pillars were solidly grounded in the insights of our Judeo-Christian heritage" had "strayed to the far country of racism and militarism." God's judgment would not tarry. "Tomorrow may be too late," King cautioned.[15]

The Apologetic Church

Billy Graham shared King's concerns about race in America. He had stopped holding segregated crusades as early as 1952, two years before the Montgomery bus boycott. He cited a sociologist who predicted in 1965 when race riots tore through Los Angeles that America would be plunged into a race war within a few years. As was often the case, Graham urged not civil rights legislation but rather "a vital personal experience with Jesus Christ on the part of both races" that would tear down "the middle wall of partition" until there is "no black, white, yellow, or red." Otherwise, he feared social chaos in which "the racial tensions will increase, racial demands will become more militant, and a great deal of blood will be shed."[16]

Not everyone was as apocalyptic as Graham, but people of faith often equated America's race problem with sin and judgment. This could be seen when Mike Huckabee, then governor of Arkansas, argued on the fortieth anniversary of the desegregation of Little Rock High School in 1997 that Arkansas had struggled with economic deprivation in part because of its failure to fully repent of its past. Like Graham, Huckabee called for a spiritual awakening. "Government can do some things, but only God can change people's hearts," he noted. "Essentially, it's not just a skin problem; it's a sin problem." Comparing the people of Arkansas to the children of Israel, he said, "In many ways Arkansas and the rest of the nation have wandered for forty years in the wilderness as it relates to race relations." The time had come to repent. "And I think today we come to say once and for all that what happened here forty years ago was simply wrong," Huckabee said. "It was evil, and we renounce it."[17]

In 1995, in a similar impulse, the Southern Baptist Convention issued a formal apology for its complicity in slavery, segregation, and racism. "Many of our Southern Baptist forebears defended the right to own slaves," the resolution acknowledged, and "participated in, supported, or acquiesced in the particularly inhumane nature of American slavery." The Southern Baptists confessed failing to support "legitimate initiatives to secure the civil rights of African-Americans" and apologized for "condoning and/or perpetuating individual and systematic racism." The resolution denounced racism as a "deplorable sin" that "profoundly distorts our understanding of Christian morality." [18]

In 2012 the Southern Baptists elected New Orleans pastor Fred Luter as the first black president in its history. The SBC's repentance for its racial past was part of a broader shift among religious conservatives to make racial reconciliation a priority. In the 1990s, the Christian men's group Promise Keepers worked through black churches and featured African-American preachers at its men's events, which packed stadiums nationwide, while the Christian Coalition's Samaritan Project raised $1 million to rebuild black churches burned by the forces of hatred and bigotry.

Critics argued these apologies were too little, too late, pointing out that white evangelicals had been on either the sidelines or the wrong side of the struggle for civil rights, and their past silence undermined their moral authority when they reentered politics in the 1970s. This charge was not entirely fair. Pat Robertson, for instance, hired an interracial couple to appear on his television program in the 1960s, and the charismatic renewal broke down barriers within evangelicalism that divided blacks and whites, in keeping with the multiracial roots of the Pentecostal movement.

But, sadly, it was true that some of the same Christians who called for civic engagement over abortion in the 1970s took a different position when the issue was civil rights. In 1964, Jerry Falwell preached against the political involvement of black churches at the forefront of the civil rights movement and criticized President Johnson for urging Christians in the South to support passage of the Civil Rights Act. The

Congress on Racial Equality (CORE) targeted Thomas Road Baptist Church for protests and sit-ins. (Falwell would later say that his stand against civil rights was among his greatest regrets.[19]) More common was the approach of Billy Graham, who was sympathetic to the civil rights movement and befriended Martin Luther King, preaching a revival in New York City with him in 1957. King understood that their roles, while different, were ultimately complementary. "You stay in the stadiums, Billy," King told Graham, "because you will have far more impact on the white establishment than you would if you marched in the streets." And so Graham did.[20]

The Less-Than-Great Society

Did slavery and segregation contribute to the persistence of a permanent minority underclass in America? The question has vexed social scientists for decades. In 1965, Daniel Patrick Moynihan, then assistant secretary of labor, argued that there was a definitive connection between the breakdown of the black family and poverty.

Pointing to what he characterized as the emasculation of the African-American male by the brutal practice of separating him from his wife and children during slavery and the humiliation of segregation, Moynihan argued that "these events worked against the emergence of a strong father figure" and that, as a result, "the Negro family made but little progress towards the middle-class pattern of the present time." The report found that female-headed households comprised one-fourth of all African-American families, while the rate of out-of-wedlock births among blacks had skyrocketed to 23.6 percent. Today that statistic seems almost quaint, but Moynihan warned of a "tangle of pathology" typified by "Negro youth growing up with little knowledge of their fathers," educational attainment plummeting, crime and delinquency rampant, and the inner cities filled with slums lacking jobs or intact families.

The consequences, Moynihan claimed, would be catastrophic: "There is one unmistakable lesson in American history. A community that allows a large number of men to grow up in broken families, dominated by women, never acquiring any stable relationship to male authority, never acquiring rational expectations about the future—that community asks for and gets chaos."[21]

The Moynihan report unleashed a national furor. Critics accused him of perpetuating stereotypes of blacks, blaming the victim, even racism. *Time* magazine called him a "renegade liberal" while conservatives cheered his findings, mislabeling him a "neoconservative."[22] Moynihan had taken the problem of poverty and turned it on its head, arguing that social conditions determined economic status.

A few months earlier, in his 1965 State of the Union address, Lyndon Johnson had called for the creation of a "Great Society" free from the scourge of poverty, racism, and social inequality. In lofty language, he challenged Congress to make the American dream accessible to everyone:

> We worked for two centuries to climb this peak of prosperity. But we are only at the beginning of the road to the Great Society. Ahead now is a summit where freedom from the wants of the body can help fulfill the needs of the spirit. We built this Nation to serve its people. We want to grow and build and create, but we want progress to be the servant and not the master of man. We do not intend to live in the midst of abundance, isolated from neighbors and nature, confined by blighted cities and bleak suburbs, stunted by a poverty of learning and an emptiness of leisure. The Great Society asks not how much, but how good; not only how to create wealth, but how to use it; not only how fast we are going, but where we are headed.[23]

Johnson vowed to double the resources devoted to the war on poverty, extend the minimum wage, tackle disease, save America's inner cities, provide affordable housing to the poor, improve education, and reduce crime. In a flurry of reform not seen since the New Deal, Johnson—perhaps the most skilled legislative leader ever to occupy the Oval Office—rammed through Congress the Voting Rights Act, Medicare, Medicaid, the Elementary and Secondary Education Act, the Clean Air Act, the Fair Housing Act, and the creation of the Office of Economic Opportunity. It was the apex of liberal triumphalism, when many believed that if the government threw enough resources at a problem it could solve it. Ironically, in the same speech, LBJ called for across-the-board income tax cuts and spending cuts to eliminate wasteful spending. His 1969 budget would be the last to balance for thirty-nine years.

At the time Johnson launched the Great Society, roughly 15 percent of the American people lived in poverty. In a fateful move, his administration decided to sidestep the controversy swirling around the Moynihan Report, shelving plans to address the plight of the family and ignoring Moynihan's recommendations. When the White House sponsored a high-profile conference on civil rights, aides excluded the topic of the disintegration of the family from the agenda to avoid provoking the ire of liberal critics.[24]

Anti-Poverty Programs

In the forty-nine years since LBJ's declared war on poverty, the United States has spent a total of $15 trillion dollars on anti-poverty programs.[25] In spite of those massive expenditures, and in some cases because of them, the poverty rate has not moved. According to the U.S. Census Bureau, 15 percent of the American population lives below the poverty level, including more than one out of every five children. We declared war on poverty, and poverty won.[26]

The grand experiment to reduce poverty by redistributing wealth was an utter failure. Today the median household income has fallen 8 percent from four years earlier, and from 2009 to 2010, fully 28 percent of the U.S. population fell below the poverty line. Median household income remains stubbornly low. The only group that has done well is the most prosperous. The top quintile of Americans in terms of wealth have seen their average net worth double, while the bottom fifth has seen their incomes fall and their indebtedness rise.[27] The wealth gap between whites and minorities has grown wider under the first African-American president than at any time in our history; today, the average white family has nearly six times the wealth of the average African-American family.[28] This disparity in education, income, and wealth, as well as the growing gulf between the haves and the have-nots, remain unfinished business for our country, but we can only bridge that gulf by addressing the social and behavioral sources of poverty.

A major factor contributing to poverty remains rising illegitimacy, which has grown worse since Moynihan wrote his report. The out-of-wedlock birth rate of 23.6 percent among African-Americans that shocked Moynihan a half century ago now stands at 73 percent, while among Hispanics it is 53 percent, and among whites the out-of-wedlock birth rate is 29 percent, higher than it was for blacks in the 1960s. Not surprisingly, the epidemic of illegitimacy closely tracks the decline in marriage over the past fifty years, as detailed in chapter 8.

"These demographic trends are stunning," notes a recent report by the Urban Institute. While concluding that the decay of the traditional family across all ethnic groups indicates causes not confined to the black community, the report found "the consequences of these trends may be felt disproportionately among blacks as black children are far more likely to be born into and raised in father-absent families than are white children."[29]

The rise of the suburbs, the failure of court-ordered busing, and the resegregation of society have fueled these trends, creating urban pockets in which families have disintegrated, fathers are absent, and there are few economic institutions (banks, shopping malls, and the like) that many whites take for granted. William Julius Wilson has demonstrated that in certain sections of America work has literally disappeared, creating urban landscapes devoid of jobs, quality schools, opportunity, and access to basic services.[30]

This is the civil rights issue of our time. If we, as the faith community, take the lead on extending educational and economic opportunity to all, it will not only help lift millions out of multigenerational poverty, but we will have renewed our moral authority for other issues as well.

Cultural Inequality

In *Coming Apart*, Charles Murray documents the gulf separating the well-to-do and poor in America, due primarily to the decline of marriage and high out-of-wedlock birthrates. The result is a virtual life sentence to economic disenfranchisement for the working class. As discussed in chapter 8, marriage is the most successful anti-poverty program in history. The data paints a stark picture. According to the U.S. Census Bureau, only 9 percent of married couples with children are poor, while over 40 percent of absent-father households are below the poverty line.[31]

This shift in values and public policy began with the Great Society. "The reforms of the 1960s jump-started the deterioration," argues Murray. "Changes in social policy during the 1960s made it economically more feasible to have a child without a husband," obtain public assistance without having to work, engage in criminal behavior without fear of punishment, and generally "easier to let the government deal with the problems in your community that you and your neighbors" used to handle. In the end, the Great Society failed because it tried to assign to the federal government responsibility for the care and nurture of children that only an intact family, built on a durable, committed marriage, is equipped to bear. As Murray notes, "the greatest source of inequality in America now is not economic; it is cultural."[32]

"You always have the poor with you," Jesus told His disciples (Mark 14:7). Poverty did not begin with the disintegration of the family. Racial and ethnic hatred, corruption, social injustice, poor government policies, educational disadvantages, and other factors have all played a role in poverty throughout history. But the phenomenon of the Great Crossover, in which education and class divide, joins the already growing racial gulf separating the rich from the non-rich.[33] As sociologist Kay Hymowitz notes, "The Great Crossover marks the moment at which unmarried motherhood moved from the domain of our poorest populations to become the norm for America's large and already flailing middle class."[34]

A healthy, vibrant middle class has been essential to the success of the American experiment. Can the United States survive without a prosperous, growing middle class? The answer is almost certainly no.

Lifting those trapped in poverty into prosperity and strengthening the middle class is one of the moral imperatives of our time.

We in the faith community are uniquely suited to address this issue, because our faith provides us a moral as well as a fiscal critique of economic policy.

A New Agenda Needed

This is what social conservatives did in the 1990s leading up to the election of the Republican Congress under Newt Gingrich. Marvin Olasky, author of *The Tragedy of American Compassion*, offered a critique of welfare and other government programs designed to help the poor, criticizing them for consigning multiple generations to hopelessness and dependency. Meanwhile, Republicans on Capitol Hill like Senators Dan Coats and Rick Santorum in the Senate and J. C. Watts in the House worked to translate this social science into a coherent reform agenda to help the poor. In his maiden address as Speaker of the House, Newt Gingrich referred to Olasky's book and put poverty front and center, connecting it to the welfare and entitlement reform proposals in the Contract with America.

The Christian Coalition supported welfare reform on the grounds that it codified the principles of work, personal responsibility, and subsidiarity. Welfare reform moved two million people from poverty and dependency to work and self-reliance. It was the most sweeping change in a federal entitlement program since the Great Society. The child tax credit also helped to alleviate poverty. As mentioned in chapter 7, George W. Bush doubled the child tax credit to $1,000 in 2001. It has probably been the most successful single anti-poverty program undertaken at the federal level in the past four decades, lifting nine million people out of poverty.[35]

We now need a new anti-poverty, pro-prosperity agenda for the twenty-first century, one that recognizes the centrality of marriage and intact families. People of faith must speak with a prophetic voice to politicians of both parties, calling on them to show respect for what the Bible calls "the rights of the poor" (Proverbs 31:9 ESV) and to "take up the cause of the fatherless" (Isaiah 1:17 NIV). This message will not always be popular, and it will likely not win plaudits from the political left or right. We have already seen how some Republicans, deficit hawks as well as supply siders (of which I consider myself one), resisted the child tax credit as too costly or insufficiently pro-growth.

The left criticizes the pro-poor agenda of religious conservatives for an alleged lack of compassion because our approach does not rely on the failed strategies of higher taxes and more bureaucracy. But there is no contradiction between free markets and lifting people out of poverty. As Arthur Brooks has argued in *Road to Freedom: How to Win the Fight for Free Enterprise*, the best way to lift people out of poverty is to create good jobs at good wages in the private sector.[36] Government has a role, but it is a subsidiary and limited role, as Catholic social teaching has argued and as the failure of the war on poverty demonstrated.

Spiritual Poverty

Material poverty can also reflect a deeper spiritual apathy, a poverty that afflicts the soul, both for individuals and society. This is especially true in the United States, with its exaltation of the go-getter, "keeping up with the Joneses," and celebration of the purely materialistic aspects of the American dream. We run ourselves ragged pursuing larger houses, bigger and faster cars, and fatter retirement funds, most of which we will never live to enjoy. We seek that which ultimately does not satisfy, trying to fulfill our needs with things rather than by serving God and others. We chase after material wealth when what we really need is food for the soul.

"Man shall not live on bread alone, but on every word that proceeds out of the mouth of God," said Jesus (Matthew 4:4). We need food, clothing, and shelter, but even more we urgently need to know God and find His purpose for our lives. It is this yearning of our souls that must be our highest priority. "Blessed are the poor in spirit, for theirs is the kingdom of heaven," said Jesus (Matthew 5:3).

This is what Pope Francis I referred to when he spoke of the "true meaning of poverty," proclaiming, "How I long for a poor Church for the poor!" The first pope from Latin America, Francis lived and worked in some of the miserable slums in the Western hemisphere, and he regards addressing poverty as one of the Church's highest callings. Yet in urging this focus, he has emphasized not just material but spiritual poverty as well, calling on believers to become like Christ, "who abased Himself, made Himself poor to walk with us on the road. And this is our poverty: the poverty of the flesh of Christ, the poverty that the Son of God brought us with His Incarnation."[37]

As believers, we should see the struggle against racism and poverty in spiritual terms, emulating Jesus, who encouraged all to come to Him. When Jesus—a Jew—spoke to the woman at the well, a half-breed Samaritan despised by many Jews of the time, He was being very intentional (John 4:7–10). Jesus boldly demonstrated that the kingdom of God is for everyone and that racial and ethnic bigotry has no place among those who love God. (In the next chapter we'll look at how bigotry toward Jews indicates spiritual darkness.) If this is our mission and purpose, we can heal our land, transcend our painful past, and experience a spiritual awakening.

Action Points

1. Get involved in a ministry that helps the least and the left behind. You will find many fine organizations to choose from, but the main thing is to get involved. I get involved by serving on the advisory board of Safehouse Outreach, a ministry that helps the poor and homeless of Atlanta (www.safehouse outreach.org).
2. Discuss with your mayor, city council, or other local leaders the need for shopping, banking, and key retail services in parts of your town or city that lack them.
3. To help those families trapped in failing schools, support the expansion of charter schools and greater educational choice in your state.

CHAPTER 10

Choosing the Chosen People

During a recent visit to Amsterdam my wife, Jo Anne, and I toured the Anne Frank house, walking through the cramped rooms of the secret annex where Anne, her family, and her friends hid from the Nazis for two years during World War II. Here eight people slept, ate, wept, argued, and celebrated birthdays; here Anne grew into a young woman. I walked past the wall where Otto and Edith marked their daughter's growth with a pen (Anne grew over two inches while in hiding) and past the map Otto used to track the progress of the Allies as they marched to Berlin. I also saw the pictures of Hollywood stars, clipped from fan magazines, that Anne used to decorate her bedroom, and I walked into the small attic where she received her first kiss.

At the end of the tour, we saw a glass case that displayed Anne's red-and-white checkered diary. Quotations from its pages covered the walls, and one in particular stopped me in my tracks. "One day this terrible war will be over," she had written on April 9, 1944. "The time will come when we will be people again, and not just Jews! We can never be just Dutch or just English, or whatever, we will always be Jews as well. But then, we'll want to be."

I wondered if seventy years after her death Anne's hopes had been realized. Is living as a Jew today the fulfillment of her desire to be "people again, and not just Jews"? I fear it is not.

In the lexicon of human suffering, there are chilling names that remind us of humankind's capacity for evil: Auschwitz, Bergen-Belsen, Dachau, and Buchenwald. The Holocaust could not have occurred without the silence, acquiescence, and cooperation of those who capitulated in the face of this inhumanity. Some miscalculated, not believing that Hitler would ever deliver on his promise to ethnically cleanse Europe. Some acted out of fear, knowing the Nazis persecuted whomever they did not brutalize or exterminate. Others curried favor with those in power.

Tragically, the church was not exempt from such behavior. As Eric Metaxas has documented in his outstanding biography of Dietrich Bonhoeffer, the Protestant church in Germany and much of Europe fell for Hitler's deceitful assurances of fidelity to Christianity and his empty promise of respect for the church's independence. The same was true of the Roman Catholic Church. Fifty years later, Pope John Paul II formally apologized for the Catholic Church's failure to rise up more aggressively in opposition to the Nazis.[1]

Given that Hitler's anti-Semitic views were readily accessible to anyone who cared to read *Mein Kampf* and to listen to his countless public speeches, why did the world fail to act until it was too late?

Bringing the question to the present day, why has the international community failed to act forcefully enough to stop Iran from spreading terrorism, attempting to wipe Israel off the map, and seeking nuclear weapons? There are multiple answers, but the main reason is they fail to realize that anti-Semitism is a central feature of evil wherever it is found. If one could devise a test for evil, anti-Semitism would be found at its core.

Those of us who are faithfully seeking God's purpose in our time must be aware that resisting anti-Semitism and supporting Israel are essential features of the spiritual awakening needed in America and the West.

A Surge in Anti-Semitism

Today waves of anti-Semitism sweep the globe from the Middle East and Europe to North America. The goal is to remove Jews from society and to eliminate the State of Israel.

Mahmoud Ahmadinejad, the former president of Iran, called for "the elimination of the Zionist regime"[2] and denounced Israel as a "stinking corpse" on the sixtieth anniversary of its modern founding.[3] In August 2013, in a speech on Al-Quds Day, an annual tradition created by Ayatollah Khomeini to target the "usurper Israel," Ahmadinejad's successor, Hassan Rouhani, referred to Israel as a "wound" on the "Muslim body," with some translations saying it needed to be "removed."[4] When asked if the Holocaust occurred, Rouhani replied that he was not a historian.[5] Former Egyptian president Mohamed Morsi referred to Jews as "pigs and dogs" and vowed to withdraw Egypt from the Camp David accords. In June 2013, a Cairo-based Hamas leader called on Hezbollah to remove fighters from Syria and instead focus on killing Jews in Israel.[6]

Small Jewish communities in the Middle East that have survived for centuries are being obliterated as radical regimes gain strongholds in countries like Egypt and Syria and as religious and ethnic violence sweeps through destabilized countries like Iraq. Egypt alone has seen its Jewish population decline from tens of thousands to just a handful over the past several decades,[7] and Iraq has seen its Jewish population drop from over one hundred thousand to what the *New York Times* recently called a "fearful few."[8] In Baghdad, the number of Jews is estimated to be in the single digits, not even enough to gather a *minyan* of ten men for certain rituals.[9]

In South America, the Chavez regime presided over a surge in anti-Semitism in Venezuela. For years, Venezuela's Jews have seen businesses and synagogues ransacked and vandalized while then-President Chavez developed a chummy relationship with Iran and openly challenged Israel's right to exist.[10] In a letter to the editor of the *New York Times*, the Anti-Defamation League wrote that "anti-Semitism is being used as a political tool" in Venezuela and that "anti-Semitic canards of Jewish control . . . have been propagated for millennia in politically unstable environments."[11]

Children in public school in France cannot wear yarmulkes, and Jewish schools have been the targets of multiple violent attacks over the past several years, the most serious of them being a 2012 attack on a school in Toulouse that killed three Jewish children and a rabbi.[12]

Switzerland, Norway, Sweden, Iceland, Denmark, Poland, and New Zealand have subverted human rights for animal rights by adopting variations of kosher slaughter bans, and almost half of Britons favor such a ban.[13] This is not the first time Europe has experimented with prohibiting kosher slaughter; it was one of the first legal moves of Hitler's Third Reich, then enforced on countries that Germany invaded.[14]

The Jewish religious practice of circumcision has also come under attack. Numerous European countries have toyed with restrictions or bans on circumcision. Nearly half of Germans support a ban on ritual circumcision, and in the spring of 2012, a German court upheld such a ban, arguing the practice infringes on a child's "fundamental right to bodily integrity." Shortly thereafter, a German rabbi who performed the ritual was hit with a criminal complaint and a fine. Another German rabbi called the move "the most serious attack on Jewish life in Europe since the Holocaust," and the ban was later overturned.[15]

America Not Immune

The United States experienced its own attempt at anti-Jewish legislation in the summer of 2011, when a ban on circumcision landed on the ballot in San Francisco. A group of self-labeled "intactivists" managed to gather enough signatures to get the ban on the ballot, arguing that they were lobbying for "genital autonomy" and "male-genital-integrity rights."[16] A superior court stopped the effort, ordering the proposed ban removed from the ballot, and Governor Jerry Brown prevented similar efforts that cropped up across the state from coming to fruition by signing a bill that prohibited local bans on circumcision.[17] While this intervention was laudable, the fact that it was needed at all is deeply disturbing, making it abundantly clear that America is not immune from the wave of anti-Semitism rearing its ugly head in Europe.

False claims about Jewish influence in society and alleged Jewish control of banks, the government, and the media are classic hallmarks of anti-Semitism. Recently, rhetoric about alleged Zionist control of the financial and political system has reemerged on the American political scene. The outrage over the so-called top 1 percent of earners that arose from the Occupy Wall Street Movement featured anti-Semitic language, in part because Jews tend to be overly represented among top earners. Because the Occupy Movement targeted financial firms such as Goldman Sachs and picketed the homes of Wall Street financiers, many of whom were Jewish, its anti-Semitic overtones were undeniable.

The Israel Test

George Gilder has argued that antipathy for Jews and Israel, stripped of its more pathological aspects, represents at base a hatred for democracy and capitalism.

As the only healthy and functioning democracy in the Middle East with a capitalist economy, Israel is the embodiment of Western civilization's best values. Gilder calls this the "Israel test," in which an individual or a country's attitude toward democratic values and free enterprise can be determined almost solely by its attitude toward Israel.

"At the heart of anti-Semitism is resentment of Jewish achievement. Today that achievement is concentrated in Israel," observes Gilder. "Obscured by the usual media coverage of the 'war-torn' Middle East, Israel has become one of the most important economies in the world, second only to the United States in its pioneering of technologies benefitting human life, prosperity, and peace." As a consequence, Gilder argues, any political philosophy that holds a "dogmatic belief that nature favors equal outcomes fosters hostility to capitalism and leads inexorably to anti-Semitism."[18]

Such was the case with fascism. Although often falsely portrayed in history textbooks as representing the far right in Germany, the Nazis (an abbreviation for *National Socialists*) were socialists who overlaid a left-wing program of state-run enterprise with a populist veneer of *Weltanschauung* ("room to grow") and anti-Semitism. The same was true of the Occupy Wall Street Movement with its slurs against Jewish bankers and businessmen. And while anti-Semitism did not begin with the rise of democratic capitalism, its modern manifestations have consistently and prominently featured a deep-seated resentment of Jews for the intelligence and industry that caused them to prosper as merchants, bankers, and entrepreneurs in capitalist economies. From the Jewish stereotypes found in Shakespeare and other popular literature in Elizabethan England to the Dreyfus affair, the caricature of the Jew as a greedy, unscrupulous profiteer more loyal to his tribe than his country has been one of the most virulent strains of anti-Semitism, from the pogroms in Russia to the Holocaust.

Today we in the U.S. are failing the Israel test. Disdain for Jews and allegations about their influence on the financial system, the government, and the media spills over even in our supposedly polite society. A 2012 report by the Anti-Defamation League found a dramatic increase in anti-Semitic incidents on college campuses, including spray-painting swastikas on the buildings of Jewish fraternities and vandalizing menorahs.[19]

This fashionable form of anti-Semitism even creeps into the classroom and faculty. Two professors of international affairs at the University of Chicago, Stephen Walt and John Mearsheimer, published an academic study in 2007 attributing the U.S. decision to invade Iraq to "the unmatched power of the Israel lobby." They begin with a provocative question: Why would the U.S. set aside its own security interests in order to advance those of the state of Israel? In their bizarre interpretation, a foreign policy cabal made up of academics, media executives, members of the American Israel Public Affairs Committee (AIPAC), conservative Christians, and neoconservatives at the Pentagon and State Department sacrificed American national security and plunged the nation into an ill-advised war. Setting aside momentarily the absurdity of this argument—a "Jewish lobby" that includes evangelicals, newspaper editors in New York, and policy analysts at Washington think tanks is such definitional nonsense as to be meaningless—it is a dangerous and slippery slope to allege that U.S. soldiers died on foreign battlefields because of a Jewish lobby. Such anti-Jewish attitudes eventually lead to persecution and marginalization.[20]

Israel Support Left Behind

These views can be found on the extremes of both left and right, but they are becoming most common on the left. Representative Jim Moran, a Democrat from Virginia, claimed in 2007 that Jewish influence was to blame for the U.S. invasion of Iraq, comments so outrageous he earned a rebuke from his party's leaders on Capitol Hill.[21] When Representative Cynthia McKinney of Georgia lost a Democratic primary in

2002 after making controversial comments about Israel, her father publicly blamed her defeat on "the Jews. J-E-W-S. Jews."[22]

Today's Democratic Party bears little resemblance to the party of Harry S. Truman and Henry "Scoop" Jackson, who respectively recognized the State of Israel and imposed sanctions on the Soviet Union because of its persecution of Jews. A recent poll asked if U.S. policy should favor Israel, favor the Palestinians, or treat both the same. Among Democrats, only 18 percent said America should favor Israel (compared to 52 percent of Republicans). When asked for whom they had more sympathy, only 34 percent of Democrats chose Israel (compared to 67 percent of Republicans).[23] Among self-identified liberals, pro-Israel sentiment is even lower.

This is a dangerous trend that poses a long-term threat to the historically bipartisan support for Israel by the United States. When Democrats drafted their party platform at the 2012 national convention in Charlotte, N.C., the document dropped pro forma language expressing support for Israel that had been included in past platforms as a matter of course. A storm of criticism erupted, forcing party officials to scramble to reinsert the pro-Israel language—a move delegates greeted with boos and catcalls.

Perhaps this explains why both Barack Obama and then-Speaker of the House Nancy Pelosi embraced the Occupy Movement, praising its attacks on capitalism and entrenched wealth while ignoring its public expressions of anti-Semitism. This is not to suggest that Obama or Pelosi shared the anti-Semitic views of Occupiers, but it does underscore the disturbing chasm separating the party's liberal activist base from its leaders when it comes to supporting Israel.

An Anti-Israel President?

Obama personifies this trend. When he ran for president in 2008, he said he would meet with Mahmoud Ahmadinejad during the first year of his presidency without preconditions. After taking office, Obama recorded a special video greeting to the Iranian people and wrote a personal letter to Ahmadinejad seeking rapprochement between the United States and Iran.

Obama's past raised troubling questions about where he stood on support for Israel. One of his earliest supporters in Illinois was Rashid Khalidi, a Palestinian activist holding extreme anti-Israel views. Khalidi suggested that "because of his unusual background, with family ties in Kenya and Indonesia, Obama would be more understanding of the Palestinian experience than typical American politicians."[24] It is not fair to subscribe Khalidi's views to Obama—all politicians have supporters on the fringe. But it is fair to hold Obama accountable for his own record as president, and his support for Israel has been tepid at best.[25] Consider the following:

- In his Cairo speech in June 2009, Obama compared Israeli sovereignty over the West Bank (the biblical regions of Judea and Samaria) to an illegal occupation.[26]
- In March 2010, during a visit to Israel ostensibly designed to restart negotiations between Israelis and Palestinians, Vice President Joe Biden condemned a routine announcement from the Israeli housing minister of construction projects in existing settlements, saying it "undermined trust."[27]
- When Israeli Prime Minister Benjamin Netanyahu visited the White House in 2010, Obama left him cooling his heels in a conference room with staff while he retired upstairs to the living quarters for dinner, insulting the leader of one of America's most reliable allies in the world.[28]
- During a speech on the Middle East in May 2011, Obama called for returning Israel to indefensible 1967 borders that exclude Jerusalem as its capital. After a public outcry, Obama clarified his remarks and added obligatory language about "appropriate land swaps" to pacify supporters of Israel.[29]
- The Obama administration submitted a budget request to Congress in 2012 that called for cutting in half U.S. funds for Israeli missile defense—this at a time when Israel faced the threat of rocket attacks from Hamas in Gaza and Hezbollah in Lebanon as well as the midrange missile technology developed by Iran.[30]

- In 2013 Obama nominated former U.S. Senator Chuck Hagel as secretary of defense. Hagel had voted against tougher sanctions against Iran, was one of four senators to refuse to sign a letter condemning anti-Semitism in the Muslim world, and chaired an organization that denounced Israel for practicing "apartheid."[31]

Taken together, these actions reveal Obama as the most anti-Israel president in my lifetime, if not modern U.S. history. For an American president to be this insensitive to the security needs of Israel at a time of such bloody turmoil in the Middle East is tragic, and it would have been unimaginable even a decade ago.

Anti-Semitism and Evil

Throughout history a dark vein that runs through almost every form of evil is hatred of the Jew. Whether that evil has taken the form of European fascism, communism, the Ku Klux Klan, the Aryan Nation, or Islamic radicalism, a common denominator is always hatred of the Jews and Israel. Why is this?

One possible explanation came from the late Richard Halverson, longtime chaplain of the U.S. Senate, who said at a meeting I attended in Washington, "The most visible and demonstrative proof of the existence of God in the world is the survival and present-day existence, against all odds, of the Jew." If God chose the Jews as His covenant people and selected them to receive His revelation, promising to bless and prosper them, then those who hate God will by definition have antipathy toward Jews, even to the point of persecution.

Since this is the case, then anti-Semitism is not just a concern for Jews and their allies. It is a concern for all people in every nation who yearn for political and religious pluralism and economic freedom, because anti-Semitism is a vital warning sign, a certain symptom of a deeper intolerance that will eventually violate the liberty and deprive the rights of all persons. No political movement that stigmatizes Jews has respected the rights of everyone else. Ethnic hatred and discrimination may begin with Jews, but it never ends there.

Hitler exterminated six million Jews, but he also killed six million others, including gypsies, communists, gays, Christians, and the disabled. Stalin killed an estimated fifty million people in a genocide that far exceeded the czarist pogroms of pre-Bolshevik Russia, murdering political opponents as well as Jews. The Nazis and communists hated each other but shared in common a pathological anti-Semitism that revealed a deeper evil at the core of their belief system.

In the midst of a great anti-Semitic retrogression, we cannot lose hope. The Bible puts it this way: "For the kingdom is the LORD's and He rules over the nations" (Psalm 22:28). Those who hope in Christ must remember that even as evil prospers, God is still on the throne and His plans and purposes will not be frustrated forever. Hitler killed himself in a bunker in Berlin, and Stalin's tyrannical system of government failed. The new wave of anti-Semitism will not prevail. In this, as in all things, we can rest on the promises of God. But we must also remain steadfastly vigilant in resisting it.

Consider the modern state of Israel. For most of recorded history, stretching from the destruction of Jerusalem by the Romans in AD 70 until the end of World War I, the Holy Land was a depopulated backwater of the Middle East. For centuries Jerusalem was overrun by every world power, its walls in ruins, the Jews scattered throughout the world, the Jewish hope of returning to their homeland apparently gone. Today the desert blooms because of the Jewish people's industry, entrepreneurship, and faith in God's promises. Modern irrigation techniques have made agriculture thrive, desalination will soon make Israel self-sufficient for its water supply, and the same technological advances that have fueled fracking in the U.S. have unleashed an oil boom in the Holy Land, with oil rigs dotting the Mediterranean Sea.

Today one can visit the Western Wall at dusk on Friday and see observant Jews praying and dancing at the arrival of the Sabbath, window-shop at high-end stores, eat at fine restaurants, and gaze upon the ancient walls of Jerusalem lit up against the night. In Tel Aviv one can walk the bustling streets, drop in on the night spots of a hip culture, and visit the offices of cutting-edge high-tech companies.

Israel now boasts one of the most vibrant economies in the world. What seemed impossible just sixty years ago has happened before our eyes, because with God all things are possible. "Pessimism is a luxury that a Jew can never allow himself," said Golda Meir. The same might be said of Christians and any other friend of the Jewish people and of Israel.

Shared Values

What is it about America that caused Jews, persecuted in other parts of the world, to cross oceans and enter through the golden door of opportunity? It cannot simply be pluralism and religious tolerance, for they can be found elsewhere in varying degrees. It is also, in part, America's conception of itself as the New Jerusalem. In addition to the United States identifying with Israel as a nation with a special destiny, America has welcomed people fleeing persecution and seeking refuge—including Jews. This was the case from America's earliest days. In 1790 the Jewish congregation in Newport, Rhode Island, wrote to President George Washington inquiring after his views on their right to practice their religion free from discrimination and harassment. They hoped that Washington's vision for America included them. "May the Children of the Stock of Abraham, who dwell in this land, continue to merit and enjoy the good will of the other Inhabitants," Washington replied.[32]

America's identification with Israel deepened after the attacks of September 11, 2001. When terrorists turned passenger planes into missiles, targeting New York and Washington, most Americans learned for the first time what it was like to live in constant fear of terrorism. On that day cable news networks ran video of protestors in Gaza dancing in the streets and chanting, "Death to America." It was difficult not to feel a closer identification with the Israelis.

Some moments in history are hinge points. Lexington and Concord, Waterloo, Fort Sumter, Pearl Harbor—all these marked turning points that separated the world that came after from all that preceded it. The attacks of September 11 were such a moment, ushering in a new period of conflict and challenge to the West, uniting

Israelis and Americans in a common struggle against terrorism and the nations who sponsor it, and deepening the bonds between the two countries. The truth is, Americans were always Israelis in a sense, with the U.S. and Israel sharing a commitment to democracy, respect for human rights, self-determination, faith in God, and freedom, including economic freedom. They just didn't fully realize it until the terrorists reminded them.

Righteous Gentiles

On the same day I toured Anne Frank's house, my wife and I visited the ten Boom family house in Haarlem, a short train ride from Amsterdam. Corrie ten Boom and her family were Dutch Reform Christians who joined the underground resistance to the Nazis, a tale of courage immortalized in the book and film *The Hiding Place*. I stood in the small space behind a false wall in Corrie's bedroom where Jews hid, a place so ingenious the Nazis never found it. Corrie and her family were arrested and shipped to concentration camps, where her father and sister later died. Many Jews who survived the Holocaust did so because of the charity displayed by Christians.

My friend Abraham Foxman, the executive director of the Anti-Defamation League, was sheltered in what is now Belarus by his Polish Catholic nanny whose family protected him from the camps by pretending he was their own son. There are countless such stories. At Yad Vashem, the Holocaust museum in Jerusalem, there is a garden and path dedicated to the Righteous Gentiles who harbored Jews during World War II. Many of them died in camps themselves. What motivates someone to lose their own life to save another? Jesus said, "Greater love has no one than this, that one lay down his life for his friends" (John 15:13). In the case of many believers, it was Jesus' example that inspired them.

Some people claim that evangelicals befriend Jews and support Israel because of their theological view of the end times and their belief that the return of the Jews to Israel is a prelude to the Second Coming. The ten Booms prayed for peace in the Holy Land as early as the 1840s, not because they believed the return of the Jews to Israel was imminent (it was not), but because the Bible commands us to "pray for the peace of Jerusalem" (Psalm 122:6). End-times theology did not motivate Victor Kugler and Johannes Kleiman to help the Frank family, a choice that led to their arrest and confinement in a concentration camp. Dietrich Bonhoeffer did not go to his death before a Nazi firing squad because he held to some convoluted notion that Jesus would not return until the ingathering of Jews to Israel. Yet critics continue to repeat the smear that evangelical support for Israel is a smokescreen for their eschatology. Evangelicals, charged *Nation* magazine, only support the Jewish state as a "biblical imperative" because they believe "Israel is the future site of the Rapture."[33]

Today's righteous Gentiles are not motivated primarily by their eschatology. A 2002 survey by the Tarrance Group found that a majority of U.S. evangelicals (56 percent) support Israel because it is a democracy and America's most reliable ally in the Middle East, while only little more than a third of evangelicals said they supported Israel because it is prophesied as the place of the Second Coming.[34] The most common reasons believers cite for supporting Israel are, first, the fact that it is the historic homeland of the Jews and, second, the need to provide a place of refuge for Jews after the Holocaust. This explains evangelicals' skepticism about the land-for-peace formula that has driven the peace process. It also explains why they treat the anti-Semitic pronouncements of the leaders of Iran, Hamas, Hezbollah, and the Muslim Brotherhood as deadly serious, not the rantings of mere demagogues.

If George Gilder is right and Israel is a modern-day Rorschach test of one's respect—or lack thereof—for democracy, free markets, and free minds, then support for the Jewish state is one of the moral imperatives of our time.

As men and women of faith, we must place among our highest priorities the opposition of anti-Semitism and bigotry in all its ugly forms, no matter how apparently benign and innocuous. We must understand that evil begins with the marginalization of Jews but always grows like a cancer until it threatens the liberty of all—including Christians around the world, even Christians in America.

Action Points

1. Read Genesis 12 and Romans 11. After reading these scriptures, do you agree that the Jews are God's chosen people?
2. Join and support a pro-Israel organization such as Christians United for Israel (www.cufi.com), the American Israel Public Affairs Committee (www.aipac.org), or the Faith and Freedom Coalition (www.ffcoalition.com).
3. Participate in a structured interfaith dialogue with Jewish individuals and organizations in your community. Break bread over a meal or go out for coffee to discuss points of agreement as well as disagreement.

CHAPTER 11

The War on Christianity

On a mild, sunny morning in March 2011, Shahbaz Bhatti was shot eight times while leaving his mother's home in Islamabad. He was the only Christian minister in Pakistan. He had devoted his life to the rights of religious minorities, and at the time he was the federal minister for minority affairs, a role he accepted in order to help uplift the downtrodden and marginalized.

Five hundred kilometers away, Asia Bibi, a Christian mother of five, still sits in a Pakistani prison awaiting execution. Her crime? Sharing a drink of water with a Muslim. Coworkers claimed that Bibi insulted the Prophet Muhammad. She was convicted of blasphemy and sentenced to death by hanging.[1]

In northeast Cairo in April of 2013, Mahrous Hana Tadros was killed when a mob stormed St. Mark's Cathedral. A local imam had urged Muslims to "kill the Christians" and rid Egypt of "infidels." Hundreds of Christians huddled in the cathedral as a violent mob attacked it with rocks, bottles, guns, and Molotov cocktails, killing dozens.[2]

In Iran, pastor Yousef Nadarkhani was arrested in October 2009 after he complained about mandatory Islamic instruction in the schools. An Iranian court found him guilty of the crime of "apostasy" and sentenced him to death. After international pressure grew, the Iranian Supreme Court released him, but Yousef continued to be harassed by the government.[3]

A wave of persecution has swept across the Middle East. As Senator Rand Paul observed, "Today, Christians in Iraq, Libya, Egypt, and Syria are on the run—persecuted or under fire—and yet we continue to send aid to the folks chasing them." Paul decried the fact that "while they burn the American flag and the mobs chant 'Death to America,' more of your money is sent to these haters of Christianity."[4]

Why does our government fail to defend Christians around the world against terror and violence? Clearly, it is not a priority in U.S. foreign policy.

Protecting Christians is not a priority, in part, because our government shows such little respect for the rights of Christians here at home. A war on Christianity has been under way in the U.S. for some time, fought not with bullets or tear gas but with court rulings, government policies, and a culture that stigmatizes and denigrates those with faith in Jesus Christ.

To be sure, unlike believers in Egypt or Pakistan, Christians in America do not fear being murdered or our churches burned because of our faith. But violence is always preceded by rhetorical and judicial hostility, and there is ample evidence that a dangerous and insidious form of religious persecution has taken root in the United States. This war on Christianity began decades ago with court decisions marginalizing religious speech, creating what Richard John Neuhaus called "the naked public square" and Yale law professor Stephen L. Carter termed a "culture of disbelief."

If we do not combat hostility toward Christianity outside of our nation's borders, by the time we finally rise up, it may be too late. That is why it is so critical that we Christians make our voices heard now; we need to fight back in the battle against Christian values and those who hold them.

The Establishment Clause

It is ironic that there is hostility toward Judeo-Christian principles by our own government. After all, America began as a religious nation. The Northwest Ordinance of 1787 even allowed the use of government funds for the distribution of religious material in the western territories, asserting that "religion, morality and knowledge being necessary to good government and the happiness of mankind, schools and the means of education shall forever be encouraged."

For most of our history, the consensus was that the First Amendment forbade the establishment of an official church but did not require the removal of religious faith from our customs, institutions, public rituals, or civic discourse. Even liberal Supreme Court Justice William O. Douglas observed, “We are a religious people whose institutions presuppose a Supreme Being.”[5]

Beginning in the 1960s, however, this agreement on accommodating religious speech began to fray. In *Engel v. Vitale* (1962), the Supreme Court struck down the Regents’ prayer in New York State. It was the beginning of open hostility toward any government policy that supported faith-based activity. In *Lemon v. Kurtzman* (1971), the justices outlawed Pennsylvania’s practice of providing the same textbooks to students at Christian schools as in public schools.

The justices didn’t stop there. They created a complex, virtually indecipherable three-part test to determine whether a statute violated the Establishment Clause: whether it had a secular purpose, whether it advanced or inhibited religion, and whether it created excessive entanglement between government and religion.[6] This “Lemon test” reduced Establishment Clause jurisprudence to a fog, creating confusion and making legislators reluctant to enact any policy that accommodated religion.[7]

Judicial bias against religion also led the Supreme Court to strike down a nonsectarian prayer offered by a rabbi at a Providence, Rhode Island, middle-school graduation service in *Lee v. Weisman* (1992). The rabbi’s prayer, which hardly constituted a fiery sermon, included the following language:

> God of the Free, Hope of the Brave, for the legacy of America where diversity is celebrated and the rights of minorities are protected, we thank You. May these young men and women grow up to enrich it. For the liberty of America, we thank You. May these new graduates grow up to guard it. . . .
>
> May our aspirations for our country and for these young people, who are our hope for the future, be richly fulfilled. Amen.[8]

Graduation prayers have been a celebrated tradition in America for centuries. We now know from the private papers of Justice Harry Blackmun that Anthony Kennedy changed his vote during the deliberations, troubled by the majority opinion affirming the rabbi's prayer. What bothered Kennedy was the fact that the school principal had given the rabbi a pamphlet containing guidelines for public prayers, guidelines such as using inclusive language and showing appropriate sensitivity to the faith—or lack thereof—of those in attendance. Kennedy deemed the principal's action an attempt by a government official to influence the prayer.

The Basis of Our Laws

Our founders would not recognize such an interpretation of the First Amendment. Our nation testifies on its currency and coins that "In God We Trust"; inaugurates presidents by having them take an oath placing a hand on the Holy Bible and praying, "So help me God"; and offers a prayer before each session of Congress. Supreme Court justices sit beneath a mural that portrays Moses presenting the Ten Commandments.

We cannot survive as a free nation if we force our citizens to leave their faith at the courthouse door. As Russell Kirk observed, "the corpus of English and American laws" will not endure "unless it is animated by the spirit that moved it from the beginning: that is, by religion, and specifically by the Christian religion."[9]

Why is this so? Because Western civilization is based on the notion that civil law should reflect the order of nature and of nature's God. Laws against murder, laws against perjury, and laws against theft and fraud find their inspiration in the Ten Commandments and the Mosaic law. These religious precepts do not provide the constitutional justification of our laws, but they are surely their moral foundation. To require the censoring of any reference to that religious tradition is to destroy the very foundations of our society.

Governmental Hostility

Judicial persecution of religion is only one aspect of the war on Christianity. In April 2013, a military official told Army Reserve soldiers in Pennsylvania that evangelical Christians and Roman Catholics should be categorized with al Qaeda as "extremists." That same month the Pentagon blocked access on military bases to the website of the Southern Baptist Convention, apparently because government filters banned it due to "hostile content." Meanwhile, the Pentagon announced that proselytizing was banned, meaning Christians could be subject to disciplinary action and even court-martial simply for sharing their faith with others.[10]

This anti-Christian hostility is not confined to the military. Consider just a few episodes in which simple expressions of Christian faith have been subjected to official government persecution:

- In New York a middle school indefinitely suspended a student. The crime? Wearing rosary beads for religious reasons in violation of the school's dress code. The American Center for Law and Justice filed a lawsuit, and although the school refused to reverse the suspension, it settled, cleared the student's disciplinary record, and paid court costs and legal fees.[11]
- When Audrey Jarvis, a liberal arts major at Sonoma State University in California, showed up for work at a student orientation fair in June 2013, she was wearing a gold cross pendant. A supervisor ordered her to remove it, saying it might offend others. Jarvis refused; her supervisor did not allow her to work in a public area. Only after a public outcry did college officials say there was a mistake and deny any policy against religious-themed jewelry.[12]
- A professor at Florida Atlantic University instructed students to write "Jesus" on a piece of paper and stomp on it as part of a lesson on symbols and culture. When a Mormon student refused, the college punished him with academic disciplinary charges. Only after the Liberty Institute, a religious liberties legal group, intervened were the charges against the student dropped.[13]
- In 2013 an atheist checked into a cabin at a Georgia state park to celebrate his son's birthday and found a Bible in a drawer. After he complained, the state's Department of Natural Resources removed all Bibles from state park inns and lodges.

Only after the state attorney general determined no public funds were expended were the Bibles returned.[14]

- In Collier County, Florida, the school board refused to allow a Christian organization to distribute Bibles on "Religious Freedom Day" despite no tax dollars or public officials involved.[15]
- A federal court struck down an innocuous "Motorists Prayer" for the safety of drivers on North Carolina highways printed on maps paid for by the state's Department of Transportation, arguing that the desire for highway safety was vitiated by the separation of church and state.[16]

The common thread in each of these episodes is the treating Christianity as a pathology, as if it is offensive and threatening to others. And there is a haunting similarity between the use overseas of blasphemy laws to silence Christians and the various executive and legal rulings in the United States that keep Christians from expressing their faith in the public square.

Cultural Ridicule

The government persecutes Christians at will in part because popular culture demeans and denigrates them, making them objects of scorn and ridicule. Bill Maher, whose comedy program is carried by HBO, has compared the Roman Catholic Church to the Taliban, the Ku Klux Klan, and Hamas; he has equated the pope with cult leaders; and he has argued that religious people suffer from a "neurological disorder."[17]

Not to be outdone, in February 2013—during the holy season of Lent—NBC's *Saturday Night Live* featured a sketch titled "Djesus Uncrossed," a spoof of Quentin Tarantino's film *Django Unchained*, in which Jesus hacks innocent people to death and guns down those who do not worship Him. Says a voice-over: "He's risen from the dead . . . and he's preaching anything but forgiveness." The *Los Angeles Times* called it "the single most offensive skit in SNL history," and retailer Sears pulled its advertising from the show after complaints from viewers.[18]

Smearing Christians is a familiar theme in Hollywood. In the opening episode of season eight of the hit Fox animated series *Family Guy*, Stewie and Brian travel to other universes, including one that boasts remarkable scientific advancement because "Christianity never existed." In season ten, an episode entitled "Tea Peter" portrays faith-based Tea Party activists as racist, anti-Semitic anarchists who allow their teenage daughters to have sex with older men.

There are notable exceptions to the anti-religious bent of the media, but they are dwarfed by the dominant trend. When the Discovery Channel broadcast the miniseries *The Bible*, produced by reality-show creator Mark Burnett and his wife, Roma Downey, it received the highest ratings of any cable program of the previous year. So impressive was the audience response that NBC announced it would air a sequel. Sparked in part by the box-office success of Mel Gibson's film *The Passion*, which grossed more than $300 million worldwide, Hollywood has a new openness to faith-based themes and stories, exemplified by Walden Media, which produced *The Chronicles of Narnia* movies and *Amazing Grace*, and EchoLight Studios, headed by former presidential candidate Rick Santorum, which is producing a dramatic film based on the biblical story of Joseph and his multicolor coat.

Obama's Insensitivity

After Barack Obama took office, it became rapidly apparent his domestic agenda included policies reflecting insensitivity to religion, if not outright hostility. In a move that went over the heads of the media but sent off alarm bells among religious folk, Obama began in his public rhetoric to replace the phrase *freedom of religion* with *freedom of worship*.

The use of the phrase was deliberate. Freedom of religion has many facets—such as speech, attire, and public rituals—that form something bigger than formal worship alone. Worship is but one facet of religious life. The president first replaced *religion* with *worship* in his memorial remarks for the victims of the 2009 Fort Hood shooting, an attack carried out by a deranged Muslim fanatic.

What followed was a string of incidents in which the president and Secretary of State Hillary Clinton used *freedom of worship* instead of *freedom of religion* in high-profile remarks about the administration's human rights agenda. One of those speeches was given in China, a nation where house churches are routinely raided and women are regularly forced to abort their children.

And President Obama was steel-eyed in opening his 2013 Religious Freedom Day speech with the words, "Foremost among the rights Americans hold sacred is the freedom to worship as we choose."

When the president of the United States speaks, his words matter. They are weighed carefully by diplomats and the courts, parsed by supporters and opponents alike, and studied in foreign capitals. To repeatedly and deliberately reduce the right to freedom of religion to the narrow act of worship is irresponsible, and the change in wording constitutes an assault on the First Amendment.

Obama's insensitivity about religious faith has revealed itself in awkward ways and at inopportune moments.

- At a 2008 fund-raiser in San Francisco, Obama was captured on an audio recording criticizing religious folks who "cling to guns or religion" because of "antipathy of people who aren't like them."
- President Obama said while on foreign soil that the United States was no longer a Christian nation.
- He opposes the World War II Memorial Prayer Act of 2013, originally introduced by Senators Rob Portman and Joe Lieberman, which proposes that FDR's D-Day prayer be included in the World War II Memorial. This prayer calls on the American people to "devote themselves in a continuance of Prayer . . . let words of prayer be on our lips, invoking God's help to our efforts."
- Obama ridiculed Congress for passing a 2011 resolution affirming that our national motto is "In God We Trust." When asked whether he supported a proclamation honoring our

motto, he replied, "I trust in God, but God wants us to help ourselves by putting people back to work." This resolution was sparked by Obama's repeated and erroneous claiming that America's motto is *E Pluribus Unum*, translated "Out of many, one." Congress has declared by law that "In God We Trust" is the nation's official motto.

- Obama has made a similar practice of misquoting the Declaration of Independence, eliminating the reference to God. He did so first in a speech to the Congressional Hispanic Caucus and again at a Democratic Party fund-raiser in October 2010.

These are not merely verbal miscues or gaffes. When George W. Bush misspoke, the media jumped on his occasionally jumbled syntax as proof of an inferior intellect. Obama taught constitutional law at the University of Chicago, yet he misquotes our nation's motto and founding document without a word of criticism from the media elite. As Jeffrey Anderson of the *Weekly Standard* noted, there are only two plausible explanations: either Obama "isn't very familiar with the most famous passage in the document that founded this nation," or he "doesn't subscribe to the Declaration's rather central claim that our rights come from our 'Creator' (also referred to in the Declaration as 'Nature's God' and 'the Supreme Judge of the World')".[19] The latter is correct.

This judgment may seem harsh until one considers the Obama administration's policies, for his rhetoric buttresses policies that treat religious belief as a private affair that has no place in the public square. One was the employment case of the Hosanna-Tabor Lutheran Church that went before the Supreme Court. The Obama administration took the bizarre position that churches do not have the right to hire or dismiss their own ministers. The case involved a teacher who filed an EEOC complaint alleging disability-based discrimination when the church fired her after rescinding her ministerial call. The church, represented by the Becket Fund for Religious Liberty, argued it should be allowed leeway in choosing its ministers. The Obama administration became the first in U.S. history to argue that churches had no such right, leaving incredulous the Supreme Court justices—even liberal Obama appointee Elena Kagan. The Supreme Court ruled 9-0 for the church, but if the Obama administration had its way, the First Amendment's right to free exercise of religion would have been destroyed.[20]

Mandate against Religious Freedom

After ramming Obamacare through Congress, the Obama administration mandated that all employers, regardless of religious objection, pay for contraception, sterilization, and abortion-inducing drugs in employee health-care plans. The mandate offered the most narrow religious freedom exemption in federal history, excluding only a few, narrowly defined religious entities. This edict made a mockery of the administration's claims in negotiations with pro-life Democrats like Representative Bart Stupak of Michigan that Obamacare would not use taxpayer funds to pay for or promote abortion. It also showed how ill-advised was the "eat me last" strategy of some faith-based groups (the U.S. Catholic Bishops Conference among them) who lobbied for the passage of Obamacare on compassionate social policy grounds and hoped the health-care plan's bureaucratic overreach would not trample on their right to practice their faith.

The Obama administration granted only one exception to the regulation for a religious charity: if it served only members of its own faith. If an evangelical homeless shelter provided beds only to evangelicals, or a Catholic hospital admitted only Catholic patients, it was exempt. But if a charity provides food to all the hungry, clothing to all the naked, and housing to all the homeless, it will now be forced to violate its own religious teaching.

The backlash against the mandate was unified across faiths. In a move of remarkable ecumenism, the president of Wheaton College, a leading evangelical institution, penned an op-ed column with the president of Catholic University, one of the nation's finest Catholic schools, blasting the mandate. Then, in "An Evangelical-Catholic Stand on Liberty," Philip Ryken and John Garvey wrote that while "American Evangelicals and Catholics have not always been the best of friends" and disagree about the morality of certain provisions of the mandate, they stand together in the view that their respective universities "should have the freedom—guaranteed by the United States Constitution—to carry out our mission in a way that is consistent with our religious principles."[21]

Faced with a firestorm of protest, the administration tried to walk back the mandate. Obama officials with deeper ties to the Catholic community—like former White House Chief of Staff Bill Daley and Vice President Joe Biden—dodged blame by leaking to the press that they had argued against the mandate, only to lose out to feminists within the administration, led by Valerie Jarrett. Scrambling to contain the damage, the White House announced a meaningless administrative "fix" in which insurance companies, not religious charities, would cover the objectionable services by issuing "free" rider policies to employees. This was a fig leaf. Biden chose simply to misrepresent his own policy, claiming in the televised vice presidential debate with Paul Ryan, "No religious institution—Catholic or otherwise, including Catholic Social Services, Georgetown Hospital, Mercy Hospital, any hospital—none has to either refer contraception, none has to pay for contraception, none has to be a vehicle to get contraception in any insurance policy they provide. That is a fact. That is a fact."[22]

It was not a fact, and the U.S. Conference of Catholic Bishops issued a statement the morning after the debate calling Biden to task for misleading the American people. The falseness of his claim was made clear when the Obama administration issued its final rule on a Friday afternoon in June 2013, on the eve of a congressional recess, hoping to attract as little media attention as possible. The "rider" policy had magically disappeared, replaced by an even more porous firewall between religious charities and the objectionable services, in which insurance companies and claims processors provide contraceptive and abortion-inducing medication free of charge to all employees. The problem was the premium dollars paid by employees and employers alike were entirely fungible, especially for charities that self-insure. Apparently assaulting the consciences of millions of Americans does not bother the Obama administration.

As constitutional scholar James Capretta pointed out, there was "no public policy rationale for the HHS mandate, because the products and services covered by it are already widely and readily available, and heavily subsidized by the government for those with low incomes. The administration is imposing this requirement for entirely ideological reasons."[23]

The mandate triggered a wave of lawsuits from more than one hundred different plaintiffs of different faiths. These employers face fines under Obamacare of up to one hundred dollars per employee per day. Lawyers from the Department of Justice have hopscotched across the country to argue in federal court that private employers like the Green family, who started the now twenty-one-thousand-employee-strong company Hobby Lobby out of their basement, must check their religious rights at the door. I had the opportunity to meet Steve Green and his family when the Faith and Freedom Coalition presented him with its Leadership in Business award in June 2013. He impressed me as a man of uncommon faith and integrity. Days before the Obama administration issued its final rule, Hobby Lobby won an important preliminary victory: a federal court issued an injunction ruling that the company would not be required to implement the policy while it fought in court. Hobby Lobby also won a stay of the mandate while it litigated. The Obama Justice Department fought even this, appealing to the Supreme Court to overturn the injunction.

IRS Harassment

These lawsuits are not the only time the Obama administration has had to defend its harassment of people of faith. As the Internal Revenue Service scandal began to unfold, it became clear that religious groups had been targeted for persecution.

Hundreds of Christian organizations, pro-life groups, Jewish and pro-Israel groups, and Tea Party groups were caught in a dragnet based on their public policy views and religious beliefs. When the IRS inspector general issued a report detailing the abuses, organizations such as Christian Voices for Life, Family Talk Action, the Billy Graham Evangelistic Association, and Billy Graham's son

Franklin Graham's Samaritan's Purse came forward with their own horror stories of IRS harassment. A BOLO ("be on the lookout") list encouraged IRS bureaucrats to flag the tax-exempt applications of organizations that educated citizens about the Constitution and the Bill of Rights. Another criterion for slow-walking an application was if the group's purpose was "to make America a better place." The leaders of a Christian group in Iowa were asked to describe the content of their prayers and told that their tax-exempt status would be denied unless the entire board of directors signed a pledge agreeing not to pray in front of abortion clinics. Others were asked to list the books they read, to provide copies of their personal Facebook postings, or to list their friends.

In a familiar pattern for the Obama administration, the White House declaimed any knowledge of the abuses, falsely claimed that the targeting of Christian and Tea Party groups was done by a handful of rogue agents at an IRS office in Cincinnati, vowed to fully cooperate with the Congressional investigation, and ordered the Justice Department to conduct its own inquiry into possible criminal misconduct. Months later, no Christian group or Tea Party group had even been contacted by the FBI. The American Center for Law and Justice, which represented some of the groups subjected to harassment, filed a class-action suit against the IRS seeking monetary damages.

None of this should come as any surprise to those who have dealt with the IRS. The agency's persecution of Christian groups has grown worse under Obama, but it did not begin with him. From the time I started serving as executive director of the Christian Coalition in 1989 until I left in 1997, the IRS never granted its application for tax-exempt status. Given the fact that we were organized as a 501(c)(4) social welfare organization whose primary objective was to influence public policy and educate Christian voters, this delay was a deliberate attempt to hinder our fund-raising and leave us under a cloud of legal scrutiny. During the same period dozens of IRS agents occupied offices at the Christian Broadcasting Network, Jerry Falwell's *Old-Time Gospel Hour*, and Liberty University, poring over tens of thousands of documents in search of some violation of the law. This was pure harassment. After my departure, the IRS denied Christian Coalition's tax-exempt status. The organization which then transferred its assets to a newly christened Christian Coalition of America.

Similar abuses occurred at the Federal Election Commission. Lois Lerner, the head of the tax-exempt division who invoked her Fifth Amendment right against self-incrimination during the IRS scandal, led the FEC's Enforcement Division from 1986 to 2001. During her tenure, the FEC sued the Christian Coalition for $5 million, the largest lawsuit in the history of the agency. Our offense? Registering Christians to vote and distributing nonpartisan voter guides in churches to educate voters on where candidates stood.

In techniques of harassment that would become familiar during the IRS scandal, FEC attorneys grilled members of my staff about what transpired at Coalition prayer meetings, who attended prayer gatherings, and the church memberships of various activists. Pat Robertson was asked during a deposition about the details of his prayers with U.S. Senate candidate Oliver North and President George H. W. Bush, while North was asked about whether he knew Robertson was praying for him.[24] The FEC subpoenaed over one hundred thousand documents and conducted eighty-one depositions during the seven-year investigation. The Christian Coalition won the case in federal district court, but not until it had spent $2 million in legal and administrative costs defending itself.

The harassment of the Christian Coalition by the FEC and the IRS's persecution of Christian groups should have been a warning to believers in America that their rights are in jeopardy. Sadly, few paid attention because those actions didn't directly affect them. Hopefully the IRS scandal will alert Christians in this country that their own government is treating them like second-class citizens. The recently proposed IRS regulations governing voter-education activities by grassroots Christian groups—including banning the distribution of nonpartisan voter guides in churches—should be a wake-up call that our First Amendment rights are in jeopardy.

It may be hard to believe that in America today Christians are routinely asked by federal agencies under penalty of perjury and imprisonment about their personal prayers, fined millions of dollars, and dragged into court for merely exercising their right as citizens to register to vote and to participate in the political party of their choice. But this is the nature of the culture's war on Christianity. From the courts to the bureaucracy, from the entertainment industry to academia, from the media to corporate boardrooms, belief in Jesus Christ is a modern scarlet letter.

Less Violent but Hostile Nonetheless

The only difference between the war on Christianity here and abroad are the tactics, including the degree of violence. The same pattern prevails in Europe, where pastors can now be fined or jailed for alleged hate speech if they preach about homosexuality.

While he professes to be a Christian, Obama has devoted great energy seeking to establish cordial relations with those who express hatred for Jews, Christians, and the United States. In his 2009 address in Cairo, he spoke movingly about growing up as a boy in Indonesia and hearing the familiar call to morning prayer. He sought common ground and mutual understanding with the Islamic world.

On one level this effort was admirable, but in practice Obama's "new beginning" with the Muslim world proved disastrous. From providing aid to a government in Egypt run by the Muslim Brotherhood (until it was deposed by the military in July 2013), to sending U.S. tax dollars and arms to jihadist rebels in Syria who have harassed and killed Christians, to claiming at a news conference in Turkey that America was not a Christian nation—Obama's administration has displayed astonishing hostility to the free exercise of religion by Christians.

Obama's policies and public statements, therefore, raise serious questions about the true nature of his core beliefs and values. Who is he and what does he really believe? Knowing the answer to this question helps us understand the opposition. And the answer may surprise you.

Action Points

1. Read Matthew 10:24–39 and reflect on Jesus' teaching regarding the certainty of the persecution of His disciples.
2. Support First Amendment legal organizations that defend the rights of Christians in the public square, including the American Center for Law and Justice (www.aclj.org), the Alliance Defending Freedom (www.alliancedefendingfreedom.org), Liberty Counsel (www.lc.org), or the Becket Fund for Religious Liberty (www.becketfund.org).
3. Educate yourself about your rights as a believer and an American citizen. A good start would be *Good Tidings and Great Joy* by Sarah Palin, which discusses the war on Christmas.[25]

CHAPTER 12

The Liberal Messiah

I first met Barack Obama when he was a freshman state senator from the south side of Chicago, in elected office for less than a year. On a rainy night in September 1997, we were part of a seminar being held on the second floor of a foreboding gray stone building on the campus of Harvard University. The polished, smooth, and confident Obama the world knows today is not the man I encountered. I met a younger Obama, skinny as a rail, a little rough around the edges, solicitous to a fault, flattering, a man on the make. Not many had yet heard of Barack Obama, but that would soon change.

Months earlier I had gotten a call from my friend Vin Weber, a former congressman from Minnesota, asking me to join him in a working group on social capital at the John F. Kennedy School of Government. Even though I had just started my consulting firm and didn't really have the time, I agreed, partly because of my friendship with Vin and partly because the event would be run by renowned social scientist Robert Putnam, author of *Bowling Alone*. I found Putnam's work intriguing. His thesis is that the lack of social cohesion caused by so many people in the United States living alone, disconnected from family and community (thus the phrase "bowling alone"), makes it more difficult for Americans to come together to solve social problems. Getting to know Barack Obama was happenstance, but I wondered later if it wasn't a divine appointment or occurrence. Most people had no idea who the politician from Illinois with the funny name was until he spoke at the 2004 Democratic Convention in Boston.

In the course of my career, I had spent decades walking the halls of state capitols to survey the political horseflesh and see who might make a good congressional or statewide candidate. In my home state of Georgia, I encountered Paul Coverdell, Johnny Isakson, Roy Barnes, Sonny Perdue, and Julian Bond when they were state legislators. All became governor or senator except Bond, who ran for Congress unsuccessfully and then became chairman of the NAACP. Every state legislator dreams of being governor someday, but not many have the intellect, ambition, guts, and interpersonal skills to go the distance.

Obama had *it*—whatever it is. Whip-smart, handsome, articulate, and fiercely ambitious, Obama had the total package, and he was in a hurry. Those who claim he is a poser who can only read words off a teleprompter are wrong. I saw him in action when he had no notes or teleprompter and found him to be uncommonly intelligent, gracious, and well spoken.

Memorable Encounter

The working group included some high-powered figures, including George Stephanopoulos, who had just left the Clinton White House, and Steve Goldsmith, the mayor of Indianapolis. But Obama stood out for the force of his personality and his oversized ambition. Indeed, he wore his ambition with an ease that bordered on arrogance, and his high self-regard was combined with unshakeable self-assurance, something the world would become familiar with later. There was no doubt he was planning to run for higher office, and he seemed to be running already, though for what exactly was not clear, I suspect, even to him.

I liked Obama, but he had a tendency to seek to impress with intellectual airs, peppering his conversation with the jargon of the academy and social sciences. Later, after he was elected president, journalist David Maraniss published a book that included excerpts of love letters Obama had sent to a college girlfriend, and I found the sophomoric references to T. S. Eliot and Yeats familiar. The Obama I knew spoke earnestly in academic and liberal clichés like "raising consciousness," "structural inequality," and working for "redemptive social justice." He was the most committed liberal who could be considered politically viable I had ever encountered. Once during a break in the proceedings, he pulled me aside and smoothly told me I would be surprised at how many things he and I agreed on. He was right.

Yet something made me uneasy about Obama. In the end, I reluctantly concluded his charm was deceitful. The flowery language, grip and grin, intellectual pretense, jargon and buzz words, and obsequiousness were all designed to obscure rather than reveal who he was and what he believed. In a word, he was disingenuous. This is not exactly a rare character trait in politicians. But in Obama's case there was something deeper and more concerning than the usual politician's salesmanship. I suspected there was something deliberately misleading about him, and that his compelling personal narrative, exotic and multiracial background, and soaring eloquence distracted from his actual beliefs and intentions. At the time I assumed his extreme views would limit his rise. I could not have been more wrong.

Rhetorical Fog

After the seminar ended, Putnam issued a report that few read until Obama ran for president. Though Obama and I never crossed paths again, I followed his career. In 2002 he challenged Congressman Bobby Rush in a primary, losing badly. Two years later he ran for the U.S. Senate, languishing in the back of the pack for most of the campaign, an asterisk in the polls. Then someone leaked the divorce records of Blair Hull, the wealthy Democratic front-runner (some claimed it had been done by Obama's campaign), revealing allegations by his ex-wife of physical abuse. The Hull campaign imploded, and Obama won the primary unscathed. Next his Republican opponent's sealed divorce records were made public, revealing salacious details that forced him to withdraw from the race. Though the GOP recruited Alan Keyes as a stand-in, for all practical purposes Obama walked into the U.S. Senate in the general election.

Despite his leading such a charmed existence, I was certain Obama's decision to run for president in 2008 was a mistake and that his ambition would exceed his grasp. But once again Obama proved to be both lucky and good. Hillary Clinton ran one of the worst campaigns for president in the previous forty years, failing to grasp how angry the left was over her vote to authorize the war in Iraq and how much liberals hungered for a true champion, not another "third way" Democratic Leadership Council clone of the Clinton variety. Her abysmal campaign gave Obama an opening, and he seized it.

When Obama ran on "hope" and "change," promising "we are the change we have been waiting for," I recognized it immediately. The same opaque language and rhetorical fog I had heard in the Harvard seminar years before tripped smoothly off his tongue to adoring crowds who hung on his every word, including some who fainted in his presence. There were no red states or blue states, Obama assured us, only the United States.

He claimed to have worked across party lines in the Illinois state senate on bipartisan issues like ethics and health-care reform, when in fact he had a fiercely partisan voting record. As a legislator Obama voted against the death penalty for cop killers, against legislation requiring medical intervention to save the life of a child born alive during an abortion, and for raising taxes. His Senate voting record displayed the same pattern, and he was rated the most liberal member of the U.S. Senate by *National Journal*.[1] No matter, for with Obama, style always trumps substance, and rhetoric always replaces the record. Facts and failure may shame other politicians into a reassessment of their policies, but not Obama. In his case, misleading the public is not a function of ego or a personality flaw. It is a deliberate strategy designed to tickle the ears with pleasing words while doing things radical and transformational.

Learning Religious Language

Nowhere was this truer than in Obama's God-talk. John Kerry lost the evangelical vote four to one to George W. Bush in 2004. The first major-party Roman Catholic nominee for president in forty-four years, Kerry even managed to lose the Catholic vote. Exit polls showed "moral values" determined the voting decision of one out of every four voters, and they voted more than three to one for Bush. Against the backdrop of this political wreckage, fixing the party's "religious problem" became an obsession for Democrats. George Soros and other liberal donors contributed to liberal evangelical groups like Sojourners to develop a religious language for liberals that stressed poverty, climate change (relabeled "creation care"), and "the common good."[2] A professor of linguistics from the University of California at Berkeley met with Nancy Pelosi and Democratic strategists, teaching them how to frame issues in moral terms.[3] But one Democratic politician who needed no tutoring was Barack Obama.

Obama arrived in Chicago from New York City in 1985 as a community organizer funded by a grant from Developing Communities Project, and he set about to organize local activists.[4] His initial results were lackluster, in part because he had no connections in the churches that served as the locus of life in the black community.

Obama met with Toni Preckwinkle, a Chicago alderwoman from the south side, and she took him under her wing. Preckwinkle suggested Obama join Jeremiah Wright's Trinity United Church of Christ, the largest and most influential African-American church in the region. "It's a church that would provide you with lots of social connections and prominent parishioners," she pointed out. "It's a good place for a politician to be a member."[5] Wright guided Obama's personal spiritual journey, serving as a mentor and father figure. It was under Wright's counsel that Obama made a commitment to Christ; married his wife, Michelle; and learned the religious language that would serve him in his political career—at least until the controversy over Wright's unorthodox theological and political views exploded in April 2008.

A sermon by Wright inspired the title of Obama's autobiography, *The Audacity of Hope*. It informed his faux sensitivity to the views of faith-based voters, such as stating that their views on abortion were worthy of a fair hearing even as he took the opposite view. By the time Obama addressed the Sojourners' "Call to Renewal" conference in 2006, he was ready to road test religious themes he later used in his campaign for the presidency. His aim was to refute the charge that the Democratic Party had become a captive of secular liberals and was hostile to religion. Obama deftly challenged not only the religious right but also the secular left. He decried liberals for seeming uncomfortable and even intolerant about the religious faith of millions of Americans. His criticism was withering:

> At worst, there are some liberals who dismiss religion in the public square as inherently irrational or intolerant, insisting on a caricature of religious Americans that paints them as fanatical, or thinking that the very word "Christian" describes one's political opponents, not people of faith. . . . I think we make a mistake when we fail to acknowledge the power of faith in people's lives—in the lives of the American people—and I think it's time that we join a serious debate about how to reconcile faith with our modern, pluralistic democracy.[6]

It was the most pro-religion message by a Democratic presidential aspirant since Jimmy Carter, and it had the desired effect of wowing pundits and charming religious leaders on the left and right. But like most of Obama's oratory, it added up to nothing. Indeed, as we saw in the previous chapter, once in office Obama proved less sympathetic to the values of religious folk than any president in our lifetime. Like the soothing words he shared in the Harvard seminar, the Sojourners speech obscured his true intentions, namely an aggressively progressive, secular agenda that sublimated religion to a greater good—as he defined that good.

Pattern of Hostility

No administration in modern times has been more hostile to the public expression of religious faith than Obama's. Beyond the anti-Christian bias of the Obamacare charitable mandate, his administration's assertion that the First Amendment does not protect the right of churches to select ministers of their choosing, and the targeting of Christian and pro-life groups by the IRS (covered in chapter 11), consider these facts:

- Obama declined to hold public services in the White House commemorating the National Day of Prayer, which had been the practice of his predecessors.
- In September 2011, his Department of Health and Human Services terminated funding to the U.S. Conference of Catholic Bishops for its extensive program to assist victims of human

trafficking and modern-day slavery. The reason? Objections to Catholic teaching on abortion and contraception.[7]

- In 2013 Obama's inaugural committee forced pastor Louie Giglio, whose Atlanta church was nationally known for its efforts to combat sex trafficking, to withdraw from delivering a prayer at the inaugural ceremony after an audio recording surfaced of a sermon Giglio delivered in the mid-1990s referencing biblical teaching on homosexuality. When it came to praying at Obama's second inaugural, no pastor holding to an orthodox view of Scripture had need to apply.
- His Justice Department canceled a $30,000 grant to a program for at-risk youth because it allowed voluntary, student-led prayer, and the oath recited by its young charges mentioned God.[8]
- He advocated passage of a version of the Employment Non-Discrimination Act prohibiting private employers from declining to hire gays and lesbians that granted no exemption for religious ministries and charities.
- The Defense Department canceled an appearance by Franklin Graham of Samaritan's Purse at a National Day of Prayer observance because of Graham's alleged anti-Muslim bigotry.
- Obama's campaign removed a reference to God from the Democratic Party platform and only moved to reinsert it after news outlets reported the exclusion and controversy erupted. In rushed proceedings at the party convention in Charlotte, North Carolina, the name of God was reinserted to boos from the delegates.

Each of these acts of bias against public expressions of faith may have an explanation, but taken together they reveal a pattern of hostility directed at the right of religious people to fully participate in civic life. They also reveal the lie of Obama's posturing prior to the 2008 election and his comforting assurances that he deplored the Democratic Party's past insensitivity toward religious belief. Obama's God-talk, like all his other talk, bore no resemblance to what he actually did as president or the policy agenda he pursued.

Forward—Over the Cliff

The media greeted Obama's 2012 reelection by proclaiming the dawn of a liberal renaissance. "His victory signaled the irreversible triumph of a new, 21st-century America: multiracial, multi-ethnic, global in outlook and moving beyond centuries of racial, sexual, marital and religious tradition," concluded Howard Fineman in the *Huffington Post* in a postelection analysis that was typical.[9] It didn't turn out that way.

Within six months Obama's agenda was on life support, and the triumphalist claims of a new liberal majority sounded delusional.

His attempt at a "grand bargain" on federal spending went nowhere in spite of a series of dinners at which he attempted to charm a group of Republican senators. His claims that air safety would be at risk due to budget cuts at the Federal Aviation Administration if the sequester of federal funds that his administration had proposed took effect proved false. The sequester happened, and life went on—with no airplanes dropping from the sky. His claims that the sequester would slow down economic growth were equally false: the economy actually grew at a faster pace after the cuts in federal spending occurred.[10] Obama's sinking fortunes were not helped when overzealous aides lashed out at the *Washington Post*'s Bob Woodward after he accurately reported that the sequester originated from the White House.[11] And after a lobbying effort to which Obama lent his full prestige and political capital, including some campaign-like stops around the country, a relatively modest compromise background-check bill cosponsored by Republican Pat Toomey of Pennsylvania failed in the Democratic-controlled Senate when five Democrats (some up for reelection in 2014 in red states) opposed it.[12]

Obamacare, meanwhile, began to strain under its own weight. The Supreme Court had upheld Obamacare under the federal government's taxing power in 2012 but gave states the right to opt out of Medicaid expansion and other mandates in the law. Twenty-five states opted out of Medicaid expansion and declined to set up state health insurance exchanges. Consumers in those states were sent to the national Obamacare insurance exchange website, which proved a disaster.

Built at a cost of over $600 million by fifty-five contractors over a three-year period, the Obamacare exchange website was so dysfunctional that it would not allow consumers to log on for weeks, and when they finally did, the site provided inaccurate information.

More than five million people had their health insurance policies canceled because they did not meet Obamacare's coverage mandates. Obama had counted on these provisions to cover up to half of the uninsured population. According to *National Journal*, "it's increasingly clear that the minor loss [on Medicaid] is punching a major hole in the law's primary ambition."[13] When the Obama administration delayed the employer mandate that required businesses to provide insurance to their employees and exempted members of Congress and their staffs, Senator Max Baucus of Montana, a key author of the law, called it "a slow train wreck."

Scandals at the IRS, Justice Department, and State Department buffeted Obama and pulled down his approval ratings. The Justice Department subpoenaed the phone records and e-mails of reporters (and, in one case, a reporter's parents), and Attorney General Eric Holder appeared to commit perjury when he denied knowledge of the practice in testimony before Congress.[14]

Journalists who had heralded Obama in 2008 discovered he simply wasn't up to the job. MSNBC's Chris Matthews, who once said an Obama speech had sent "a thrill up my leg," pointedly asked, "What part of the presidency does Obama like? He doesn't like dealing with other politicians. That means his own cabinet. That means members of the Congress, either party. He doesn't particularly like the press. . . . He likes going on the road and campaigning, visiting businesses, like he does every couple days somewhere in Ohio or somewhere. . . . He doesn't seem to like to be an executive."[15] Maureen Dowd echoed his complaint: "The silver-tongued campaigner has turned out to be a leaden salesman in the Oval Office. On issues from drones to gun control to taxes to Syria, the president likes to cite public opinion polls to justify his action or inaction." Obama is "incapable of getting in front of issues and shaping public and Congressional opinion with a strong selling job."[16]

How to explain the failure of a man celebrated by so many as the liberal messiah? The chasm separating his rhetoric from his governance is now undeniable to all. As the character played by Dan Aykroyd in the film *Ghostbusters* said, "I've been in the real world. They demand results." For the first time in his career, a president whose prior professional experience as a law professor and community organizer ill prepared him for the responsibilities of high office is being asked to deliver results, and it is not a pretty sight. Consider the following:

- Obama pledged to close the military prison complex where the U.S. houses terrorists in Guantanamo Bay, Cuba, in his first year in office. It remains open at this writing.
- He promised not to raise taxes on anyone making less than $250,000 per year, and then he did so with the tax increases enacted under Obamacare.
- Obama stated throughout the 2008 campaign that he believed marriage should be a union between a man and a woman. Then he flip-flopped and came out for same-sex marriage in May 2012.
- He vowed to limit campaign spending and accept federal funds for the general election. Then he rejected the funds in both 2008 and 2012. Obama went on to raise a record $1.75 billion in contributions, effectively driving a stake through the heart of Watergate-era campaign finance reform.
- Obama attacked social welfare organizations for being engaged in politics, calling them a threat to democracy and an invitation to foreign influence of U.S. elections. He then set up a group himself and allowed administration officials to appear at special briefings for top donors.
- He criticized the National Security Agency's terrorist surveillance program begun under George W. Bush. Then he expanded it.

All presidents change their mind, but in Obama's case, equivocation has become an art, and according to Gerald Seib of the *Wall Street Journal*, the explanation lies in his sheer complexity. "Simple people aren't often elected presidents," Seib argues. "Instead, presidents tend to come in complicated packages."[17] The implication is that Obama is a paradox, a jumble of contradictions, and an enigma whose true character is known only to him.

Nowhere was Obama's deliberate dissembling and deceit more evident than in his oft-repeated promise, "If you like your health-care plan, you can keep your health-care plan, period." This was a central argument for Obamacare: it would not affect anyone already insured. As Obamacare took effect, it became evident this promise was either intentionally misleading or an outright lie. Millions of consumers received cancellation notices, and when they sought comparable policies, they discovered they cost thousands of dollars more. With his poll ratings plummeting and Democrats in revolt, Obama flip-flopped and vowed to make an administrative fix allowing those who liked their current policies to keep them for at least another year. Obamacare was the central domestic legislative achievement of his presidency, but his major promise to the American people was false, costing him trust and credibility he may never regain.

Good leaders set a clear path, show the way forward, and provide friend and foe alike with clarity and consistency that, like a northern star, can be reliably followed. We need leaders who say what they mean, who do what they say, and whose rhetoric provides a road map for how they will lead and where they will take the country. In this essential test of leadership, Obama has failed miserably, and I would suggest that failure has been deliberate insofar as he could not allow the American people to have insight into his genuine beliefs and intentions.

Outdated Rhetoric

On April 23, 2007, Barack Obama delivered his first major foreign policy address as a presidential candidate at the Chicago Council on Global Affairs. At the time he had been in the U.S. Senate for twenty-seven months.[18] He faulted George W. Bush for pursuing a "foreign policy based on a flawed ideology" and the misplaced belief that "tough talk can replace real strength and vision." Bush "may occupy the White House," Obama argued, "but for the last six years, the position of leader of the free the world has remained open. And it's time to fill that role once more."[19]

Obama's arrogance had little justification, given the fact that he had vocally opposed the surge of forces in Iraq earlier in the year, claiming it might actually make things worse.[20] Instead, the surge reduced sectarian violence, dramatically improved security, and dropped the number of U.S. casualties to their lowest level since the invasion of Iraq in March 2003. In his most important foreign policy assessment as a U.S. senator, Obama was wrong.

Obama called Iraq "an unnecessary diversion" inspired by "old ideologies and outdated strategies." But he had told a different story earlier. At the Democratic National Convention in Boston in July 2004, Obama demurred when asked how he would have voted on authorizing military action against Iraq, saying he did not have access to the classified intelligence reports. Nevertheless, he promised that a new approach—namely, unilateral withdrawal—would increase the chance of peace in the region: "Now it's our moment to lead—our generation's time to tell another great American story. So someday we can tell our children that this was the time when we helped forge peace in the Middle East."[21]

Once again, Obama's soaring rhetoric bore no resemblance to reality. On his watch, Egypt descended into civil war and chaos. Hezbollah tightened its grip on Lebanon. Syrian President Hafez al-Assad waged war against his own people, including bombing civilian population centers and using chemical weapons to wipe out more than a hundred thousand innocent lives. In Gaza, the Iranian-backed terrorist group Hamas threatens to overwhelm Fatah in the control of the Palestinian territories. Iran is poised to obtain a nuclear weapon, with an estimated three thousand centrifuges at nuclear installations in Fordo and Natanz, and has provided intermediate-range missiles to Assad.[22] Jordan has been destabilized by an influx of an estimated 250,000 refugees from the bloodshed in Syria, with a total of four million persons displaced within Syria. Obama established a "red line" for U.S. military intervention if Assad used chemical munitions, procrastinated when Assad did exactly that, failed to assemble an international coalition or gain the support of the United Nations, and then sought congressional approval of military strikes after claiming he did not need it. By every reasonable measure, the Middle East is a bloodier and more dangerous region than when Obama took office.

The media and even some conservatives greeted Obama's reelection as if it signaled a ringing endorsement of the progressive agenda, from government-run health care to higher taxes. That was not the case. Obamacare remains deeply unpopular, economic growth sluggish, Obama's approval ratings lackluster, and his response to challenges in Egypt, Syria, and Russia feckless. His second term could lead to a repudiation of government overreach and a revival of conservatism, just as disappointment with the Vietnam War and the Great Society under Lyndon Johnson paved the way for the emergence of a center-right majority.

As the spiritual cycle turns, a triumphant moment for a political movement may in fact be the beginning of its end. If enough believers today pray and work for a restoration of common-sense values, we can ignite an awakening that will be the beginning of the end of America's false messiah's brand of progressivism. However, it will require taking a stand, as we shall see in our last section.

Action Points

1. Commit to praying daily for our nation's leaders. Pray for leaders who say what they mean, who do what they say, and whose rhetoric provides a road map for how they will lead and where they will take the country.
2. Read 2 Chronicles 7:13–14. Believers often cite this passage in hopes that other people will turn from their wicked ways. But make this verse personal: In what ways do you need to humble yourself, pray, seek God's face, and turn from your wicked ways? Cling to God's promise that when you do, He will hear your prayers, forgive your sin, and heal our land.
3. Contact your church or call a few friends and host a prayer meeting focusing on the spiritual needs of our nation. As you pray, consider specific ways that you and your fellow believers can help ignite an awakening that will be the beginning of the end of Obama's brand of progressivism.

Part 3

Awakening

CHAPTER 13

Reenergizing the Party of Lincoln

Obama's election as president signified a historic moment in America overcoming its painful past of slavery and segregation. His life and career would not have been possible without those who opposed slavery and gave rise to the Republican Party. Among them was Abraham Lincoln. In one of the most consequential decisions of his political career, Lincoln walked away from the Whig Party in 1856 and helped form a new political party to fight the gravest evil of his time. This move would change the direction of America, taking it to a new level of greatness.

Raised in an impoverished family on the Kentucky frontier, Lincoln scraped his way to political prominence through hard work. Although a self-taught man, he found himself prepared and able to practice law, win election to the legislature, and serve in Congress. Lincoln believed deeply in the Whig platform of internal improvements, tariffs, individualism, and the nonextension of slavery. But as his opposition to slavery hardened, Lincoln gradually became convinced America could not survive half-slave and half-free.

Still considering himself a Whig at heart, Lincoln watched his party disintegrate over the issue of slavery.[1] On Washington's birthday in 1856, Lincoln joined a gathering in Decatur, Illinois, a gathering of Free-Soilers, abolitionists, anti-slavery Democrats, and Conscience Whigs to form the Republican Party. "Of strange, discordant, even hostile elements, we gathered from the four winds," he later recalled. One thing united them: moral revulsion over slavery. Just four years later Lincoln received the Republican presidential nomination as a dark horse candidate and was elected president.

Ronald Reagan grew up in a working-class, Irish, Democratic family during the Depression. A committed liberal at the time, he cast his first presidential ballot for Franklin D. Roosevelt, and he actively campaigned for Harry S. Truman in 1948 as president of the Screen Actors Guild. But as the Cold War unfolded and he wrestled with the evil of communism, Reagan's views evolved and he became more conservative. In 1960 he joined Democrats for Nixon, and by 1964 when he delivered "The Speech" on behalf of Barry Goldwater's presidential campaign, Reagan had become a Republican. In later years, he would remark, "I didn't leave the Democratic Party; the Democratic Party left me."

Call for True Conservatism

Both Lincoln and Reagan became Republicans because of the party's moral clarity on the defining issue of their times: slavery for Lincoln and communism in the case of Reagan. Unique among all major parties in the history of Western civilization, the Republican Party was founded to right a wrong, ameliorate evil, and remove the stain of sin from the American body politic.

The GOP has succeeded best when it has acted in accordance with this heritage by offering a moral critique of social ills and putting forward bold solutions, and it has usually failed when it has allowed itself to be seen as the party of Wall Street, mostly concerned with protecting big business and the wealthy rather than the working class.

This theme played a central role in the party's defeat in 2012, when the Obama campaign attacked Mitt Romney's business background in private equity, alleging he was unconcerned with the plight of the middle class.

Some have argued Reagan and Lincoln would not recognize the Tea Party–infused, religiously flavored GOP of today and could not win its presidential nomination.[2] But that conclusion requires ignoring the core beliefs of both men. As we saw in chapter 5, Reagan was at heart a moralist who took his Christian faith seriously and encouraged the entry of men and women of faith into the Republican Party. Historians have long wrestled with whether Lincoln was an orthodox

Christian, but there is no doubt that he felt a commonality with anti-slavery evangelicals and saw God's hand in the Civil War. In any case, the question is ahistorical. Could John F. Kennedy, a staunch anti-communist who sent the first U.S. armed forces to Vietnam and favored across-the-board tax cuts, win the Democratic Party nomination today? It is a little like asking whether Ted Williams could hit today's pitchers. We simply don't know.

What is known is how the Republican grassroots responded to the 2012 defeat, and it was the exact opposite of the reaction of the media and the Republicans inside the Beltway. While GOP strategists in Washington responded with hand-wringing and self-criticism, debating whether to put new toppings on the pizza or change the pizza box of their party, the grassroots called for authentic conservatism. A December 2012 *Washington Post*–ABC News poll asked voters if the Republican Party was too far to the right and out of touch, needing to adopt new policies; or if it had the right policies but needed new leaders. Among all voters, 58 percent said the party was too far to the right and out of touch. But among Republicans, only 23 percent said the party needed new policies, while 64 percent said it needed better leaders who could communicate more effectively.[3] In other words, the party's supporters have not responded to the 2012 defeat with self-doubt or by moving to the left or the middle.

Part of this is the result of simple math. Conservatives constitute roughly 75 percent of Republican primary voters. Evangelicals play a similarly supersized role in Republican primaries. Self-identified evangelicals comprised 51 percent of the vote in the GOP presidential primaries, according to exit polls. This was the highest level of participation ever recorded for voters of faith in the GOP presidential primaries.[4] A 2013 survey by the Pew Research Center found that Tea Party members make up 37 percent of all Republican voters and cast 61 percent of the votes in 2012 primaries for which network exit polls were conducted.[5] These voters are not persuaded by calls for more moderate, centrist candidates who appeal to ticket-splitting voters by trimming their ideological sails. They want leaders in the model of Senators Ted Cruz of Texas, Rand Paul of Kentucky,

Mike Lee of Utah, and Marco Rubio of Florida.

This is the likely future of the Grand Old Party: bold, unapologetic conservatism of a reformist bent—not hunkering down in the mushy middle. By recognizing this reality and becoming more active in the Republican Party, as leaders and candidates as well as voters, people of faith can ensure that it remains true to its principles.

Circular Firing Squad

This desire for bold conservatism is the opposite of the perspective of many Republicans in Washington. The attitude of these Washington Republicans contributed in part to the Republican National Committee's well-intentioned but misguided "autopsy," a ninety-eight-page report that examined the 2012 defeat and made suggestions to improve the party. There was much in the report—such as its calls for more advanced technology, the use of social media, and a superior ground game—that made good sense. But the report ignored moral and social issues other than to imply that the party should reconsider its support for traditional marriage: the report discounted the vital and energetic role played by voters of faith.

In a similar vein, many of their fellow Republicans pointed to U.S. Senate nominees Todd Akin in Missouri and Richard Mourdock in Indiana as examples of failed candidates who allowed themselves to be drawn into awkward discussions of whether abortion should be legal in the case of rape, blaming them for the GOP losing single and young women in 2012—this in spite of the fact that women voters did not list abortion high on their list of issues that determine their voting behavior. (The fact that Senate candidates in Ohio, Montana, North Dakota, and other battleground states lost in spite of establishment support received nary a mention.) Republicans too often respond to defeat by organizing themselves into a circular firing squad.

Those individuals who stand up for conservative principles are met with the same firing-squad response. Sarah Palin, the GOP vice-presidential nominee in 2008, was not even invited to speak at the Republican National Convention in Tampa four years later. Democrats display no reticence in featuring controversial figures at their convention, people like civil rights leader Reverend Al Sharpton, Teamsters president James P. Hoffa, and Planned Parenthood Federation of America and the Planned Parenthood Action Fund president Cecile Richards. Sometimes Republicans don't seem to understand that a political party has many roles. The presidential nominee requires broad appeal to the entire electorate, while others motivate and mobilize the grassroots, often stirring controversy and opposition. Their name is not on the national ballot, but their ability to energize voters is necessary. Too often—and to its own detriment—the Republican Party keeps its strongest allies at arm's length. A political party that lets its opponents pick its friends shouldn't be surprised when it doesn't have many.

Party Loyalists

Many evangelicals and Tea Party activists today decline to identify with either party, and that's one reason more people identify themselves as evangelicals or conservatives than Republicans in the U.S. today.[6] But this is a mistake as well. Party loyalty does not debase one's citizenship; it is a healthy and enhanced expression of our civic engagement, and it provides solidarity with others who share common values. There is a big difference between blind partisanship and a healthy loyalty to a party based on one's beliefs and values.

Lincoln and Reagan were both party loyalists who supported the candidates and the platform that aligned with their views. If evangelicals, faithful Catholics, and their allies retreat from party involvement, their voice will become muted in government, their role in the primaries and caucuses that choose party nominees will be reduced, and in many cases they will be forced to support the lesser of two evils in general elections.

Social reform movements usually win one of the major parties to their cause before winning the country. When the African-American Mississippi Freedom Democrats were seated as delegates at the 1964 Democratic National Convention in Atlantic City, it was an important victory for the civil rights movement. The adoption of a pro-life plank at the 1976 Republican Convention in Kansas City signaled the ascendancy of the pro-family movement even as Reagan suffered a narrow defeat for the nomination to President Gerald Ford. The ability of anti-slavery evangelicals to keep the Republican Party focused on opposition to slavery during the mid-1850s set the course that led to the Emancipation Proclamation. No social movement can govern the country until it can win within a major political party.

But if it would be wrong for men and women of faith to retreat from involvement in the political parties, they commit a graver error if they allow the church to become a special interest group beholden to one party. A constituency that gives its loyalty and votes to a party regardless of its candidates' stances on the issues, their ethics, or their competence will be taken for granted and, in the case of evangelicals, risk losing credibility.

The church is not the Republican Party at prayer. The church is Christ's bride. Christians must speak with a prophetic voice, fearing God and no man, sparing neither party nor politician.

Jesus said of His disciples: "They are not of the world, even as I am not of the world" (John 17:16). Believers are in the world but not of the world; and as American citizens, men and women of faith should be in a party but not of the party. They should have the attitude of sojourners: they are on a spiritual journey through a strange land, carrying a passport from another kingdom. Their involvement should be a witness to others, driven by passion and patriotism, not a desire for power. And they must be prepared to leave if necessary—as Lincoln did when he forsook his beloved Whigs and Reagan gave up on the Democratic Party—over nonnegotiable issues of principle.

Third Party Failures

Some have suggested that people of faith should abandon the GOP and form a Christian or conservative third party. But third parties have usually been a fool's errand. In American history they have rarely won a healthy share of the vote, and most slid into irrelevance within a few elections of their founding.

Frances Willard, president of the Women's Christian Temperance Union, broke with the Republican Party over its lack of support for the temperance cause and helped found the Prohibition Party, but the party's presidential nominees never garnered more than two million votes in a national election. A decade later, agrarian rebels offended by Democratic foot-dragging on regulating banks and railroads founded the Populist Party. Running on a revolutionary platform in 1892 that included a graduated income tax and direct election of senators, the Populist ticket received barely one million votes. In 1896 the Democratic Party nominated William Jennings Bryan, a thirty-six-year-old free silver champion, and adopted many of the Populists' demands in its platform, so the Populists nominated Bryan as well but chose firebrand Congressman Thomas E. Watson of Georgia as his running mate. They lost badly again, and the failure of fusionism contributed to the Populist Party's demise.

The twentieth century is riddled with third parties led by strong personalities with lofty aspirations but no strategy for victory. Teddy Roosevelt's Bull Moose Party in 1912, Robert La Follette's Progressive Party in 1924, Strom Thurmond's Dixiecrats in 1948, George Wallace's American Independent Party in 1968, and Ross Perot's Reform Party in 1992 and 1996 all won few, if any, seats in Congress. Roosevelt's 27 percent of the vote was the highest share ever received by a third-party candidate, exceeding the total of 23 percent won by President William Howard Taft. But it was largely a cult of personality centered on Roosevelt, and when he rejoined the GOP in 1916, the party disintegrated.

Another personality-centered party was the Reform Party, founded in 1992 by Ross Perot. I got to know Perot and urged him to consider joining forces with the Republican Party on the condition that they support term limits and a constitutional amendment requiring a balanced federal budget. Perot was intrigued but took a different course. Within a matter of years, the Reform Party was plagued by internal discord, ideological confusion, and multiple lawsuits. Perot could have had an enduring impact on national politics, with a Reform caucus in the House of Representatives of fifty to one hundred members and the ability to act as a power broker in choosing Republican nominees in 1996 and 2000. But by taking the third-party route, the Reform Party found itself co-opted by the Republican Party while receiving nothing in return, with two-thirds of Perot voters casting their ballots for GOP congressional candidates in 1994.

Ralph Nader ran on the Green Party ticket in 2000 and 2004, and many Democrats still blame him for siphoning off enough votes from Al Gore to elect George W. Bush. This is another danger of third parties: they split the vote of one party and push the other party to victory, the opposite of their intended effect. Nader, once one of the most prominent and admired liberals in the country, saw his influence wane as a result of his quixotic presidential bids.

The futility of third parties derives to some extent from our system of government. Unlike European parliamentary systems, U.S. parties receive no seats in Congress based on their share of the national vote. Roosevelt, Wallace, and Perot all would have had many seats in Congress under a parliamentary system; in the U.S. they won few or none. If the Constitution had not determined that members of Congress would represent single-member districts, a Christian political party could elect as many as seventy-five to a hundred members of the House and ten to twenty U.S. senators in today's electorate, playing a role similar to that of orthodox Jewish parties in Israel. But in the American system, one must win 50 percent plus one of the vote or walk away empty-handed.

The American people have never shown much enthusiasm for single-issue, narrowcast, or ideological parties. Unlike Europe, where ideological schisms have dominated political life since medieval times, Americans prefer broad-based political movements that allow for accommodation, compromise, and cooperation. This aversion to partisanship found expression in Madison's famous warning about "factions" in the *Federalist Papers* and Washington's denunciation of parties in his farewell address, in which he urged the people to "mitigate and assuage" the party spirit "to prevent its bursting into flame, lest, instead of warming, it should consume."[7]

Because it began as a third-party movement, the Republican Party embraced abolitionists, Conscience Whigs, anti-slavery Democrats, free blacks, abolitionists, Free-Soilers, anti-Masonics, and temperance advocates. As much as they were divided on key issues, these groups were united in their opposition to slavery and, even more, in their commitment to freedom. As Eric Foner has demonstrated, the Republican Party's ideology of "free soil, free labor, and free men" was not just a negative critique of slavery but an optimistic vision of a prosperous America expanding westward, with a market economy that gave freedom to all and granted the opportunity to everyone for upward mobility, regardless of race or ethnic background.[8]

Evangelicals, the Tea Party, and the GOP

Today's GOP is a patchwork quilt of Chamber of Commerce business advocates, libertarians, evangelicals, moderates, defense hawks, Second Amendment activists, and Tea Party members. The moderates, who ruled the party's national nominating system virtually unchallenged from 1936 until 1964, lost their influence as the nation's population shifted South and West. It is no accident that Mitt Romney was the first Republican presidential nominee from a Northern state since Thomas E. Dewey in 1948. Still, the establishment remains formidable because of its fund-raising ability, which has grown in importance as the cost of winning the nomination has increased to $100 million in recent years.

Evangelicals poured into the GOP in the 1970s and 1980s like new wine entering old wineskins. In 1976, millions of born-again voters cast their ballots for Jimmy Carter; in 1980, nearly two-thirds of the evangelical vote went to Ronald Reagan.[9] It was the most significant demographic shift in the U.S. electorate since the rise of the union vote and the ethnic Catholic vote in the 1930s and then, in the 1960s, the African-Americans' switch in loyalty from the Republican to the Democratic Party. As they transitioned from Reagan Democrats to Republicans, millions of evangelicals switched their party registration to vote for Pat Robertson in 1988 and went on to support social conservative presidential candidates like Pat Buchanan, Mike Huckabee, and Rick Santorum. This represented a return by conservative Protestants to their Republican roots.

The influx of evangelicals into the GOP, driven by cultural issues such as abortion and marriage, created tension. The Republican Party wants the votes of evangelicals, but party leaders are often uncomfortable with their exuberance, religiosity, and moral agenda. Democratic Party officials have displayed no such double-mindedness as they lock arms with union bosses or the pro-abortion set. Some Republican leaders are afraid to be seen with their evangelical best friends—who have cast more votes for the party's candidates in the past quarter century than any other constituency in the electorate. Perhaps they take these voters for granted, not realizing that evangelicals will simply stay home in the absence of candidates running on platforms that embody their values. Trepidation at being barbecued on the media spit for associating with religious folk plays a role too. Obama need not fear media criticism as he hangs with "cool" friends like Jay-Z, Beyoncé, Oprah, or Eva Longoria.

Tea Party activists have been greeted with the same mixture of ambivalence and dread. The establishment bemoaned the poor performance of Tea Party candidates like Christine O'Donnell in Delaware, Sharron Angle in Nevada, and Ken Buck in Colorado. (The victories of Rand Paul in Kentucky, Marco Rubio in Florida, Ron Johnson in Wisconsin, and Mike Lee in Utah are ignored.) The tension over Tea Party activists and their agenda in the Republican Party is a reprise of a similar reaction when evangelicals entered the party. This reaction comes in part because of considerable overlap in the two constituencies. A Pew Research Center analysis in 2011 found that two-thirds of the voters who self-identified as Tea Party members hold conservative views on issues such as marriage and abortion, while 69 percent of white evangelicals identified with the Tea Party.[10]

David Brody of the Christian Broadcasting Network coined the term "Teavangelicals" to stress their commonality. "Think of Teavangelicals as a large subset of the Tea Party movement," argues Brody. "The truth of the matter is that Tea Party libertarians cannot win without evangelicals by their side. Conversely, evangelicals can't do it alone either."[11]

This statistical reality has led some to assert a direct link between the Tea Party Movement and religious conservatives.[12] But the overlap between the two constituencies is one of demographic happenstance.

Both evangelicals and Tea Party supporters tend to be married, churchgoing, middle-class, and well-educated, centered in the South or Midwest. A survey conducted for the Faith and Freedom Coalition in 2010 found that 47 percent of all evangelicals considered themselves members of the Tea Party.[13]

The confusion among pollsters and political analysts over the relationship between Tea Party activists and evangelicals is also due to their misunderstanding of what drives people of faith into the civic arena. While motivated by moral concerns, they are not single-issue voters. Their concerns about family breakup are intertwined with opposition to government overreach and high taxes. To these voters, runaway spending and the deficit are moral issues. They see no dichotomy between social and fiscal issues because their worldview applies equally to economic and cultural concerns. Their principles are summed up in the Declaration of Independence, the Constitution, and the writings of the founders that stress the individual liberty, a virtuous citizenry, limited government, and morality derived from faith in God.

Democrats and Civil Rights

In her book *Team of Rivals*, Doris Kearns Goodwin revealed Abraham Lincoln as a canny, practical politician and provided a road map of sorts for Barack Obama's assembling a "team of rivals" in his cabinet, including Hillary Clinton and thrilling both their supporters. (Obama even cited the book in his selection of his cabinet: just as Lincoln had chosen former rivals Salmon P. Chase and William H. Seward, Obama had chosen Hillary.)[14]

Moviegoers of both parties packed into theaters in 2012 to see Steven Spielberg's biopic of the sixteenth president, only to experience a dramatic reminder that it was Republicans who had stood for emancipation and civil rights, while Democrats had defended slavery and second-class citizenship for blacks. MSNBC's Chris Matthews wanted to know: "Which party would Abraham Lincoln join today? Would he still be a Republican after all the talk about state's rights and honoring the Confederacy?"[15]

Media commentators ignore the fact that Democrats led the opposition to civil rights for most of America's history. Republicans led the way in passing not only the Thirteenth, Fourteenth, and Fifteenth Amendments that secured emancipation, equality before the law, and the right to vote for black Americans, but also the Civil Rights Acts of 1866 and 1875. These constitutional amendments and the 1875 legislation did not receive a single Democratic vote.

When black students integrated Little Rock High School in 1957, the federal troops called out to protect them were sent by a Republican president, Dwight Eisenhower; a Democratic governor refused to protect them. That same year, at Eisenhower's urging, Congress passed the first civil rights act in eighty-two years, and an overwhelming majority of Republicans in both chambers voted in support. The 1964 Civil Rights Act was modeled after the 1875 law, which was struck down by the Supreme Court in 1883. It passed the Senate with the indispensable support of Republican leader Everett Dirksen, who helped overcome a Southern filibuster by delivering the votes of 82 percent of the Republican caucus; 80 percent of the "no" votes in the Senate came from Democrats.[16]

One of the six Republican "no" votes was cast by Barry Goldwater, the 1964 GOP presidential nominee, with consequences felt ever since. Lyndon Johnson reportedly remarked after signing the civil rights bill that it would cost Democrats the South for two generations. The reverse was also true: Republican candidates did well among black voters for nearly a century after the Civil War, but in 1960 John F. Kennedy won 70 percent of the African-American vote. With Goldwater's opposition to the 1964 Civil Rights Act, the black vote swung more heavily to the Democrats, and today its candidates routinely win 90 percent or more of the black vote.[17]

Yet the status of blacks in the Democratic Party is a cautionary tale. What has the African-American community gotten in return for its loyalty to the Democrats? Not much. Obama infrequently addresses race and poverty, has appointed few African-Americans to his cabinet, and bristles at critics like the public intellectual Cornel West and television host Tavis Smiley, who urge him to take the lead on racial justice. African-American unemployment during Obama's presidency has averaged 15 percent, roughly twice the national average, while black youth unemployment hovers near 50 percent.[18]

Obama's lack of leadership has sparked criticism from members of the Congressional Black Caucus and others in the minority community. "When Barack Obama leaves the White House in January 2017," notes Bruce Dixon of the Black Agenda Report, African-Americans will have "T-shirts and buttons and posters, the souvenirs. That will be the good news. The bad news is what else we'll have . . . and not."[19]

More Than Special Interest

Evangelicals should learn from this example. Like African-Americans, they have largely been active in one party, and, like them, evangelicals risk losing influence if that party takes their votes for granted. Also like African-Americans, evangelicals will lose their prophetic voice if they are seen as merely a special interest group of pleaders.

The evangelical challenge is made more difficult by the fact that the Democratic Party under Obama has taken positions opposed to religious freedom. At times the Democratic Party has sought political advantage by demonizing and attacking evangelicals for their faith, or suggesting that they are intolerant of women's health concerns. But the Democrats' decisions must not determine our course.

Men and women of faith should speak to issues and values above party, and our involvement in the grassroots of either party should be for the primary purpose of increasing our witness and maximizing the impact of our citizenship. Believers should not be shallowly or narrowly partisan, and we should work with Democrats wherever possible on those issues on which we agree, which has been possible in the past in such policy areas as the child tax credit, education reform, support for Israel, pornography (which many feminist Democrats oppose), and abortion. As both U.S. parties have followed in the footsteps of European parties and become more ideological, their officeholders more beholden to party discipline, and their followers more polarized, this cooperation across party lines is more difficult today—but it is still possible.

Just as Republicans supported civil rights long before Democrats did, Republicans also took the lead in supporting women's rights. As we saw in chapter 4, support for women's suffrage in the nineteenth and early twentieth centuries was strongest among evangelical women and advocates of temperance. Largely as a consequence of their activism, the Republican Party became the first major political party to formally support women's suffrage. The Nineteenth Amendment was first proposed by a Republican from California and defeated by a Democratic-controlled Congress. Almost forty years and multiple defeats by Senate Democrats later, Republicans had taken control of both chambers of Congress, enabling them to pass the amendment, introduced again by a Republican, despite strong opposition from Democrats and even President Woodrow Wilson, referred to by women's suffrage activists as "Kaiser Wilson."[20] Of the thirty-six state legislatures that subsequently ratified the Amendment, nearly three-quarters were controlled by the GOP. It should come as no surprise, therefore, that the first woman elected to Congress was a Republican.

The Most Nonpartisan Leader Ever

The most nonpartisan leader who ever lived was Jesus. He numbered among His disciples a tax collector for the Roman Empire and a member of a political party (the Zealots) dedicated to the violent overthrow of Rome. It is unlikely this was a coincidence. By being seen among the people with followers like both Matthew and Simon the Zealot, Jesus made clear that His kingdom was not of this world and that the gospel did not belong to any political faction.

More broadly, Jesus' gesture demonstrated that He did not come to earth as a political savior and that eternal salvation does not come through politics.

Yet that does not absolve His followers from participating in the political process. In fact, we are called to do so, despite how difficult and arduous politics can be. Parties and factions may at times seem evil, but they are a necessary evil in a free society. They can also be a positive and valuable force, and as we have seen, they have had an enormous impact for good throughout history when they have advocated and fought for what was right.

So whether as a Republican or Democrat, get involved, make a difference, and stand for what is good and honorable and worthy of praise. This stand will involve supporting new public policies that can improve the lives of all our citizens. It is to that agenda that we now turn.

Action Points

1. Get involved in the political party of your choice at the local level. Start by attending your precinct caucus and regular county party meetings.
2. Run for and get elected party precinct chair in your precinct or neighborhood. This is the most essential building block of your local party organization.
3. Recruit party volunteers and donors from the faith community to join your precinct volunteer network or to run for precinct chairperson in their own neighborhood. Good folks to recruit include members of your social network, Bible study, discipleship group, or Sunday school class. Share the material in this chapter so they understand the importance of party involvement.

CHAPTER 14

A Bold Pro-Family Plan

For much of its history, the religious conservative movement devoted its energies to abortion, pornography, gay rights, and school prayer. This focused activism served as a much-needed corrective in a political culture that had ignored family breakup and moral decline for far too long. Today social conservatives cast a wider net and work on taxes, poverty, support for Israel, human trafficking, immigration, and education reform.

To take just one example, the more than two thousand references in the Bible to money and finances lay out clear principles on avoiding debt, diversified investing, charitable giving, and honesty in business. This led *Forbes* magazine to ask, "Is the Bible the Ultimate Finance Guide?"[1]

Biblical financial principles also apply to government. If we applied biblical precepts to fiscal policy, we could rein in runaway spending, reduce the debt, balance the budget, and end the immoral, confiscatory policies that will force higher taxes on future generations. The Bible likewise includes principles for education, immigration, health care, and poverty.

It is time for us to put forward a new agenda to restore America to moral and economic greatness. I call this agenda the Bold Pro-Family Plan. It addresses prison reform, immigration, and divorce laws, but as that name suggests, the agenda begins with the family.

The Crisis of the American Family

Imagine bringing your newborn baby home from the hospital and finding a bill in your mailbox for $301,790. According to a recent study by the U.S. Department of Agriculture, that is what it costs (after inflation) a middle-income couple to raise a child to age eighteen—and that does not include the cost of college.[2] To send a child to a public college or university with in-state tuition, add another $195,592.[3] (A private or out-of-state college would cost much more.) That brings the grand total to educate, raise, and nurture a child to adulthood for a middle-class family to a staggering $497,382.

This cost increases every year, and anyone who has gone to the grocery store or pulled up to a gas pump in recent years knows the painful reality of rising costs that average families face. The price of gasoline has doubled since 2000, forcing many moms and dads to choose between getting to work and driving their child to soccer practice or gym class. The cost of child care has increased twice as fast as median family income and now averages about $1,000 per child per month. Health-care costs have risen at a similarly rapid rate, taking up nearly one-fifth of the cost of raising a child.

Furthermore, putting food on the table has never been costlier. Food prices have risen more than at any time in the previous twenty years, in part due to the high price of oil because transportation and energy are major contributors to the cost of food. Two other factors in rising food prices are the diversion of a portion of the U.S. corn crop to meet government ethanol mandates and the Federal Reserve's inflationary money policy, which drives up the cost of commodities like wheat, oat, and barley. Rising food prices sparked riots in Mexico in 2009, fueled the Arab Spring in 2011, hobbled humanitarian organizations feeding the poor in sub-Saharan Africa, and squeezed working-class families as well as victimized the poor in the U.S.

At the same time that expenses have been rising, middle-class family income has fallen. After adjusting for inflation, median family income has fallen since 2007 by more than $4,000.[4] Unemployment remains high, and many newly created jobs are either part-time or pay less than the jobs they replaced. Facing higher costs for health care, gasoline, food, and education while their incomes decline, many have delayed marriage and childbearing. (A similar demographic contraction took place in the 1930s during the Great Depression, lasting through World War II until the baby boom began in 1946.)

The economic crisis that began in 2007 is now the crisis of the American family. Therefore, helping working-class families must become one of the top priorities of the pro-family movement. Some individuals, though, might question whether the economic well-being of the family should concern a social reform movement motivated by moral concerns. My response is this: while man may not live by bread alone, he cannot live without bread.

When Jesus entered a village, He met the needs of the people right where they were, including their need for food, water, and health. In fact, Jesus' standard for righteousness is based on how much we help meet the physical needs of the hurting: "For I was hungry, and you gave Me something to eat; I was thirsty, and you gave Me something to drink; I was a stranger, and you invited Me in; naked, and you clothed Me; I was sick, and you visited Me; I was in prison, and you came to Me" (Matthew 25:35–36). This is a call to evangelize, not a political platform, yet it is striking how much Jesus emphasized meeting people at the point of their need.

As believers, we must do this good work in the trenches of our society: we must go into the cities, towns, rural areas, and wherever else needs exist and meet those needs as an act of compassion and a witness to our faith. But meeting people's basic needs should also inform our public policy agenda. If people lack the ability to provide for their children and give them a good education, then more than just the fate of the family is at stake; the survival of the American dream is at stake.

Reducing the Tax Burden

The financial pressure on middle-class families with children is worsened by a crushing tax burden. In 1948 the federal tax code's $600 standard deduction for children protected 42 percent of per capita income. As a result, the average family in the U.S. immediately after World War II paid just 2 percent of their adjusted gross income in federal income taxes. If the exemption had kept pace with inflation, it would have been valued at $13,260 in 1990, and $23,728 for a family of four in 2013.[5] Instead, the dependent exemption is only $3,650 and protects just 7 percent of median household income.[6] In the last six decades, a combination of bracket creep, higher income taxes, higher payroll taxes, and inflation eating away at the value of the standard deduction has dramatically increased the tax burden on families.

Today, when one adds in payroll taxes, federal and state income taxes, and property and sales taxes, the typical family's marginal tax rate is 40 to 50 percent.[7] This is more than the average family spends on housing, clothing, and food combined. Most middle-income families in the U.S. are in the 15 percent or the 25 percent tax brackets. But when one factors in payroll taxes for Medicare and Social Security (13.3 percent), state income taxes (which average 4.3 percent but go as high as 9 percent in some states like New York and California), and state and local property and sales taxes, the government is actually taking more of the average family's income than it did before the Reagan tax cuts.

The situation will only get worse. The looming entitlement bubble will lead to either a dramatic hike in payroll taxes or a cut in benefits. (Some estimates predict that without entitlement reform, the payroll tax will double by 2050.[8]) Payroll taxes fall hardest on working families because they are not offset by the dependent exemption. Reducing payroll tax rates will be difficult in light of the current fiscal situation in Washington, but more of a family's income must be protected from taxes.

Since the Reagan era, Republicans have focused on pro-growth cuts in marginal tax rates. The economic model known as the Laffer curve theorizes that the greater incentive to work and save created by lower rates will spur growth, create jobs, and actually generate more tax revenue. High tax rates perversely reduce revenue. The Reagan economic boom confirmed Laffer's theory. Ever since, Republican presidential candidates have made tax cuts a central feature of their economic platform. In 2012 Mitt Romney proposed both a 20 percent across-the-board cut in income tax rates and the repeal of the death tax.

But replicating the economic growth and job creation of the Reagan tax cuts is more difficult today. Reagan's tax cuts reduced the top marginal tax rate from 70 to 50 percent, increasing the amount retained on the next dollar earned by taxpayers in the highest bracket by over 40 percent. Cutting today's top rate of 40 percent back to the Bush-era level of 35 percent will not create the same incentive to work, save, and invest for either the wealthy or middle-class families, most of whom are in the 15 and 25 percent tax brackets.

Robert Stein, a Treasury Department official under George W. Bush, has pointed out that "taxpayers are not simply workers, employers, and investors. Economic man is also a family man, and the next generation of tax reform should address the distortions and burdens our fiscal policy imposes on American families."[9] As fertility rates fall, the burden of raising future workers, entrepreneurs, and taxpayers will fall on the shrinking number of couples who bear and raise children.

What is the value of these future workers to our country? The present value of lifetime Medicare and Social Security tax payments for a typical American child born today is $150,000. Because the solvency of these programs depends on new workers paying into them, Stein argues, "Those who do not raise children are, in effect, enjoying a partial free ride at the expense of those who do."

To reduce the tax burden on the family, Congress should take the following actions:

- Enact a refundable child tax credit of $4,000 to reduce the tax burden on American families. Under current law, combining the $1,000-per-child tax credit with the dependent exemption, the average American parent can offset the cost of each child by approximately $1,550.[10] Given the cost of raising children, this is insufficient. The $4,000-per-child tax credit should have no income limit, treat each child the same, and count against both income and payroll taxes.
- Eliminate the marriage penalty. The Bush tax cuts reduced the marriage penalty by doubling the single standard deduction for married taxpayers who file jointly and indexing it for inflation, but the marriage penalty remains. Congress should eliminate it for all married taxpayers, and that policy could amount to thousands of dollars for taxpayers who file jointly and own a small business.

- Enact a $2,000 "baby bonus" tax credit for married couples who have children. We should treat children as a blessing, not a burden to society. France provides payments to couples who have children, fueling a rise in its fertility rate to 2.03, the highest of any European Union nation save Ireland. The fertility rate for Europe as a whole is only 1.5, while Germany's is only 1.36. The U.S. needs a similar policy. Despite the influx of immigrants who usually have more children, the U.S. fertility rate is at a twenty-five-year low of 1.89.[11] A "baby bonus" would send a strong signal to American citizens that our country values children and treats them as an asset to be celebrated, not a financial liability to be avoided.
- Provide tax incentives for companies that offer pro-family policies such as generous maternity-leave benefits and child-care facilities. Businesses that offer paid maternity leave of six weeks or more should receive a reduction in the employer share of payroll taxes to offset that cost, as should companies that provide employees with quality, subsidized on-site daycare or stipends for child-care costs. Given the number of women now in the workforce, we must transcend the false divide separating women who work at home from those who work at the office. We must make the U.S. workplace family-friendly.

Religious Freedom

As we saw in chapter 11, a war on Christianity rages worldwide, from violence in the Middle East to the confiscation of Bibles and rules against religious jewelry here in the United States. One of the most fearsome weapons of anti-Christian bigotry at home has been the Internal Revenue Service. The IRS scandal revealed an institutional hostility toward Christianity that has been endemic at the agency for decades.

While the situation has grown worse under the current administration, IRS abuse did not begin and will not end with Barack Obama. The First Amendment guarantees the right of every American to practice their faith free from government harassment or persecution, but this promise has been denied by bureaucratic meddling, government overreach, and the ongoing effort to restrict tax-exempt status in an attempt to intimidate the Christian community.

Congress should act swiftly in the following areas to reclaim the constitutional guarantee of religious freedom:

- Pass a Freedom of Houses of Worship Act that allows any church or ministry to engage in insubstantial political activity without fear of losing its tax-exempt status. Currently the Internal Revenue Code removes tax-exempt status for any religious group that expends even one penny on political advocacy. This provision was inserted in the tax code in 1954 by Lyndon Johnson in order to punish religious conservative broadcasters in Texas who opposed his reelection. Its enforcement has been unfair and biased, and the time has come to end the government's ability to harass and persecute Christians through its power to tax.
- Enact a Freedom of Speech and Association Act that reaffirms the right of citizens to engage in legal political activity under the auspices of social welfare organizations—organized under Section 501(c)(4) of the Internal Revenue Code—as long as the political activity does not exceed more than 40 percent of the organization's revenue in a three-year period. Under current law, a social welfare group such as the National Right to Life Committee or the Sierra Club can engage in political advocacy as long as it is not the organization's primary purpose and does not comprise a substantial portion of its activity or income. What constitutes "primary" and "substantial" in the activities of an organization is highly subjective, and the IRS has applied the law in ways that are unfair, ways that restrict the First Amendment rights of millions of Americans. The Obama administration's new IRS regulations will further deny free speech rights for millions of Americans who are members of social welfare and lobby groups. Providing a bright-line standard of 40 percent of an organization's revenues over a three-year period (to prevent the IRS from selecting a single

election year to measure political involvement, as it has done in the past) would protect the right of the American people to petition the government.

- Repeal the Religious Charity Mandate under Obamacare that requires religiously affiliated hospitals, schools, colleges, and other charitable institutions to provide health-care services, such as abortion and contraception, that contradict the teachings of their faith. As much of a disaster as Obamacare has proven to be to the U.S. economy and the American health-care system, its most egregious provision is a bureaucratic edict that violates the religious freedom of millions of Americans, forcing them under penalty of massive fines to engage in the taking of innocent human life.

Empowering Health Care

In August 2013, Newt Gingrich addressed the Republican National Committee and urged that instead of focusing solely on repealing Obamacare, the GOP should offer a positive alternative. The party, he argued, had a problem with a culture of negativity.[12] Rush Limbaugh weighed in, arguing that he saw nowhere in the Constitution where the federal government was required to provide health care to anyone. Some Republican House members also objected, pointing out that they had several times introduced legislation outlining an alternative to Obamacare. But this legislation has not had a single hearing or been considered in committee, much less voted on by the full House.

Repealing Obamacare should be a major legislative priority of social conservatives for a number of reasons. First, we simply cannot afford it. The estimated cost of Obamacare by the Congressional Budget Office has now soared to $1.8 trillion, from the original estimate of $980 billion. If the histories of Medicare and Medicaid are any guide, the cost of Obamacare can be expected to explode in the decades to come if it remains in place. The government's initial forecast of the cost of Medicare at the time of its passage in 1965 was $12 billion annually by 1990. In fact, in that year Medicare cost

$110 billion, *ten times* the original forecast.[13] Obamacare will also harm consumers by driving up the cost of health insurance premiums.

Second, Obamacare violates religious freedom and assaults the conscience of millions of Americans. The Independent Payment Advisory Board under Obamacare sets reimbursements for health-care providers that will lead to rationing of care and deep cuts in payments for certain procedures; this endangers seniors, the disabled, and the infirm. Finally, the subsidies for abortion that are both implicit and explicit in the law, including forcing private insurers to cover "comprehensive women's health care services," will lead to more abortions.[14] The Alan Guttmacher Institute has found that one-fourth of the women who have a Medicaid-funded abortion would carry their child to term in the absence of that government subsidy. Based on that statistic, the Obamacare subsidies could lead to as many as three hundred thousand more abortions performed in the U.S. annually.[15]

As people of faith, however, we should say what we are *for*, not just what we are *against*. After we have repealed Obamacare, we should replace it with a market-oriented, patient-centered reform that lowers insurance premiums, reins in health-care costs, and increases the efficiency and responsiveness of the health-care system. Here are some suggestions that Congress should pass, some of which are included in the Empowering Patients First Act, introduced by Representative Tom Price (R-GA), himself a physician and orthopedic surgeon:

- Establish a national high-risk insurance pool that enables those with previous conditions to purchase health insurance with subsidies from the states and the federal government.
- Create a national market for affordable health insurance by allowing consumers to purchase their insurance across state lines. Under current law health insurance companies must jump through bureaucratic hoops and comply with confusing state-by-state regulations and mandates, forcing many insurance providers to simply pull out of many states. Creating a national market such as that which exists for auto and home insurance will increase competition and drive down premiums.

- Make federal Medicaid subsidies to states contingent upon those states allowing the marketing of health insurance policies that cover basic primary, preventative, and catastrophic care at affordable rates. Health insurance premiums have skyrocketed in part because medical groups have lobbied legislatures to pass state mandates requiring insurers to cover chiropractors, optometrists, acupuncture, cosmetic surgery, dentists, orthodontists, and psychiatrists. Only ten states permit "mandate-lite" affordable policies, but a majority of states have at least forty coverage mandates, and some states have more than sixty mandates. These mandates require expensive policies that drive up premiums for healthy middle-class families. A 2013 report by the Council for Affordable Health Insurance found that there are 2,271 health insurance mandates at the state level that increase health insurance premiums as much as 50 percent.[16]
- Restore the cuts in Medicare and revoke the regulations of Medicare Advantage under Obamacare that are intended to strangle the program. Medicare Advantage, currently utilized by 13 million seniors, gives seniors more choices and increases competition. Medicare Advantage also provides a glide path toward the privatization of Medicare, which is why Obama and the left have had their sights on its destruction since its passage in 2003.
- Enact tax credits for the purchase of basic health insurance by individuals on par with that offered to employers, making insurance affordable and fully portable. The practice of offering health insurance as an employee benefit began during World War II when a wage freeze prevented employers from increasing pay. But in the economy of the twenty-first century, when the average worker changes jobs as many as ten times during his or her career, health insurance should not be tied to the workplace. The tax credits should also be offered to those on Medicare and Medicaid to give them an opportunity to consider private insurers as they seek the best policy for themselves.

- Pass medical malpractice reform at the state and federal levels that reduces junk lawsuits against doctors and hospitals while protecting the patient's right to seek judgments in cases of legitimate negligence or misconduct. Doctors should be granted safe harbor from malpractice lawsuits if they follow generally accepted clinical guidelines for patient treatment. This protection will cut down on defensive medicine practiced by millions of doctors in order to avoid a potential lawsuit and standardize treatment without regard to the subjective, hindsight judgments of juries and trial lawyers.[17] The cost savings will be substantial. Sixty percent of the doctors in a recent survey said they ordered additional tests or consultations solely to protect themselves against a malpractice claim. A study by the Department of Health and Human Services found that the annual cost of defensive medicine adds up to between $70 and $126 billion a year.[18]

A New War on Poverty

One of the best ways to improve health is to improve the standard of living for more Americans by reducing poverty. Currently, 46.2 million Americans are living in poverty, the largest number in our nation's history.[19] As we saw in chapter 9, the top-down, one-size-fits-all war on poverty waged for fifty years has failed. But what will replace it? The first answer is to restore personal responsibility. Society should not be called upon to pay people to drop out of school, engage in criminal behavior, sire children out of wedlock, and refuse to work. Subsidizing this conduct simply leads to more of it.

Yet we cannot be passive in the face of so many who are suffering in poverty. On the one hand, poverty is a part of the human condition, a reality of a fallen world. Jesus said, "You always have the poor with you, but you do not always have Me" (John 12:8). But believers are not called to accept this condition. We are called to provide assistance to the least, the lost, and the left behind through personal action as well as sound public policy. The pro-family movement must therefore offer a compassionate and effective alternative to the failed welfare state.

Nothing we do in the public policy arena is more vital than our personal involvement in ministries and organizations that help the poor. The Great Commission can be summed up in three simple phrases: love God, love your neighbor, and make disciples of all nations. This means loving everyone, regardless of economic status, ethnic background, or nationality. As World Vision president Richard Stearns recently put it, "That love, when demonstrated to the world through acts of kindness, compassion and justice, is revolutionary; and when we become the agents of it, we make credible the message of a Savior who transforms men and women for eternity."[20]

This personal involvement in helping the poor must be our focus. We cannot repeat the mistake of our brothers and sisters on the left who deemphasized individual acts of mercy and tried to transfer to the government those tasks best performed by churches, synagogues, and charities.

We need a new war on poverty waged with more effective weapons and a better strategy. Government's role will be vital but limited, focused on providing a hand up, not a handout. Here are some of the most effective measures that Congress can enact:

- Pass the next generation of welfare reform by enacting work or school-attendance requirements for recipients of food stamps and other federal benefit programs for the poor. The work requirements under the Temporary Assistance to Needy Families (TANF) program—suspended by the Obama administration by executive order—should be reinstated. Unemployment benefits should be limited in duration and tied to job training. Studies have demonstrated that federal unemployment benefits subsidize joblessness and act as a cash-subsidy disincentive to seek employment.
- Enact charitable choice that allows individual taxpayers to earmark up to $1,000 on their tax return for a private or religious charity involved in working with the poor. The list of options could include but not be limited to homeless shelters, food banks, GED-equivalency training, job training and placement, after-school programs, and the like. The

government should encourage consumer ratings—based on evaluations by clients as well as donors—of the most effective charities and display that information on a website.

- Pass a separate $1,000 tax credit for charitable giving for taxpayers earning less than $100,000 per year in order to encourage support for faith-based and charitable organizations. Because the charitable giving deduction is based on one's tax bracket, the incentive is greatest for the highest earners. A $1,000 tax credit will encourage middle- and lower-income households to support those charities that are doing the best work in their communities to help the poor.
- Reenergize the Office of Faith-Based Community Initiatives, diminished during the Obama years, by increasing support for local groups fighting poverty, especially health-care clinics that provide free or subsidized care to the poor and undocumented populations. There are currently thousands of community health clinics in the U.S., many operating with no government subsidies whatsoever. According to the Congressional Budget Office, even if Obamacare had been fully implemented, there would still be over thirty million people in the U.S. without health insurance.[21] Many of these are families who need access to health care without having to go to the emergency room. Community-based health care is the best solution for them. Such health care avoids the bureaucratic inefficiency of Obamacare at the same time that it meets a genuine need for care at the local level.
- Provide charters and choice in education. Barack Obama once said, "The best anti-poverty program around is a world-class education."[22] He was right, but his policies have not advanced this goal. Most recently, for instance, the Department of Justice sued the state of Louisiana for offering a school choice program that benefits poor and minority children. Under the program, over eight thousand Louisiana children attended charter schools and parochial schools or benefitted from online educational options, and the results were higher test scores

as well as a higher graduation rate. (The Justice Department eventually dropped the suit.) We should provide expanded school choice beyond existing programs in Louisiana, Florida, and the District of Columbia through the creation of federal scholarship pilot programs in major cities plagued by crime, poverty, and drugs. The D.C. Opportunity Scholarship program has been remarkably successful, with thousands of applicants applying for under fifteen hundred scholarships to attend the school of their choice. In this program the graduation rate has exceeded 90 percent.[23] This program should be expanded to other major cities to help those who have been left behind by a failed education system.

A Pro-Life Agenda

In the 1960s and 1970s, feminists and their allies claimed that abortion-on-demand would put an end to back-alley abortions in which quack doctors preyed on women, endangering their health and in some cases their lives. They won the case if not the argument, and by a single act of judicial fiat, *Roe v. Wade* imposed on all fifty states the most liberal abortion laws in the Western world.

But as the gruesome case of Dr. Kermit Gosnell in Pennsylvania made abundantly clear, abortion-on-demand did not end back-alley abortions; it merely gave them a new name: reproductive health. Gosnell killed women in his care, performed forced abortions on teenage girls, murdered children born alive on the operating table by snipping their spines with scissors and stuffing them in shoe boxes, and violated standards of cleanliness and medical procedures that would not be acceptable in a rural clinic in a Third World country.

The Gosnell case laid bare the moral bankruptcy of the abortion-on-demand policy. His victims were overwhelmingly minority and immigrant women far removed from the largely white, prosperous precincts of modern feminism. Yet after the Gosnell trial, when states like Texas and North Carolina moved to ensure clinic safety and require abortionists to have visitation privileges at an accredited hospital—a pretty low standard in the medical profession—the media and the left cried foul.

Wendy Davis, a feminist Democratic state senator from Houston, donned her pink tennis shoes and launched a one-woman filibuster of the pro-life bill in Texas, becoming a cause célèbre on the left. (The bill later passed and was signed into law by Governor Rick Perry.) But the policies she defended—late-term abortions and unsafe abortion clinics—were neither noble nor especially liberal.

The legal regime of abortion-on-demand cannot abide because it troubles the nation's conscience and contradicts its ideals. As Father Theodore Hesburgh, an iconic liberal and former president of Notre Dame University, put it, "It is difficult to explain how a moral America, so brilliantly successful in confronting racial injustice in the sixties, has the most permissive abortion laws of any Western country."[24] And while Hesburgh provided cover for pro-choice, Catholic Democrats like Mario Cuomo, those who have acted as apologists for abortion at every stage of a pregnancy see their position whittled away, not only by remarkable advances in neonatal care and ultrasound technology, but also by significant shifts in public opinion.

In 2012 Gallup found for the first time since it began surveying the issue that a larger percentage of the American people identified themselves as "pro-life" than "pro-choice."[25] Similarly, a CNN poll in 2012 found that 52 percent of the public is pro-life, a statistic favoring making abortion illegal in most or all circumstances.[26] The pro-abortion lobby knows this is the case, which is why it tries to shift the debate to the more complicated cases of rape and incest. But the overall trend in public support for common-sense restrictions on abortion continues unabated. In 2011 eighty-three pieces of pro-life legislation were passed at the state level, more than three times the number passed in 2010.[27]

The pro-life momentum is most noticeable among young people, who grew up under *Roe* and who question it more readily than their baby-boomer parents do. A survey by the National Abortion Rights Action League found that 51 percent of pro-life millennial voters (ages 18 to 29) ranked abortion as an important issue in their voting behavior, compared to only 26 percent of pro-choice millennials.

The intensity is now firmly on the pro-life side. Commenting on the crowd at a March for Life in Washington, Nancy Keenan, president of NARAL Pro-Choice America, exclaimed, "I just thought, my gosh, they are so young. There are so many of them, and they are so young."[28] Fading support for abortion among America's youth contributed to her decision to step down from NARAL.[29]

Life is a gift from God, and we ordain government to protect it. The ultimate solution is passing a constitutional amendment that protects human life or persuading the courts to rule that an unborn child is a person under the Fourteenth Amendment of the Constitution. Either will be difficult in the short term. Even so, we can enact pro-life laws that protect both women and their unborn children from exploitation.

Consider these elements of a pro-life agenda that are achievable in the short term:

- Pass state and federal laws against abortions after the twentieth week of pregnancy ("late-term abortions"), because at that point many children can survive outside the womb. The House of Representatives passed the Pain-Capable Unborn Child Protection Act in 2013 only to see it die in the U.S. Senate. Hopefully this law can be passed by a pro-life House and Senate after the 2014 elections and sent to President Obama's desk for his signature. If he vetoes it, he will only bring into fuller relief the fact that pro-choice politicians defend the indefensible, as was the case with Bill Clinton's veto of the Partial-Birth Abortion Ban in 1995. The ban on partial-birth abortion eventually became law, and we must not rest until the late-term abortion ban is made into law as well.
- Establish "women's right to know" laws requiring that women be fully informed of the emotional and physical health consequences of an abortion, that they know the stage of their pregnancy and therefore the developmental point of their unborn child, and that they receive an ultrasound allowing them to see their child in the womb. The pro-abortion lobby has vigorously objected to laws requiring an ultrasound, comparing

it to rape because an ultrasound in early stages of pregnancy involves a transvaginal procedure. But ultrasounds are standard before any abortion to determine the gestational stage of pregnancy and often after an abortion to ensure that no part of the fetus remains in the mother's womb. Furthermore, Planned Parenthood guidelines require transvaginal ultrasounds in the early stages of pregnancy. One study found that 83 percent of Planned Parenthood affiliated clinics *always* performed a transvaginal ultrasound, while 16 percent usually did. Only 1 percent never did so.[30]

- Enact clinic safety standards at the state and federal level that ensure that a case like that of Kermit Gosnell can never happen again. Many clinics are unsanitary abortion mills that prey on minorities, immigrants, teens, and the poor. Clinics that perform abortions should be required to have a qualified physician with hospital visitation privileges on-site, to have certified attending nurses present, and to meet the highest standards for sanitation and legal liability.
- End taxpayer subsidies provided to Planned Parenthood, the largest abortion provider in the Western world, by the states and the federal government. Planned Parenthood has put its own financial interests ahead of the women it claims to represent, as documented by undercover activists Lila Rose and James O'Keefe. A 2011 report from Americans United for Life alleged incidents at Planned Parenthood clinics of assisting in child sex trafficking, failing to report child sexual abuse, misleading women, and misusing taxpayer funds.[31] The organization has also been involved in alleged massive Medicaid fraud. In 2013 Planned Parenthood paid $4.3 million to settle claims by a former employee and whistle-blower that it billed Medicaid for services it never provided women, including birth control and STD tests.[32] Yet at a time when the government cannot pay its bills, taxpayers subsidized Planned Parenthood with an estimated $542 million—45 percent of all its revenues.[33] We cannot afford Planned Parenthood anymore.

Fixing a Broken Justice System

In general, conservatives have favored tough measures to ensure law and order, while liberals have suffered politically when perceived as soft on crime. But between the two extremes of locking the prison door and throwing away the key and blaming society for crime is a third way. It is a redemptive, biblical solution to the problem of crime that convicts the offender, offers restitution to the victim, and relies on rehabilitation and reform rather than punishment.

Today the criminal justice system is broken. States now spend $50 billion maintaining prisons that all too often warehouse criminals until they can return to our streets and neighborhoods, rejoin gangs, and commit ever more sophisticated crimes. One out of thirty-three adults is under correctional control, and an estimated 40 percent of them will return to prison within three years after their release. In the minority community, the numbers are even more shocking. One out of every three African-American males born in 2001 will likely end up in jail or prison, and these prisons are nothing more than training grounds for criminals. Unless the public takes action, this prison-industrial complex threatens to chew up more taxpayer dollars. The cost of housing an inmate in state prison in California is now almost $50,000 per year, more than it would cost to send him to Harvard University.

Does society benefit more by having offenders make restitution to victims and society, or by imprisoning them for long sentences that make it harder for them to find jobs and become productive members of the community when they get out? In recent years organizations like Justice Fellowship, founded by Chuck Colson, and initiatives like Right on Crime have put forward a promising agenda to reform the criminal justice system by reducing mandatory minimum sentences for nonviolent, first-time offenders and stressing instead the use of drug courts, early intervention, and counseling to get these people's lives back on track.

Here are a few reforms that should be implemented at the state and federal level:

- Establish special drug courts to adjudicate the cases of first-time drug offenders. Require mandatory counseling to deter these individuals from a life of chemical dependence and crime. Encourage the use of faith-based organizations in this counseling. Faith-based organizations have a proven record of greater success than other institutional programs.

- Enact restitution laws for nonviolent property crimes that require offenders to make restitution to their victims as well as to society. Include in these restitution laws procedures allowing victims to confront offenders in court as well as mandated and supervised opportunities with faith-based organizations for the offender's repentance and reconciliation.
- Wherever practical, shift law enforcement funds away from additional prison construction and maintenance and toward less costly and more effective community-based service by offenders, including but not limited to charitable service, education, job training, and employment.

Biblical Principles of Immigration

The current immigration system violates the American spirit of fairness as well as the rule of law, dividing families and rewarding those who break the law. We should oppose amnesty. We should provide priority status for spouses and minor children of permanent legal residents who have entered the country legally. Currently, more than one million children of legal residents are waiting for entry—and in some cases can be on those waiting lists for as long as ten years. I learned, for instance, about a Russian teenager whose mother married an American and who waited to join her. It was estimated that he would be on the waiting list for up to seven years. He was cared for by his grandmother, but after he had been on the list for two years, his grandmother died, leaving him alone in Russia. This is an indefensible situation, but it occurs every day under our current immigration system.

The best solution to our current immigration system should be based on biblical principles that show compassion for the foreigner, uphold the rule of law, secure the border, honor work, and strengthen the family. Granting amnesty to all those who have entered the country illegally undermines respect for the rule of law and punishes those who played by the rules. We also need to modernize the visa system to meet the needs of our economy and allow those who graduate from our universities to apply for a green card rather than deport them to China or India to compete with us. Many of these young people may start the next Google or Apple in their dorm room or garage. We must secure the border using fencing, drones, and technology similar to the border barrier built by Israel in the West Bank. And we should replace the failed chain migration system with one that reunites families by giving priority to children, wives, and husbands.

Marriage Matters

As I noted earlier, the faith community suffers from a credibility gap on the issue of same-sex marriage because it allowed no-fault divorce to wreak havoc on the institution of marriage. It is long past time to rectify this blind spot and make the reform of unilateral divorce the centerpiece of a pro-marriage agenda. Our current laws treat spouses as dispensable at any time, for any reason or for no reason at all, even when the spouse objects. The no-fault divorce revolution that swept the country in the 1970s fueled the doubling of the U.S. divorce rate in less than a decade.[34] Today eight out of ten marriages that end in divorce are unilaterally dissolved, meaning one partner desires to save the marriage. In most states, however, the dissenting spouse has no legal recourse and no real legal right to object to the end of the marriage. No-fault divorce is particularly harmful to women and children, who suffer the most financially in the aftermath. Little wonder that feminist leader Betty Friedan called no-fault divorce, once a feminist ideal, a "mistake."[35]

For women, the economic impact is ugly. Only about a third of the women retain the family home after a no-fault divorce (as compared with more than 80 percent in a divorce where the husband was at fault) and nearly a fourth fall into poverty (as compared to 11 percent of men). Divorced women are also more likely than men to lose their health insurance and to be poor in their old age as compared with unmarried or widowed women.[36] The negative financial impact of divorce on women has led to what some to call "the feminization of poverty." This disparate economic impact is only compounded by the fact that women are more likely to care for the children and also to suffer a number of other health-related effects of divorce.

Men also have a stake in rolling back no-fault divorce laws. Two-thirds of divorces are filed by women, and that number climbs to 90 percent among couples with a college education. Men are also far more likely to lose child-custody battles. Women are granted child custody in nearly three-fourths of cases, and 40 percent of the time men are denied the right to see their children at all. Joint custody is granted in just one out of five cases.[37] Undoubtedly there are situations involving an abusive father, but too many fathers lose the right to see their own children solely because their wives picked up and moved on.[38] Joint custody of children should be the default situation unless a spouse has demonstrated a pattern of physical and/or emotional abuse.

Divorce reform is a pressing need for society as a whole. Social science has established that children of divorce are more likely to experience chemical addiction, depression, and emotional and mental health issues. These children are also far less likely to be able to establish healthy, well-adjusted relationships with the opposite sex once they reach adulthood. Girls whose parents divorce are more likely to get pregnant out of wedlock, and the children of divorce live shorter and less happy lives than their counterparts from married households. They also have a 50 percent higher risk for divorce than children raised in intact homes with married parents.[39]

It is not, however, practical to repeal no-fault divorce laws in all fifty states. Nor is it possible to pass a law to make husbands love their wives and remain devoted to their children. Rather than restoring the legal bias to "find fault" as the basis for granting a divorce, we should begin by making it more difficult for one party to unilaterally dissolve a marriage. State legislatures should discourage unilateral divorce by implementing longer waiting periods, higher court fees, and more generous financial settlements in divorce cases where one spouse objects. Courts could also require that the primary residence of the family be reserved for the objecting spouse and the children, as well as make it more difficult for the spouse initiating that divorce to dispose of marital assets and thereby further destabilize the family. Legislatures can also establish "safe harbor" for women who gave up jobs or careers to stay at home to care for children, favoring them with more favorable asset division, alimony, and child support. We can also provide for a higher legal standard for the dissolution of marriages that have lasted more than five years and in which children are present in the home. Society has a clear interest in preserving these marriages wherever possible.

A New Pro-Family Agenda

The public policy agenda just outlined can help strengthen the family, protect innocent human life, assist the poor, and restore fiscal sanity and responsibility to Washington, D.C. It cannot create a perfect society or guarantee the spiritual awakening we've been studying. But it can measurably improve the lives of our citizens, help the least and the lost, and give the American people the good government they richly deserve. These are noble goals, all.

Establishing this new public policy agenda—this Bold Pro-Family Plan—will require hard work, patience, long-suffering, and a much better understanding of our proper role as we engage the political system both as American citizens and as Christians. The rules of the road for effective citizenship are the topic of the next, and final, chapter.

Action Points

1. Share with your friends and family the main platform planks of this Bold Pro-Family Plan. Get their reaction and feedback.
2. Write a letter or send an e-mail to your state legislators and your representatives in Congress urging action on one or more of the issues covered in the Bold Pro-Family Plan.
3. Write a letter to the editor of your local newspaper or call in to a local talk radio program and highlight one of the issues covered in the Bold Pro-Family Plan.

CHAPTER 15

A Call to Christian Citizenship

Toward the end of Jesus' earthly ministry, the Pharisees tried to trick Him into taking sides in the most heated political controversy of His day—whether Jews should submit to Rome's occupation of their land. Their challenge took the form of a question: Should they pay taxes to Caesar?

If Jesus said yes, He would be exposed as a traitor to the Jewish people and a supporter of the Roman occupation. If He said no, He would be revealed as a revolutionary and be arrested and likely executed as an enemy of Rome.

Fully aware of their scheme, Jesus answered them with a question. "Show Me the coin used for the poll-tax," He said. "Whose likeness and inscription is this?"

"Caesar's," they replied.

"Then render to Caesar the things that are Caesar's; and to God the things that are God's," Jesus answered. The Bible recounts that the Pharisees were amazed by His teaching and left disappointed, realizing they had been outmaneuvered again (Matthew 22:15–22).

This teaching was one of the most important of Jesus' ministry. It calls believers to be faithful citizens here on earth while reserving a greater loyalty to a heavenly kingdom yet to come. Jesus acknowledged the temporal role that earthly citizenship plays in maintaining the social order and promoting the common good, but He claimed that because we are made in the image of God, we owe our ultimate loyalty to Him, not to any earthly king, Caesar, parliament, or president. Just as the coin was stamped with Caesar's likeness, so are we "stamped" with God's likeness, and we are to render ourselves in body, mind, and soul to Him alone.

The image on the coin probably belonged to Caesar Tiberius, one of the most notorious rulers of ancient Rome.[1] A ruthless paranoid, vicious anti-Semite, murderer and pedophile, Tiberius governed with an iron fist. He rounded up political opponents and executed them after show trials, floating their corpses down the Tiber River as a warning.[2] Tiberius expelled Jews from Rome, threatening to enslave any who remained.[3] The Zealots rose up against him, calling for violent resistance against Rome. The Pharisees and Herodians made peace with Rome, paying taxes and submitting to Roman authority in hopes of saving their synagogues and preserving their religious practice.

Against that backdrop, Jesus' interrogators had asked if God's people should pay taxes to an occupying foreign government led by a brutal and deranged deviant. Jesus declined to ally Himself with either side, but His reply did not signal acquiescence to tyranny or a timid surrender to slavery. Rather, He expressed one of the most important truths in human history: men and women are made in God's image and endowed with certain rights and responsibilities that are not granted by any ruler and therefore cannot be denied by any ruler or rule of law.

Christ's teaching instructs believers that their civic engagement is really prayer in action, a call to conscience, an assertion of God-given rights, and a testimony of His sovereignty.

Politics: Its Possibilities and Its Limits

As people of faith, we exercise our temporal citizenship not to gain power but to witness to a higher authority. Properly understood, our citizenship is a gift from God, and we utilize it to glorify Him by defending the defenseless, giving voice to the voiceless, and asserting that our rights come from God, not any king, president, court, or congress.

Some have criticized religious folk for pouring into the civic arena in recent decades with the misplaced hope that politics could right every wrong, cure every social ill, save the family, and usher in the millennium. Certainly there were times in the late 1970s and early 1980s when, after decades of social withdrawal, the unbridled enthusiasm of religious conservatives for politics was over the top. That should be expected of any constituency that does not fully exercise the biblical responsibilities of citizenship for two generations. Their exuberance for politics resembled that of a teenager who had never seen an automobile finding a fully loaded, brand-new Mercedes-Benz in the driveway on Christmas Day.

Christians in the late twentieth century found politics fascinating in part because it was so new to them. This is not a sign that their civic engagement was wrong, but that their earlier withdrawal was a mistake. A half century of self-imposed exile rendered evangelicals rusty and awkward in exercising their citizenship. They were prone to triumphalism and heated rhetoric as they felt a naive allure to power. How could it have been otherwise? Even those who know how to drive a car will find the steering wobbly if it has been five decades since they got behind the wheel. So it was with evangelicals and politics.

Today, people of faith have a greater moral imagination when it comes to the possibilities and limits of politics. Politics cannot save the lost or inculcate moral sentiments in the unregenerate heart. But it can restrain the wicked from committing evil, an important function for those who seek to bend the arc of history toward justice. Martin Luther King once said, "It may be true that the law cannot make a man love me, but it can keep him from lynching me, and I think that's pretty important."

If, as some critics of the religious conservative movement contend, the transforming power of the gospel is more effective than politics in bringing about social change, and if winning hearts and minds is more important than winning elections or passing laws, the same could be said of any social reform movement. Did Christian suffragists who fought to give women the right to vote cure all that ailed America? Certainly not. By this argument civil rights protestors should have prayed, fasted, and read the Bible, not staged sit-ins at segregated restaurants or marches on Washington. The passage of civil rights legislation did not extinguish racism, but the civil rights movement pricked the conscience of the nation, changing hearts and minds as well as laws, and we are far better off because of their political activism.

If believers do not speak out for social justice, who will? The religious impulse to bring one's moral convictions to the civic arena is consistent with the Bible and America's heritage.

The Engaged Church

Even as people of faith enter the political arena, the church should never be beholden to any party or politician. Rather, as Catholic Archbishop Charles Chaput has urged, "pastors should encourage members of their church to become involved in [political] parties, and to do what they can to make sure the party platforms align with the Gospel and the teachings of Christ." The laity should be fully engaged in the life of their community, state, and nation. To do otherwise, Chaput argues, "is cowardice. We're supposed to avoid giving to Caesar what belongs to God, and sometimes Caesar—the government—tries to take more than it should."[4]

The late Chuck Colson saw political involvement as one aspect of engaging the culture. "We ought to be engaged in politics," Colson argued, "we ought to be good citizens, we ought to care about justice." Those who claim believers should "just take care of the church and tend to our knitting" are wrong, Colson insisted, because "there's an intelligent way to engage the culture in every area, including politics."[5]

This argument recognizes the separate and distinct roles of the clergy and the laity. The church is not a political party. It should focus on sharing the gospel, saving the lost, and making disciples. But pastors should equip their flock for effective earthly citizenship, instructing them to be informed, register to vote, contact elected officials, pay taxes, and vote. Jerry Falwell's phrase at the Moral Majority was "Get them born again, baptized, and registered to vote." Jon Zens and Cliff Bjork have criticized this equation of Christian salvation with civic engagement, asking whether "the motivation for personal evangelism becomes less a concern for men's eternal souls than for their temporal vote."[6]

But churches that teach sound biblical doctrine cannot ignore the responsibilities of citizenship, and in a free society, that means being registering to vote, being properly informed, and voting. Our forebears risked their lives and shed their blood so we might have the right to elect our leaders, and to treat that hard-earned privilege and duty lightly is to show disrespect for their sacrifice. The laity should view citizenship as prayer in action, advancing what is right and just, while at the same time glorifying God by conducting themselves with uncommon grace, diligence, civility, and moral courage.

The shortcomings of Christian political involvement, then, came primarily because of unrealistic expectations. No constituency—not evangelicals, pro-lifers, labor unions, feminists, gays, minorities, or the business community—can turn out in huge numbers on election day, elect a wave of like-minded candidates, pass some bills into law, and transform America. That is expecting more than politics can deliver in a free society, especially in America where power is divided between three branches of government and then dispersed between the states and national government as well as between civil society and government. Political activism can lead to better public policy and make America stronger and better. That is a noble goal. But politics cannot usher in the millennium.

Some believers felt profound disappointment when the election of Reagan, the Bushes, or a GOP Congress did not lead to a land of milk and honey. Now the shoe is on the other foot. After Obama's election, liberal blogs seethed with bitterness over his failure to close Gitmo, end electronic surveillance by the National Security Agency, enact single-payer health care, repeal the Bush tax cuts, pass climate change legislation, and act on other items on the progressive wish list. They learned the hard way—as evangelicals had earlier—that no one in a healthy and vibrant democracy gets everything they want.

Awakening a Slumbering Giant

Evangelical leaders who birthed the religious right faced a challenge: how to compel millions of people who had been marginalized for decades to reengage in the political arena. They could hardly do so by offering scraps from the table, and as a consequence they sometimes promised more than politics could deliver. To energize religious folk, they put forth a vision of a redeemed and thoroughly transformed society. They urged evangelicals to march out of the pews and into the precincts to "take back America" or "reclaim America for Christ." Awakening a slumbering giant requires a trumpet blast, not the sounding of a kazoo. If the clarion call at times included rhetorical flourish—and make no mistake, it did—these evangelical leaders were in good company. Throughout our history social reform movements have contained a strong dash of hyperbole. Zeal in a righteous cause is admirable, but it must eventually be leavened with knowledge and practical experience to be effective.

As we saw in chapter 3, anti-slavery leaders equated abolitionism with Christ's Second Coming, while temperance advocates like Billy Sunday compared Prohibition to the millennium. Radical feminist leaders claimed women's liberation would abolish marriage, family, capitalism, and even religion as patriarchal and oppressive institutions. "Overthrowing capitalism is too small for us. We must overthrow the whole f—ing patriarchy," vowed Gloria Steinem.[7] "Women are going to bring an end to God," promised one feminist theologian. "We will change the world so much that He won't fit in anymore."[8]

Civil rights leaders didn't call blacks to brave billy clubs, fire hoses, and jail so that too many African-Americans could remain in poverty, unsafe neighborhoods, and broken homes to this day. Martin Luther King's "I Have a Dream" speech offered a vision of a day when black children would play with white children, racism was nonexistent, and people were judged by the content of their character, not the color of their skin. In one of his final sermons, he said he had "been to the mountaintop" and seen "the promised land." That promised land for many remains distant, but King's vision still inspires. Social reformers shake the political system, and they do not speak like a U.S. senator discussing a bill in committee. To wake a sleeping dog, one must kick it, and social reformers do.

Politics has its limits—and thank goodness. Only in totalitarian states does politics consume every inch of civil society. Politics can protect our rights to vote, recruit candidates for public office, speak freely, petition elected officials, practice our religion, disseminate our views to others, and keep and bear arms. Politics can also prevent others from denying us those rights. But politics will not create a just and holy society; that must await Christ's return.

At its best, politics can—to borrow a phrase from the founders—make our society a "more perfect union," and that is a noble goal. And even if political engagement delivers none of our hoped-for outcomes, Jesus taught that our citizenship is a testimony to the fact that we human beings have certain rights and allegiances by virtue of being made in God's image. These we cannot and will not surrender or compromise, just as the early apostles refused the demand of the political authorities in their day to cease preaching about Jesus.

Called to Be a Citizen

Exercising our responsibilities as citizens can advance God's kingdom in remarkable ways. The apostle Paul was willing to die for the sake of the gospel, and he ultimately did. But when Roman soldiers detained him in Jerusalem and prepared to flog him for preaching the gospel, he defended himself by asserting his rights as a Roman citizen (Acts 22:25–29).

Roman soldiers and government officials quaked in fear when Paul asserted his rights as a citizen—and for good reason! The violation of a Roman citizen's rights could bring swift punishment. In claiming his rights as a citizen, Paul didn't appeal to Jewish law or Scripture but to Roman law, an authority that all Romans respected. Eventually he exercised the most cherished right of a citizen of Rome, appealing his case all the way to Caesar. It was this act of citizenship that carried the gospel message to Caesar's court.

Like Paul, we should not be lukewarm or halfway citizens. We have been blessed with the privilege of U.S. citizenship, which millions yearn for but may never gain. As believers, we express our gratitude for this gift with fidelity to the rights and responsibilities of American citizenship.

Six Guidelines for Being an Effective Christian Citizen and Activist

How, then, are we to respond to the Christian's call to citizenship? Let me suggest six guidelines for how to be an effective citizen and activist. Most of these guidelines are timeless, most apply to almost any democratic society, and most are found in the Bible. Following these guidelines will maximize your effectiveness as a citizen of the United States.

1. Pray

Prayer must be the foundation of our civic involvement. First and foremost, we must pray for wisdom and knowledge so we can understand the times in which we live. The Bible promises us that this is a prayer God will answer. Those who lack wisdom or who ask for it with doubting hearts will be as one on "the surf of the sea, driven and tossed by the wind" (James 1:6). When Christians poured into the political arena in the 1970s and 1980s with a moral zeal, they sometimes lacked wisdom about the political process. The Bible makes clear that zeal without knowledge is not only ineffective but can also be counterproductive (Proverbs 19:2).

We should also pray for elected representatives, judges, and appointed officials, interceding on their behalf and asking God to grant them wisdom and sound advisers. This is for their good as well as for our protection and the betterment of society. The Bible links the prayers of believers for those in authority to a peaceful society and the ability of God's people to live in godliness and tranquility. The apostle Paul urged that prayers and petitions be made for "all who are in authority, so that we may lead a tranquil and quiet life in all godliness and dignity" (1 Timothy 2:2).

We should also pray for those in elected office to be protected from the temptations inherent in public life, especially matters of finances and personal morality. Those in high office experience uncommon temptations to pride and lust, so we should pray that God will guard their hearts and their integrity.

I was once asked by television talk show host Larry King whether I prayed to God for the passage of a particular piece of legislation or the victory of my favorite candidate. While I know of no theological proscription against such a prayer, I told him I did not pray for a specific election result. At election time I ask that God's will is done, that He is glorified, and that His kingdom is advanced whatever the outcome. I have never found a time when that prayer was not answered, usually beyond my greatest hopes—and often in defeat.[9] When George

H. W. Bush lost the presidency in 1992, I was devastated. But Bill Clinton's victory and failed policies led to an explosion in Christian Coalition's membership, and I could see that the election results were a wake-up call for the faith community. I saw similar results after the 2012 elections. The spiritual cycle is always turning.

In 1998, my first election cycle as a political consultant, my client state senator Mike Fair of South Carolina narrowly lost a congressional primary to a businessman making his first run for office. I had poured my heart into that campaign, and I flew out of Greenville the next morning feeling pretty low.

Two years later, when I was working for George W. Bush during the hard-fought South Carolina presidential primary, Fair endorsed Bush at a critical time. The night before the primary, as Bush delivered his final speech of the campaign on the campus of Furman University in Greenville, Mike ran up and gave me a hug, exclaiming, "It took us two years to win, but we're going to have a big victory tomorrow!" I understood his meaning: Mike had lost, but God had a bigger plan, and a tough congressional defeat paved the way for the election of a president.

Nor was that all. The man who defeated Mike was Jim DeMint, who later served with great distinction in the U.S. Senate and who is now president of The Heritage Foundation. So we didn't really lose after all. (Jim still good-naturedly ribs me for being on the other side of his first campaign for Congress. We have since become friends and allies.)

The lesson is, God knows better than we do. What counts for success in His kingdom is not measured by the world's yardstick. In God's sovereignty and timing, there are times when victory masquerades as defeat, and vice versa. A tough loss can mean the death of our own ambitions, a pruning that enables us to bear more fruit for Him and His plan for our community, state, and country. So pray as Jesus taught His disciples: that God's will be done here on earth and that His kingdom will come even before our very eyes (Matthew 6:10). In politics, you will win some and lose some, but the cause of Christ never loses as long as we are faithful in our citizenship and trusting God for the outcome.

2. Be Informed and Educated

The Bible says, "My people are destroyed for lack of knowledge" (Hosea 4:6). This truth applies to all citizens but doubly so for people of faith, who are sometimes unfamiliar with how the political and legislative process really works.

Often when I speak at a church, I will ask everyone who knows the name of the president of the United States to raise their hand. Every hand goes up. I then ask those who know the name of the vice president and both U.S. senators to keep their hands raised. Some hands go down. Then I ask them to keep their hands raised if they know the name of their congressman or congresswoman. I start to get quizzical looks as more hands go down. By the time I get to their state senator, state representative, county commissioner, city council members, and school board members, there are very few hands still up. How can men and women of faith hope to influence the direction of their country if they don't even know who their elected officials are? We cannot influence those we do not know.

Knowledge is power. So do you know which committees your member of Congress, your senators, and your state legislators serve on, so that you know which issues they are most likely to follow? Do you know the names and have the phone numbers (preferably cell numbers) of their chiefs of staff, top political advisers, and legislative director? If not, then others, including issue organizations who hold views contrary to yours, will have more influence with these elected officials than you will.

Make it your business to know the staff and the key influencers around your member of Congress and your state legislators. Get to know them on a first-name basis. Check in with them every so often to pass on information or ask a question about where their boss stands on pending legislation. Don't wait until a critical vote on a pro-life or school choice bill to call them. By then it is too late.

Thomas Jefferson said, "If a nation expects to be ignorant and free in a state of civilization, it expects what never was and never will be." Being truly informed and educated means not relying on only one news outlet or just those news organizations that share or reinforce your ideological viewpoint for information.

I am sometimes asked, "Where do you go for news?" My answer is everywhere. To be effective, don't expose yourself only to news sources you agree with. To know your opponent's arguments, you must read them and study them.

The news sources I consult daily include the *Wall Street Journal* (I never miss the opinion pages if I can help it), *New York Times*, *Washington Post*, *Politico*, *National Review*, *National Journal*, *Daily Caller*, *Washington Times*, *Washington Examiner*, *Crisis*, *Christian Post*, *Weekly Standard*, and *Huffington Post*. I also read *Newsmax*, the *New Yorker*, *Vanity Fair*, *Time*, the *Economist*, and *World* magazine.

I watch cable news and listen to talk radio. I regularly visit the websites of The Heritage Foundation, Family Research Council, CATO Institute, American Enterprise Institute, Ethics and Religious Liberty Institute, the Urban Institute, the American Center for Law and Justice, and the Brookings Institute. In terms of columnists and bloggers, I read Charles Krauthammer, George Will, Pete Wehner, Karl Rove, Mike Gerson, Peggy Noonan, Dan Henninger, Kimberley Strassel, Jonah Goldberg, Andrew Sullivan, John Fund, Jim Geraghty, and Redstate.com. On foreign policy, my personal favorites are former United Nations Ambassador John Bolton, Bret Stephens of the *Wall Street Journal*, and David Ignatius of the *Washington Post*.

I also try to keep up with books, especially those dealing with history, public policy, and contemporary politics. I recommend reading at least one book a month on a public-policy, political, or historical topic. Some leading conservatives like Newt Gingrich and Karl Rove discuss on their websites what they are reading, and I peruse those to see which ones I am interested in reading. I also have maintained book-reading friendships and exchange book suggestions.

3. Become Involved in a Political Party

In chapter 13 we discussed the importance of parties to the political process in the United States. Suffice it to say here that the aspirations and ideals of social reform movements triumph first in a major party before they become enshrined in the laws of the nation.

George Will once observed that conservatives learned under Goldwater and Reagan that it is more important to lead a party than it is to govern the country. Will is right. Majority status comes and goes in Washington, but involvement in a political party is enduring. Whether the trade union, feminist, and civil rights movements on the left, or the pro-family, Tea Party, and pro-Second Amendment movements on the right, the first step toward advancing sound public policy is including it in the platform on which the candidates of a major political party seek office.

Involvement in a political party also credentials pro-life and pro-family activists. It is harder to demonize someone who has been elected to serve on the Republican or Democratic executive committee in their state. Get involved as a precinct chair or serve on the executive committee for the county party organization of your choice. Or get involved in a women's, youth, or minority auxiliary of a state party, which often invites speakers, lobbies on issues, and holds candidate forums.

Party involvement is also the best way to get to know candidates at the earliest stage of their political careers. Jimmy Carter began his road to the presidency on the Sumter County, Georgia, school board. Ronald Reagan trekked across California while running for governor in 1965-66, getting to know party activists like Mike Deaver and Bill Clark, who were later part of his inner circle and went with him to the White House. Barack Obama ran for Congress in 2002 against Bobby Rush in the Democratic primary and lost, but anyone who was a Democratic Party official or activist in Chicago at that time got to know Obama personally. Party involvement is a way to get to know current and future leaders of your state without being a Washington lobbyist or a well-heeled campaign contributor.

4. Build Relationships with Your Elected Representatives

We tend to think of public policy in terms of issue papers, interest groups, committee hearings, and voting records. Too often we neglect the human element. Politicians are first husbands and wives, friends and business partners, and mothers and fathers, open to the viewpoints of those whose judgment they have grown to value and respect in those roles. Not all of us can be the best friend or former law partner of a member of Congress. But we can make it our business to get to know them better as human beings.

One of the tips I teach grassroots activists is to contact their state legislators by calling them at home in the early evening when the legislature is not in session and ask to meet with them or buy them a cup of coffee to discuss pending issues. If one waits until the legislature is in session, lobbyists have descended on state capitols seeking meetings, favors, and handouts. Every trade association, industry group, and major city or county has a Lobby Day, complete with workshops, box lunches, and one-on-one visits with legislators. The slower months when the legislature is out of session is the best time to visit with your legislator and tell him or her about your values and the issues that concern you. These meetings should be informal, low-key, and conversational, designed to build a relationship based on mutual respect, not confrontation or threats.

If you invest time and energy into building relationships with elected officials or candidates, those relationships will pay dividends for years, even decades. At the urging of a friend, I once attended a fund-raiser for a state legislator and wrote a check. Over time we became friends. A few years later, he became majority leader in the state house. When he ran for Congress and was elected, the leadership in Congress asked him to help out with campaign fund-raising, where he similarly excelled. A couple of years later, I called him on his cell phone. He was on a campaign trip and riding in a rental car with the house majority leader, and he handed him the phone. After a brief chat, the leader passed the phone back to my friend. A relationship that began fifteen years earlier with a backbencher in a minority state legislative caucus rose to the highest levels of the U.S. Congress. These friendships don't guarantee policy victories, but they can ensure that the pro-family movement gets a fair hearing by those who can advance our issues.

5. Join a Public Policy Organization

Some believe that public policy organizations are part of the problem in American politics, that "special interests" make it harder for politicians in Washington to come together on a bipartisan basis to solve problems.

During the fiscal cliff negotiations in late 2012 and early 2013, the chorus of media commentators denouncing the "No New Taxes" pledge of Americans for Tax Reform reached a crescendo.[10] This criticism was exceeded only by attacks on the National Rifle Association in the aftermath of the tragic shooting by a deranged gunman at Sandy Hook Elementary School in Newtown, Connecticut. One columnist tore into the NRA for favoring "absurd, unbelievable, tragic, obscene" and "insane" public policy, an evil force seeking a "dystopian future" featuring a "tyranny of death and destruction—a tyranny of which the National Rifle Association is proud." Another columnist suggested that advocates of the right to keep and bear arms suffered from a form of mental illness.[11]

This vitriol (which, it should be noted, is rarely directed at the AFL-CIO or the Sierra Club) not only reveals an ideological bias in the media, but more troubling, contempt for the free association of like-minded citizens that is at the heart of the founders' vision for American democracy. It reached a fever pitch after the Supreme Court ruled in the Citizens United case that social welfare organizations can engage in electioneering activity. Liberals called for forcing conservative issue groups such as Americans for Prosperity and American Crossroads to disclose their donors, exposing contributors to boycotts, harassment, and personal attacks.

Under the false guise of transparency, these proposals would make it harder for free-market and social conservative groups to raise funds and therefore have a chilling effect on their ability to engage in free speech. The *New York Times* urged the Internal Revenue Service to go after Tea Party groups and others involved in "blatant abuses of tax law" and "root out political operatives who are abusing the law and conning taxpayers and voters."[12] This cheerleading led directly to the IRS scandal in which Tea Party and Christian groups were targeted for abuse and senior officials pleaded the Fifth Amendment. The cheerleading also instigated the issuing of new IRS regulations governing political activity by grassroots groups designed to force the disclosure of their donors and hamper their ability to educate and turn out voters.

The high crime that Tea Party and pro-family groups are guilty of is committing democracy. They register people to vote, educate them, and turn them out to the polls. We want to stop this? Liberal groups also raise large sums of money to mobilize citizens who agree with their views. That is their right. Issue groups enable people to enlarge their voice in government by uniting around common concerns. The four million members of the NRA have a bigger impact by operating under the umbrella of a public policy organization than acting as Lone Rangers.

The second reason issue organizations are so valuable is because elected officials rely on them for their expertise, their research, their guidance, and their counsel on pending legislation. If Americans for Tax Reform, the Ethics and Religious Liberty Commission of the Southern Baptist Convention, Concerned Women for America, the Family Research Council, or the Heritage Foundation send a letter to every member of Congress urging them to support or oppose a particular piece of legislation, their opinion carries special weight. Over time, issue groups gain brand equity in the public policy arena and are taken seriously by elected officials because of their expertise, leadership, relationships on Capitol Hill and in the various state capitals, and the size of their grassroots membership. While an individual citizen may have knowledge about a given issue, that person usually doesn't have that same level of legitimacy and credibility—which is why joining an issue group can give citizens a larger voice in the process.

Furthermore, issue groups do not bow to the party bosses. They came about because of what Alexis de Tocqueville noted 130 years ago as Americans' hunger to engage in free association for a common purpose. As long as there are Americans, they will form organizations that reflect their passions, interests, and desires.

Al Smith once observed that the only solution to what ails democracy is more democracy.[13] If the current set of issue organizations influencing the public policy debate is insufficient or inadequate, then like-minded citizens can form new organizations to better reflect their sentiments. A robust and vigorous debate—the conversation we call democracy—will be made more vibrant and colorful with more voices that mean more people have a stake in the outcome.

That is why I founded Faith and Freedom Coalition in 2009: I wanted to give Christians and their allies a voice in government and ensure they turn out to the polls in record numbers. Many outstanding organizations on the center-right are doing terrific work. Get involved in one or more of them, support them financially, and pray for their leaders. America will be a better place when you do.

6. Persuade, Don't Preach

Finally, to be effective, speak in a language that politicians, policy makers, and those who may not share our faith can hear. The Bible records in the book of Acts that the apostle Paul nearly caused a riot when he shared the gospel to a crowd in Jerusalem. But when he spoke to them in their native Hebrew tongue, they fell silent (Acts 22:1–2). We must remember that influencing those who don't already agree with us means citing authorities and making arguments they find persuasive. We can't just preach to the choir. When we believers quote Scripture or speak in "Christianese"—when we use biblical terminology and speak with religious flourish—we may fire up those who already agree with us, but we are unlikely to change many minds.

For that reason, I urge people to study both sides of an issue before they meet with an elected official or a member of their staff. Know the arguments for and against a piece of legislation frontwards and backwards. Know our opponent's arguments better than they do. And be ready with facts, statistics, results of government or academic studies, policy analysis by outside groups, and other third-party validation for our viewpoints. When discussing contentious social issues, we will find it helpful to appeal to natural law, buttressed with the findings of social science. "The Bible says it, I believe it, that settles it" may be good theology, but it isn't very effective in changing minds on Capitol Hill or in the halls of state legislatures.

Believers should always speak in a respectful tone, especially with those who don't share your viewpoint. Don't threaten, cajole, or insult others. At the Faith and Freedom Coalition, when we "score" a vote on a bill on our Congressional Scorecard, we do our best to alert staff and members of Congress in advance. We do so less to change minds than as a professional courtesy. There will be plenty of time and opportunity for disagreement later, but when you are sharing your views with elected officials or their staff, honey always works better than vinegar.

If Christians get serious about citizenship, not with promises to "take back America," but by serving others through public service, we can see good government restored in America. True reform must begin with us. During a dark period in Israel's history, the prophet Isaiah urged the people to get right with God. "Woe to the sinful nation, a people whose guilt is great," he proclaimed. "Learn to do right; seek justice. Defend the oppressed." Then God will "restore your leaders as in days of old, your rulers as at the beginning. Afterward you will be called the City of Righteousness, the Faithful City" (Isaiah 1:4, 17, 26 NIV).

Note that repentance and justice for the oppressed came before rulers who had integrity. This is a beautiful yet sobering promise. Civic leadership that builds a just and faithful society begins first with us citizens doing the right thing in our personal lives, our churches, our homes, and our communities. God will honor that brokenness and repentance by raising up just and righteous leaders of integrity who will restore our cities and our country to faithfulness.

The Awakening Must Begin with Us!

Some say that believers have politicized the gospel, turned off secular folk, and reduced the church to a political pressure group. So they counsel a season of spiritual introspection, reflection, and withdrawal from politics. But that would be a case where the cure is worse than the illness. It would no doubt be easier on our churches, our families, and our reputations if we withdrew from civic life. But it would also be an abrogation of our responsibility as citizens and believers to be a voice for the voiceless and an advocate for those who do not have one. The unborn, the poor, minority children trapped in failing schools, and mothers who fear for the safety of their children in crime-ridden neighborhoods should not have to wait for justice while we seek the self-indulgent safety of silence and retreat.

We may not be able to usher in the kingdom of God through political action, but we can combat evil, protect the innocent, and secure justice. This is the purpose of a muscular assertion of our rights as citizens. Let us finish the vital work of first repenting and getting right with God, and then we can work on restoring America to her founding principles.

Regardless of the outcome of our efforts, as we experience both victory and defeat, may we exercise our rights as American citizens with moral zeal but also with knowledge, in wisdom and patience, so that future generations may rise up one day and praise our memory because in the hour of testing we persevered. Let us act in a way worthy of the sacrifices made by those before us who gave us the precious gift of citizenship.

The spiritual cycle continues as Americans seek satisfaction and grow prideful in abundance and self-gratification. As a society, we have too often rejected God and His principles. But soon this pride will bring God's chastening, which can lead to repentance, revival, and cultural renewal.

May this movement toward renewal begin with us and then spread like a flood to our friends, neighbors, the larger society, and ultimately state capitals and Washington until America is both spiritually and economically vibrant again.

Action Points

1. Read Romans 13 and Acts 22:25–29 and reflect on their teaching about how believers can be effective citizens.
2. Call your state representative or state senator and invite him/her to coffee to get to know each other and discuss issues important to you and your family.
3. Pray for wisdom for our elected officials and all those in authority.

Notes

Chapter 1: The Spiritual Cycle

1. Greece, Cyprus, Spain, Portugal, and Italy have unsustainable public debt, and unemployment is in the 12 to 25 percent range. "Unemployment in Europe: Get the Figures for Every Country," *Guardian*, January 8, 2013, http://www.theguardian.com/news/datablog/2012/oct/31/europe-unemployment-rate-by-country-eurozone.
2. Gerren McHam, "$17,000,000,000,000," *The Foundry*, The Heritage Foundation, October 21, 2013, http://blog.heritage.org/author/gerren-mcham/.
3. Niall Ferguson, *The Great Degeneration: How Institutions Decay and Economies Die* (New York: Penguin Press, 2012), 11–20.
4. "Remarks by the President at the Planned Parenthood Conference," April 26, 2013, http://www.whitehouse.gov/photos-and-video/video/2013/04/26/president-obama-speaks-planned-parenthood-gala#transcript. Obama's symbiotic relationship with Richards while the government provides her group with $542 million in public subsidies would seem to merit journalistic inquiry, yet not a single major news organization noted the conflict of interest. Instead, the Associated Press approvingly noted, "The president lauded Planned Parenthood's nearly 100 years of providing cancer screenings, contraception and other health services for women and assured those fighting to protect abortion rights that they have an ally in him" (Darlene Superville, "Obama Backs Planned Parenthood in Political Fight," Associated Press, April 26, 2013). The media double standard is stark. In 2008 the press hounded John McCain for daring to associate with evangelical leaders like John Hagee, president of Christians United for Israel, and Rod Parsley, a prominent Ohio pastor.
5. After the shocking revelations that led to the murder conviction of Philadelphia abortionist Kermit Gosnell, the House of Representatives passed a ban on abortion after the twentieth week of pregnancy, which Democratic leader Nancy Pelosi denounced as an attempt to "ban all abortions," a deliberate lie. It is a medical fact that the unborn child responds to pain and has to be anesthetized for fetal procedures, yet commentators denounce pro-life advocates for being "antiscience" when they assert this is the case. See Annie Murphy Paul, "The First Ache," *New York Times*, February 10, 2008.

6. Andrew Sullivan, "Andrew Sullivan on Barack Obama's Gay Marriage Revolution," *Newsweek*, May 13, 2012, http://www.newsweek.com/andrew-sullivan-barack-obamas-gay-marriage-evolution-65067.
7. The *New York Times* praised him for occupying "the moral high ground on what may be the great civil rights struggle of our time," condemning his opponent for advancing "bigotry." See "President Obama's Moment," *New York Times*, May 10, 2012, New York Edition, A28.
8. Paul Hitlin, Mark Jurkowitz, and Amy Mitchell, "News Coverage Conveys Strong Momentum for Same-Sex Marriage," Pew Research Journalism Project, June 17, 2013, http://www.journalism.org/node/33731.
9. National Center for Health Statistics, Centers for Disease Control, "Births: Final Data for 2010," *National Vital Statistics Reports* 61, no. 1 (August 28, 2012).
10. California and several other states had previously legalized medicinal marijuana, allowing anyone to buy it with an easily obtained prescription.
11. Jerry Ropelato, "Internet Pornography Statistics," Internet Filter Software Review, *Top Ten Reviews*, http://internet-filter-review.toptenreviews.com/internet-pornography-statistics-pg2.html. See also http://internet-filter-review.toptenreviews.com/internet-pornography-statistics.html.
12. William Adams, Colleen Owens, and Kevonne Small, "Effects of Federal Legislation on the Commercial Sexual Exploitation of Children," U.S. Department of Justice, Office of Juvenile Justice and Delinquency Prevention, *Juvenile Justice Bulletin*, July 2010, https://www.ncjrs.gov/pdffiles1/ojjdp/228631.pdf.
13. National Council on Problem Gambling, http://www.ncpgambling.org/i4a/pages/Index.cfm?pageID=3314.
14. *The Works of Aurelius Augustine, Bishop of Hippo*, ed. Marcus Dods, vol. 1, *The City of God* (Edinburgh: T & T Clark, 1913), 336.
15. Here I am speaking of "New Jerusalem" as a metaphor, not as theology.
16. Jacques Maritain, "On the Philosophy of History," Jacques Maritain Center, University of Notre Dame, http://maritain.nd.edu/jmc/etext/philhist.htm.
17. Ronald Reagan, "Remarks at the Annual Convention of the National Association of Evangelicals," March 8, 1983, www.reaganfoundation.org.
18. David Sanders, "John Dos Passos, the Art of Fiction No 44," Interviews, *The Paris Review* 46 (Spring 1969), http://www.theparisreview.org/interviews/4202/the-art-of-fiction-no-44-john-dos-passos. Dos Passos was talking about communism, which appeared to be at its zenith even as it teetered on its last legs. Whittaker Chambers reached the opposite conclusion, writing in his memoir *Witness* that when he left the ranks of communism, he felt as if he had crossed over from the winning to the losing side.
19. Jean-François Revel, *How Democracies Perish* (New York: Doubleday, 1984), 10.

20. Read the transcript of Reagan's 1993 remarks to the National Association of Evangelicals at http://www.reaganfoundation.org/pdf/Remarks_Annual_Convention_National_Association_Evangelicals_030883.pdf.

Chapter 2: Launching a New Jerusalem

1. "The President's News Conference in Strasbourg, April 4, 2009," *Public Papers of the Presidents of the United States: Barack Obama, 2009, Book 1* (Washington, DC: Government Printing Office, 2011), 437. See also Mallory Factor, "American Exceptionalism—And an 'Exceptional' President," *Forbes*, August 31, 2010.
2. John Winthrop, "A Model of Christian Charity," speech written and delivered in 1630 aboard the ship *Arbella* voyaging to the New World, The Religious Freedom Page, http://religiousfreedom.lib.virginia.edu/sacred/charity.html.
3. Perry Miller, *Errand in the Wilderness* (Cambridge, MA: Belknap Press, 1956).
4. William Bradford, quoted in Bruce Feiler, *America's Prophet: Moses and the American Story* (New York: William Morrow, 2009), 8.
5. Nathaniel Philbrick, *Mayflower: A Story of Courage, Community, and War* (New York: Penguin Books, 2006), 173.
6. Walter Isaacson, *Benjamin Franklin: An American Life* (New York: Simon & Schuster, 2003), 111.
7. Jonathan Mayhew, quoted in Bernard Bailyn, *The Ideological Origins of the American Revolution* (Cambridge, MA: Belknap Press, 1967), 140; Marilyn C. Baseler, *Asylum for Mankind: America, 1607–1800* (Ithaca, NY: Cornell University Press, 1998), 135.
8. Samuel Seabury, letter to Alexander Hamilton, December 24, 1774, original text at http://teachingamericanhistory.org/library/document/samuel-seabury-to-alexander-hamilton/. Also see Bernard Bailyn, *The Ideological Origins of the American Revolution*, 137.
9. John Adams, quoted in Bailyn, *The Ideological Origins of the American Revolution*, 140.
10. Thomas Paine, *Common Sense*, 1776, http://www.ushistory.org/paine/commonsense/singlehtml.htm.
11. George Duffield, "A Sermon Preached on a Day of Thanksgiving," December 11, 1783; Jon Meacham, *American Gospel: God, the Founding Fathers, and the Making of a Nation* (New York: Random House, 2006), 80–81. In Duffield's telling, the God of Abraham, "who raised a Joshua to lead the tribes of Israel on the field of battle," had also "raised and formed a Washington" to lead the colonists to victory over Great Britain. As "manifest was His voice on Sinai; or His hand in the affairs of Israel of old," so, too, had "the wisdom, the power, and the goodness of God" brought about America's "deliverance; cast forth our enemy; bestowed upon us a wide extended, fruitful country; and blessed us with a safe and honorable peace."

12. Bailyn, *The Ideological Origins of the American Revolution*, 141.
13. Paul Johnson, *A History of the American People* (New York: HarperCollins, 1997), 116.
14. John Dickinson, quoted in Bailyn, *The Ideological Origins of the American Revolution*, 187; Newt Gingrich, *Rediscovering God in America* (Nashville: Thomas Nelson, 2012), xiv.
15. A. J. Langguth, *Patriots: The Men Who Started the American Revolution* (New York: Simon and Schuster, 1988), 59.
16. Peter Marshall and David Manuel, *The Light and the Glory* (Old Tappan, NJ: Revell, 1977), 268–69.
17. George Bancroft, *Bancroft's History of the United States*, vol. 7 (Boston: Little & Brown, 1838), 229.
18. George Washington, letter to Lafayette, February 7, 1788, http://founders.archives.gov/documents/Washington/04-06-02-0079.
19. James Madison, "Federalist No. 37," in Alexander Hamilton, James Madison, and John Jay, *The Federalist Papers*, ed. Jacob E. Cooke (Franklin Center, PA: The Franklin Library, 1977), 257; Catherine Drinker Bowen, *Miracle at Philadelphia: The Story of the Constitutional Convention May–September 1787* (Boston: Little, Brown, 1966), 126–27; Meacham, *American Gospel*, 87–89.
20. For a fuller view of John Adams's views on constitutional government, see David McCullough, *John Adams* (New York: Simon and Schuster, 2001), 374–81.
21. George Washington, "Farewell Address," September 19, 1796, http://avalon.law.yale.edu/18th_century/washing.asp. For a good discussion of Washington's Farewell Address, see Joseph J. Ellis, *Founding Brothers: The Revolutionary Generation* (New York: Random House, 2000).
22. Alexis de Tocqueville, *Democracy in America* (New York: Alfred A. Knopf, 1994 [originally published 1835]), 44, 308.
23. Ibid., 305–6.
24. Ibid., 307.
25. Frederick Jackson Turner, "The Significance of the Frontier in American History," paper delivered to the American Historical Society, July 12, 1893, original text available at http://xroads.virginia.edu/~hyper/turner/chapter1.html#foot1.
26. Paul Johnson, *A History of the American People*, 85–91.
27. Karen Ordahl Kupperman, "Apathy and Death in Early Jamestown," *Journal of American History* 66 (1979), 24–40.
28. For more about King Philip's War, see Eric B. Schultz and Michael J. Tougias, *King Philip's War: The History and Legacy of America's Forgotten Conflict* (New York: W. W. Norton, 2000).

29. Stephen Ambrose, *Undaunted Courage: Meriwether Lewis, Thomas Jefferson, and the Opening of the American West* (New York: Simon & Schuster, 1997), 155.
30. D. T. Max, "Twister: How Tony Gilroy Surprises Jaded Moviegoers," *New Yorker*, March 16, 2009.
31. William Grimes, *Straight Up or On the Rocks: A Cultural History of American Drink* (New York: Simon & Schuster, 1993) 44–45.
32. Daniel Okrent, *Last Call: The Rise and Fall of Prohibition* (New York: Scribner, 2011), 7.
33. Edmund Morgan, *American Slavery, American Freedom: The Ordeal of Colonial Virginia* (New York: W. W. Norton, 1975), 376–81.
34. George W. Bush, "Text of President Bush's 2003 State of the Union Address," *Washington Post*, January 28, 2003.

Chapter 3: Early Awakenings

1. *Richmond Christian Advocate*, May 27, 1847.
2. Paul E. Johnson, *A Shopkeeper's Millennium: Society and Revivals in Rochester, New York: 1815–1837* (New York: Hill and Wang, 1978), 55–58.
3. Daniel Okrent, *Last Call: The Rise and Fall of Prohibition* (New York: Scribner, 2010), 7–9.
4. Myra L. Spaulding, "Dueling in the District of Columbia," 1928, Records of the Columbia Historical Society, Washington, D.C., 120.
5. Richard Bell, "The Double Guilt of Dueling: The Stain of Suicide in Anti-Dueling Rhetoric in the Early Republic," *Journal of the Early Republic* (2009), 383–410; Ron Chernow, *Alexander Hamilton* (New York: Penguin Press, 20 04), 714–20.
6. Bertram Wyatt-Brown, "Andrew Jackson's Honor," *Journal of the Early Republic* 17, no. 1 (Spring 1997): 8; H. W. Brands, *Andrew Jackson* (New York: Anchor Books, 2005), 132–38.
7. Barry O'Neill, "Mediating National Honour: Lessons from the Era of Dueling," *Journal of Institutional and Theoretical Economics* (March 2003), vol. 159, No. 1, 241; Richard Carwardine, *Lincoln: A Life of Purpose and Power* (New York: Alfred A. Knopf, 2006), 58; Rich Lowry, *Lincoln Unbound* (New York: Broadside Books/HarperCollins, 2013), 82–84.
8. Johnson, *A Shopkeeper's Millennium,* 95.
9. Donald G. Mathews, *Religion in the Old South* (Chicago: University of Chicago Press, 1977), 68–69.
10. Whitney R. Cross, *The Burned-Over District: The Social and Intellectual History of Enthusiastic Religion in Western New York, 1800–1850* (Ithaca, NY: Cornell University Press, 1950), 224.
11. Eric Metaxas, *Amazing Grace: William Wilberforce and the Heroic Campaign to End Slavery* (New York: HarperSanFrancisco, 2007), 136.

12. Ronald G. Walters, *American Reformers*, 1815–1860 (New York: Hill and Wang, 1978), 23.
13. Harriet Beecher Stowe, *Uncle Tom's Cabin* (Boston: John P. Jewett and Company, 1852).
14. Edmund Wilson, *Patriotic Gore: Studies in the Literature of the American Civil War* (New York: Oxford University Press, 1962), 3–32; Harriet Beecher Stowe Center, "Impact of Uncle Tom's Cabin, Slavery, and the Civil War," http://www.harrietbeecherstowecenter.org/utc/impact.shtml.
15. "The Time for Prayer: The Third Great Awakening," *Christianity Today*, July 1, 1989.
16. The Frederick Douglass Papers 1, vol. 3 (New Haven, CT: Yale University Press, 1986).
17. Okrent, *Last Call*, 13.
18. William Knoedelseder, *Bitter Brew: The Rise and Fall of Anheuser-Busch and America's Kings of Beer* (New York: Harper Collins, 2012), 17–18.
19. Reverend S. Parkes Cadman, president, and Reverend Charles S. Macfarland, general secretary, Federal Council of Churches, Testimony Before the Committee on the Judiciary, U.S. Senate, 1926, reprinted in K. Austin Kerr, ed., *The Politics of Moral Behavior: Prohibition and Drug Abuse* (Reading, PA: Addison Wesley, 1973).
20. Okrent, *Last Call*, 97.
21. Ralph Reed, *Active Faith: How Christians Are Changing the Soul of American Politics* (New York: Free Press, 1996), 38–39; Okrent, *Last Call*, 38–41.

Chapter 4: Turn! Turn! Turn!

1. Mrs. Henry Peabody, "Testimony on the National Prohibition Law," Committee on the Judiciary, U.S. Senate, 69th Congress, First Session (1926), 666–67.
2. Edward J. Larson, *Summer for the Gods: The Scopes Trial and America's Continuing Debate Over Science and Religion* (New York: Basic Books, 1997), 233.
3. George Weigel, "Humanae Vitae at 45," *National Review*, July 25, 2013, www.nationalreview.com. This cyclical was drafted by Cardinal Wojtyla of Poland (who later became Pope John Paul II).
4. Gerald Kennedy, quoted in Geraldine Doogue, "The Pill: 50 Years On," December 25, 2010, http://www.abc.net.au/radionational/programs/saturdayextra/the-pill-50-years-on/2981770.
5. *U.S. News & World Report* cover story, quoted in Elaine Tyler May, "Promises the Pill Could Never Make," *New York Times*, April 25, 2010, WK13, http://www.nytimes.com/2010/04/25/opinion/25may.html.
6. R. Albert Mohler, Jr., "Why the Sexual Revolution Needed a Sexual Revolutionary," *The Atlantic*, August 23, 2012, http://www.theatlantic.com/entertainment/archive/2012/08/why-the-sexual-revolution-needed-a-sexual-revolutionary/261492/.

7. Billy Graham, *World Aflame* (New York: Doubleday, 1965), 12, 218.
8. Ibid., 20–21.
9. Norman Vincent Peale, *Sin, Sex, and Self-Control* (New York: Doubleday, 1965), 55–56.
10. Robert W. Fogel, *The Fourth Great Awakening and the Future of Egalitarianism* (Chicago: University of Chicago Press, 2000), 25–36.
11. Richard D. Land, "The Southern Baptist Convention, 1979–1993: What Happened and Why?" *Baptist History and Heritage* 28, no 4 (October 1993): 4–7.
12. Clayton Sullivan, *Called to Preach, Condemned to Survive* (Macon: Mercer University Press, 1985), 79, cited in Land, "Southern Baptist Convention," 8.
13. Paul Pressler, *A Hill on Which to Die: One Southern Baptist's Journey* (Nashville: B&H Publishing Group, 2002); Jerry Sutton, *The Baptist Reformation: The Conservative Resurgence in the Southern Baptist Convention* (Nashville: Broadman & Holman, 2000), 67–85.
14. Gerald R. Ford, "Remarks Delivered Before the Southern Baptist Convention," Norfolk, Virginia, June 15, 1976, The American Presidency Project, http://www.presidency.ucsb.edu/ws/?pid=6127.
15. Richard Viguerie, *The New Right: We're Ready to Lead* (Falls Church, VA: Viguerie, 1981), 127–29.
16. Jerry Falwell, *Strength for the Journey* (New York: Simon & Schuster, 1987), 358–60.
17. Peter Applebome, "Jerry Falwell, Moral Majority Founder, Dies at 73," *New York Times*, May 16, 2007, http://www.nytimes.com/2007/05/16/obituaries/16falwell.html?pagewanted=all.
18. Edith L. Blumhofer, *Restoring the Faith: The Assemblies of God, Pentecostalism, and the American Culture* (Champaign, IL: University of Illinois Press, 1993), 9.
19. Steve Rabey, "Fire From Above," *Charisma*, May 31, 2005, http://www.charismamag.com/site-archives/216-features/spiritual-revival/1609-fire-from-above.
20. David Edwin Harrell, Jr., *Pat Robertson: A Life and Legacy* (Grand Rapids: William B. Eerdmans, 2010), 82–85.
21. Jeffrey K. Hadden, "The Rise and Fall of American Televangelism," *Annals of the American Academy of Political and Social Science* 527, Religion in the Nineties (May 1993), 118; Jeffrey K. Hadden, "Religious Broadcasting and the Mobilization of the New Christian Right," *Journal for the Scientific Study of Religion* 26 (March 1987), 16.
22. Hadden, "Rise and Fall of American Televangelism," 120.
23. Donald R. McClarey, "Pope Paul VI and the Smoke of Satan," *The American Catholic*, December 4, 2011, http://the-american-catholic.com/2011/12/04/pope-paul-vi-and-the-smoke-of-satan/.

24. George Weigel, *Witness to Hope: The Biography of Pope John Paul II* (New York: Cliff Street Books/HarperCollins, 1999), 612–19.
25. Billy Graham, quoted in Deal Hudson, *Onward Christian Soldiers: The Growing Political Power of Catholics and Evangelicals in the United States* (New York: Threshold Editions, 2010), 257.

Chapter 5: The Reagan Revival

1. John G. Turner, *Bill Bright and Campus Crusade for Christ: The Renewal of Evangelicalism in Postwar America* (Chapel Hill: University of North Carolina Press, 2008), 190; Interview with James Robison, July 23, 2013; Interview with John Conlan, October 25, 2013.
2. Peggy Noonan, *What I Saw at the Revolution: A Political Life in the Reagan Era* (New York, Random House, 1990), 149.
3. George Will, "Reagan Revelation: At 100, Why He Still Matters," *Time*, February 6, 2011, http://content.time.com/time/magazine/article/0,9171,2044770,00.html.
4. Barack Obama, Editorial Board Interview. *Reno Journal-Gazette*, January 15, 2008.
5. Ronald Reagan, "Farewell Address from the Oval Office," January 11, 1989, http://www.reaganfoundation.org/pdf/Farewell_Address_011189.pdf.
6. Ronald Reagan and Richard Hubler, *Where's the Rest of Me?* (New York: Dell, 1965), 12.
7. Paul Kengor, *God and Ronald Reagan: A Spiritual Life* (New York: ReganBooks, 2004), 7–10, 17–26.
8. Paul Kengor, "The Intellectual Origins of Ronald Reagan's Faith," The Heritage Foundation, April 30, 2004, http://www.heritage.org/research/lecture/the-intellectual-origins-of-ronald-reagans-faith.
9. Margot Morrell, *Reagan's Journey: Lessons from a Remarkable Career* (New York: Simon and Schuster, 2011), 24–27.
10. Nancy Reagan, *I Love You, Ronnie* (New York: Random House, 2002), 87.
11. Paul Kengor, "When Reagan Spoke Truth to Soviet Power," *Wall Street Journal*, January 31, 2011, http://online.wsj.com/news/articles/SB10001424052748704698004576104483730194812.
12. Peter Schweizer, *Reagan's War: The Epic Story of His Forty-Year Struggle and Final Triumph Over Communism* (New York: Doubleday, 2003) 9–13, 25–26.
13. Kengor, *God and Ronald Reagan*, 95.
14. Ronald Reagan, "Radio Commentary on Private Schools," November 28, 1978, in Kiron Skinner, Annelise Anderson, and Martin Anderson, eds., *Reagan, in His Own Hand: The Writings of Ronald Reagan That Reveal His Revolutionary Vision for America* (New York: Free Press, 2001), 355.
15. Randall Balmer, "The Religious Right and the Abortion Myth," http://old.euba.sk/dokumenty/cnas/Interdisc%202013/Week%207%20-%20Pre-reading%20-%20Religious%20Right%20and%20the%20Abortion%20Myth.pdf.

16. Richard Viguerie, *The New Right: We're Ready to Lead* (Falls Church, VA: Carolin House Publishers/The Viguerie Company,1981), 127; Randall Balmer, *Thy Kingdom Come: How the Religious Right Distorts Faith and Threatens America* (New York: Basic Books, 2007), 7–8.
17. Mark Kilmer, "Adamantly Pro-Choice? Ronald Reagan and Abortion in 1967," Redstate, 2008, http://archive.redstate.com/stories/elections/2008/adamantly_pro_choice_ronald_reagan_and_abortion_in_1967.
18. Lou Cannon, *Governor Reagan: His Rise to Power* (New York: PublicAffairs, 2003), 208–15.
19. Ronald Reagan, "Radio Commentary on Abortion Laws," April 1975, in Skinner, et al., *Reagan in His Own Hand*, 380.
20. Paul Kengor and Patricia Clark Doerner, "Reagan's Darkest Hour: 'Therapeutic' Abortion in California," *National Review*, January 22, 2008, http://www.nationalreview.com/articles/223437/reagans-darkest-hour/paul-kengor/page/0/1.
21. Paul Kengor and Patricia Clark Doerner, *The Judge: William P. Clark, Ronald Reagan's Top Hand* (San Francisco: Ignatius Press, 2007), 65–67.
22. Ronald Reagan, "Debates Between the President and Former Vice President Walter F. Mondale in Louisville, Kentucky," The Reagan Presidential Foundation and Library, October 7, 1984, http://www.reaganfoundation.org/reagan-quotes-detail.aspx?tx=2041.
23. Viguerie, *The New Right*, 175–76.
24. "God in America: 'Of God and Caesar,'" *God in America*, PBS, http://www.pbs.org/godinamerica/transcripts/hour-six.html.
25. Brian T. Kaylor, *Presidential Campaign Rhetoric in an Age of Confessional Politics* (Lanham, MD: Lexington Books, 2012), 47.
26. Kengor, *God and Ronald Reagan*, 166.
27. "History of Federal Income, Bottom and Top Bracket Rates," National Taxpayers Union, http://www.ntu.org/tax-basics/history-of-federal-individual-1.html.
28. "Inflation 1979 by Country/Region," Inflation EU, http://www.inflation.eu/inflation-rates/cpi-inflation-1979.aspx.
29. Viguerie, *The New Right*, 128; J. Brooks Flippen, *Jimmy Carter, The Politics of Family, and the Rise of the Religious Right* (Athens: University Of Georgia Press, 2011), 316–17.
30. Carl Bernstein, "The Holy Alliance," *Time*, February 24, 1992; Carl Bernstein and Marco Politi, *His Holiness: John Paul II and the Hidden History of Our Time* (New York: Doubleday, 1997) 355-361. For a different view of Pope John Paul II's role, see George Weigel, *Witness to Hope: The Biography of Pope John Paul II* (New York: Cliff Street Books/HarperCollins, 1999), 440–42.

31. "First Inaugural Address of Ronald Reagan," January 20, 1981, http://avalon.law.yale.edu/20th_century/reagan1.asp.

Chapter 6: A Coalition of Christians

1. Cal Thomas and Ed Dobson, *Blinded by Might: Can the Religious Right Save America?* (Grand Rapids: Zondervan, 1999), 23–27.
2. Thomas B. Edsall, "Key Conservative Surrenders in Culture War," *Washington Post*, February 18, 1999, A6, http://www.washingtonpost.com/wp-srv/politics/daily/feb99/right18.htm.
3. James Gerstenzang and Robert Shogan, "Conservatives Hit Reagan on Treaty: One Calls President 'a Useful Idiot' of Soviets; Criticism of Accord Mounts," *Los Angeles Times*, December 5, 1987, http://articles.latimes.com/1987-12-05/news/mn-6395_1_president-reagan.
4. As we have already seen, the temperance movement began during the Second Great Awakening, but Prohibition did not become law until 1920, more than eighty years later. The NAACP was founded in 1909, but it would be two generations before the Democrats included a civil rights plank in its platform—and another generation before the goals of the civil rights movement were enshrined in law under Lyndon B. Johnson. In the intervening years a federal anti-lynching law was defeated, the first civil rights bill since the Civil War was gutted of enforcement powers before Congress passed it in 1957, and Senate filibusters by the Southern caucus stalled other attempts at reform. The lesson: social reform comes slowly, haltingly, and painfully, and it usually takes decades to achieve.
5. Sean Wilentz, "God and Man at Lynchburg," *New Republic*, April 25, 1988, 20; "Falwell's Farewell: Jerry Falwell Disbands Moral Majority," *National Review*, July 14, 1989, 19; Laura Sessions Stepp, "Falwell Says Moral Majority to Be Dissolved," *Washington Post*, June 12, 1989.
6. Quin Hillyer, "Poor, Uneducated, and Easily Led," *The American Spectator*, May 1, 2006.
7. Frank Rich, "Bait and Switch II," *New York Times*, April 6, 1995, http://www.nytimes.com/1995/04/06/opinion/journal-bait-and-switch-ii.html.
8. Richard L. Berke, "A Tape Reveals Pat Robertson, the Politician," *New York Times*, September 18, 1997, http://www.nytimes.com/1997/09/18/us/a-tape-reveals-pat-robertson-the-politician.html.

Chapter 7: A Man for the Job

1. George W. Bush, *Decision Points* (New York: Crown, 2010), 126–28; Ely Brown, "Florida Students Witnessed the Moment Bush Learned of 9/11 Terrorist Attacks," ABC News, September 8, 2011, http://abcnews.go.com/US/September_11/florida-students-witnessed-moment-bush-learned-911-terror/story?id=14474518.

2. Afsin Yurdakul, "He Told Bush That 'America Is Under Attack,'" NBC News, September 10, 2009, http://sys04.msnbc.msn.com/id/32782623/.
3. "Unemployed Persons by Occupation and Sex," U.S. Bureau of Labor Statistics, 2009, ftp://ftp.bls.gov/pub/special.requests/lf/aa2009/pdf/cpsaat25.pdf.
4. David Aikman, *A Man of Faith: The Spiritual Journey of George W. Bush* (Nashville: W Publishing Group/Thomas Nelson, 2004), 68–80; "The Jesus Factor: A President and His Faith," *Frontline*, PBS, April 29, 2004, http://www.pbs.org/wgbh/pages/frontline/shows/jesus/president/.
5. George W. Bush, *Decision Points*, 31–33; Aikman, 73–76; Julian Borger, "How Born-Again George Became a Man on a Mission," *Guardian*, October 6, 2005, http://www.theguardian.com/world/2005/oct/07/usa.georgebush.
6. Glen Justice, "Bush Drew Record $259 Million During Primaries," *New York Times*, September 21, 2004, http://www.nytimes.com/2004/09/21/politics/campaign/21money.html?_r=0.
7. "South Carolina Republican Debate," CNN, February 15, 2000, http://transcripts.cnn.com/TRANSCRIPTS/0002/15/lkl.00.html.
8. "Bush Wins S. Carolina Primary; McCain Promises Fight to the Finish," *Sunday Morning News*, CNN, February 20, 2000, http://www.cnnstudentnews.cnn.com/TRANSCRIPTS/0002/20/sm.01.html; "South Carolina Primary: Bush Wins Decisively; McCain Promises Fight in Michigan, Arizona," CNN, February 19, 2000.
9. Dan Keating and Dan Balz, "Florida Recounts Would Have Favored Bush," *Washington Post*, November 12, 2001, http://www.washingtonpost.com/wp-dyn/articles/A12623-2001Nov11.html.
10. Jake Tapper and Dennis Powell, "Fact Check: Health Care Plan, Gas Prices," ABC News, October 12, 2004, http://abcnews.go.com/Politics/Vote2004/story?id=160148.
11. CNN Library, "Stem Cells Fast Facts," CNN, July 5, 2013.
12. Steven Ertelt, "Bush Recalls Decision to Limit Embryonic Stem Cell Funding in New Book," *Life News*, November 9, 2010.
13. "Adult Stem Cell Research Leaving Embryos Behind," CBS News, August 2, 2010, http://www.cbsnews.com/news/adult-stem-cell-research-leaving-embryos-behind/.
14. Roll Call Vote 118, United States Senate, May 11, 2006, http://www.senate.gov/legislative/LIS/roll_call_lists/roll_call_vote_cfm.cfm?congress=109&session=2&vote=00118.
15. Roll Call Vote 237, United States Senate, October 11, 2002, http://www.senate.gov/legislative/LIS/roll_call_lists/roll_call_vote_cfm.cfm?congress=107&session=2&vote=00237.

Chapter 8: The Life of Marriage

1. http://www.youtube.com/watch?v=Ir6gEvmwQtc.
2. Jessica Gavora, "Obama's 'Julia' Ad and the New Hubby State," *Washington Post*, May 11, 2012, http://www.washingtonpost.com/opinions/obamas-julia-ad-and-the-new-hubby-state/2012/05/11/gIQAcRdoIU_story.htm.
3. "Exit Polls 2012: How the Vote Has Shifted," *Washington Post*, November 6, 2012, http://www.washingtonpost.com/wp-srv/special/politics/2012-exit-polls/.
4. W. Bradford Wilcox, "The Evolution of Divorce," *National Affairs*, November 1, 2009, 81–94.
5. Ibid.
6. "Marriage: America's Best Antidote to Child Poverty," Fact Sheet No. 112, The Heritage Foundation, September 5, 2012.
7. W. Bradford Wilcox, ed., *The State of Our Unions: Marriage in America, 2009*, The National Marriage Project at the University of Virginia, December 2009, 64, http://www.stateofourunions.org/2009/SOOU2009.pdf.
8. "Marriage Rates," University of Maryland, October 8, 1999. http://www.vanneman.umd.edu/socy441/trends/marriage.html.
9. Gretchen Livingston and D'Vera Cohn, "Childlessness Up among All Women; Down among Women with Advanced Degrees," Pew Research Center, June 25, 2010, http://www.pewsocialtrends.org/2010/06/25/childlessness-up-among-all-women-down-among-women-with-advanced-degrees/.
10. Michelle Castillo, "Almost Half of First Babies in U.S. Born to Unwed Mothers," CBS News, March 15, 2013, http://www.cbsnews.com/news/almost-half-of-first-babies-in-us-born-to-unwed-mothers/.
11. W. Bradford Wilcox, "The Great Recession's Silver Lining?" http://www.americanvalues.org/pdfs/Unions/Unions_wilcox.pdf.
12. Casey E. Copen, Kimberly Daniels, and William D. Mosher, "First Premarital Cohabitation in the United States: 2006–2010 National Survey of Family Growth," National Health Statistics Reports, no. 64, Centers for Disease Control, April 4, 2013, http://www.cdc.gov/nchs/data/nhsr/nhsr064.pdf.
13. "Cohabitation, Marriage, Divorce, and Remarriage in the United States," National Center for Health Statistics series 23, no. 22, Centers for Disease Control, July 24, 2002; Wilcox, ed., *The State of Our Unions*, 69–70.
14. Kay Hymowitz, Jason Carroll, W. Bradford Wilcox, Kelleen Kaye, "Knot Yet: The Benefits and Costs of Delayed Marriage in America," The National Marriage Project at the University of Virginia, 2013, 20, http://nationalmarriageproject.org/wp-content/uploads/2013/03/KnotYet-FinalForWeb.pdf.

15. U.S. Census Bureau, "Households and Families: 2010," April 2012, 5-6; Doris Nhan, "Census: More in U.S. Report Nontraditional Households," *National Journal*, May 1, 2012, http://www.nationaljournal.com/thenextamerica/demographics/census-more-in-us-report-nontraditional-households-20120430; Haya El Nasser and Paul Overberg, "More People Choose to Go Solo," *USA Today*, October 10, 2012, http://www.usatoday.com/story/news/nation/2012/10/10/more-people-living-alone/1625591/.
16. Robert Putnam, *Bowling Alone: The Collapse and Revival of American Community* (New York: Simon & Schuster, 2011), 66.
17. Wilcox, "The Evolution of Divorce," 81–94.
18. Greg Kaufmann, "This Week in Poverty: US Single Mothers—'The Worst Off,'" *The Nation*, December 21, 2012, http://www.thenation.com/blog/171886/week-poverty-us-single-mothers-worst#.
19. Castillo, "Almost Half of First Babies."
20. Brendan Lyle, "After Divorce, Women Rebound Faster but Stay in Poverty Longer," *Huffington Post*, October 22, 2012, http://www.huffingtonpost.com/brendan-lyle/after-divorce-women-rebou_1_b_1970733.html.
21. Ron Haskins and Isabel V. Sawhill, "Five Myths About Our Land of Opportunity," November 1, 2009, Brookings Institute, http://www.brookings.edu/research/opinions/2009/11/01-opportunity-sawhill-haskins.
22. "Text of Obama's Fatherhood Speech," *Politico*, June 15, 2008; Margaret Mead, *Male and Female* (New York: New American Library, 1962), 148, quoted in Daniel Patrick Moynihan, "The Negro Family: The Case for National Action," United States Department of Labor, March 1965, http://www.dol.gov/dol/aboutdol/history/webid-meynihan.htm.
23. "U.S. Abortion Statistics," Abort73.com, June 21, 2013, http://www.abort73.com/abortion_facts/us_abortion_statistics/.
24. See George Gilder's revised and updated edition, *Wealth and Poverty: A New Edition for the Twenty-First Century* (Washington, DC: Regnery Publishing, 2012), 103–7.
25. Paul C. Vitz, "Family Decline: The Findings of Social Science," Catholic Education Resource Center, 1999, http://www.catholiceducation.org/articles/marriage/mf0002.html.
26. Christopher Jencks, "Is Violent Crime Increasing?" *American Prospect*, December 4, 2000, http://prospect.org/article/violent-crime-increasing.
27. Adam Gopnik, "The Caging of America," *New Yorker*, January 30, 2012, http://www.newyorker.com/arts/critics/atlarge/2012/01/30/120130crat_atlarge_gopnik.
28. Paul Krugman, "Delusions of Populism," *New York Times*, July 12, 2013, A21, http://www.nytimes.com/2013/07/12/opinion/krugman-delusions-of-populism.html?_r=0.

29. Lynn Sweet, "Obama's June 15, 2008 Father's Day Speech at the Apostolic Church of God in Chicago," *Chicago Sun-Times*, June 15, 2008; Megan Slack, "President Obama Delivers the Commencement Address at Morehouse College," The White House Blog, May 19, 2013, http://www.whitehouse.gov/blog/2013/05/19/president-obama-delivers-commencement-address-morehouse-college.
30. Jeff Zeleny, "Jesse Jackson Apologizes for Remarks on Obama," *New York Times*, July 10, 2008.
31. Nana Ekua Brew-Hammond, "Absent Black Fathers: Should Our Community Discuss the Issue Publicly, or Privately?", *The Grio* (blog), June 11, 2013, http://thegrio.com/2013/06/11/absent-black-fathers-should-our-community-discuss-the-issue-publicly-or-privately/.
32. Audrey Barrick, "Study: Christian Divorce Rate Identical to National Average," *Christian Post*, April 4, 2008, http://www.christianpost.com/news/study-christian-divorce-rate-identical-to-national-average-31815/.
33. "Gay Marriage Around the World," Pew Research Religion and Public Life Project, December 19, 2013, http://www.pewforum.org/2013/12/19/gay-marriage-around-the-world-2013/.
34. Ben Brumfield, "Voters Approve Same-Sex Marriage for the First Time," CNN, November 7, 2012, http://www.cnn.com/2012/11/07/politics/pol-same-sex-marriage/.
35. Matt K. Lewis, "The IRS Admits to 'Targeting' Conservative Groups, but Were They Also 'Leaking'?", *Daily Caller*, May 13, 2013.
36. Edith Honan, "Most Americans See Gay Marriage as Inevitable: Survey," Reuters, June 6, 2013, http://uk.mobile.reuters.com/article/lifestyleMolt/idUKBRE9550VI20130606.
37. "Households and Families: 2010," United States Census Bureau, April 2012, 1–5, http://www.census.gov/prod/cen2010/briefs/c2010br-14.pdf.

Chapter 9: Overcoming Racism and Poverty

1. Lizette Alvarez, "Defense in Trayvon Martin Case Raises Questions About the Victim's Character," *New York Times*, May 23, 2013, A15, http://www.nytimes.com/2013/05/24/us/zimmermans-lawyers-release-text-messages-of-trayvon-martin.html; Jeff Burnside and Brian Hamacher, "Trayvon Martin Suspended from School Three Times: Report," NBC 6 South Florida, March 27, 2012, http://www.nbcmiami.com/news/Trayvon-Martin-Suspended-From-School-Three-Times-Report-144403305.html.
2. Madeleine Morgenstern, "Oakland Demonstrators Burn Flags, Smash Cop Car After Zimmerman Verdict," *The Blaze*, July 14, 2013, http://www.theblaze.com/stories/2013/07/14/oakland-demonstrators-burn-flags-smash-cop-car-after-zimmerman-verdict-photos/; Justin George, "Witness Claims Youth Yelled 'This is for Trayvon' in Beating," *Baltimore*

Sun, July 15, 2013, http://articles.baltimoresun.com/2013-07-15/news/bs-md-trayvon-martin-george-zimmerman-monday-20130715_1_trayvon-martin-george-zimmerman-baltimore-police.

3. Shelby Steele, "The Decline of the Civil-Rights Establishment," *Wall Street Journal*, July 21, 2013, A17, http://online.wsj.com/news/articles/SB10001424127887324448104578618681599902640.
4. Barack Obama, "Remarks by the President on Trayvon Martin," James S. Brady Press Briefing Room, The White House, July 19, 2013, http://www.whitehouse.gov/the-press-office/2013/07/19/remarks-president-trayvon-martin.
5. Lee Hawkins, "Paula Deen Switches Legal Teams," *Wall Street Journal*, July 11, 2013, B4, http://online.wsj.com/news/articles/SB10001424127887324425204578600180601333310.
6. Daniel P. Moynihan, "The Negro Family: The Case for National Action," Office of Policy Planning and Research, United States Department of Labor, March 1965, http://www.dol.gov/dol/aboutdol/history/webid-moynihan.htm.
7. Judy Faber, "CBS Fires Don Imus Over Racial Slur," CBS News, April 12, 2007, http://www.cbsnews.com/news/cbs-fires-don-imus-over-racial-slur/.
8. Edmund Morgan, *American Slavery, American Freedom: The Ordeal of Colonial Virginia* (New York: W. W. Norton, 1975), 6.
9. David W. Blight, *Frederick Douglass' Civil War: Keeping Faith with Jubilee* (Baton Rouge: Louisiana State University Press, 1989), 112–13.
10. Edmund Wilson, *Patriotic Gore: Studies in the Literature of the American Civil War* (New York: W. W. Norton, 1962), 92–97.
11. James Oakes, *The Radical and the Republican: Frederick Douglass, Abraham Lincoln, and the Triumph of Anti-Slavery Politics* (New York: W. W. Norton, 2007), 91.
12. Abraham Lincoln, "Second Inaugural Address," March 4, 1865, http://www.historytools.org/sources/lincoln-second.pdf.
13. W. E. B. Du Bois, *Black Reconstruction* (Piscataway, NJ: Harcourt, Brace, 1935), quoted in Blight, *Frederick Douglass' Civil War*, 101; Eugene D. Genovese, *Roll Jordan Roll: The World Slaves Made* (New York: Random House, 1974), 252–55.
14. Elisabeth Schussler Fiorenza, *The Book of Revelation: Justice and Judgment* (Minneapolis: Augsburg Fortress, 1998), 8.
15. Martin Luther King, Jr., "It's a Dark Day in Our Nation," sermon delivered at Ebenezer Baptist Church, Atlanta, Georgia, April 30, 1967.
16. Billy Graham, *World Aflame* (New York: Doubleday, 1965), 7–8.
17. Mike Huckabee, "Huckabee: Never Again Be Silent When People's Rights Are at Stake," remarks delivered on the fortieth anniversary of Central High School crisis, September 25, 1997, Arkansas Online,

http://www.arkansasonline.com/news/1997/sep/25/huckabee-never-again-be-silent-when-peoples-rights/; Kevin Sack, "In Little Rock, Clinton Warns of Racial Split," *New York Times*, September 26, 1997, http://www.nytimes.com/1997/09/26/us/in-little-rock-clinton-warns-of-racial-split.html?n=Top%2fReference%2fTimes%20Topics%2fPeople%2fC%2fClinton%2c%20Bill.

18. Southern Baptist Convention, "Resolution on Racial Reconciliation on the 150th Anniversary of the Southern Baptist Convention," Atlanta, Georgia, June 22, 1995, http://www.sbc.net/resolutions/amresolution.asp?id=899.
19. Jerry Falwell, *Strength for the Journey* (New York: Simon & Schuster, 1987), 289–99.
20. Billy Graham, *Just as I Am* (New York: HarperCollins, 1997), 426.
21. Moynihan, "The Negro Family."
22. "Moynihan's Memo Fever," *Time*, March 23, 1970, 17.
23. Lyndon B. Johnson, "Lyndon Johnson's State of the Union Address, Proposing the "Great Society" Program," January 4, 1965, http://www.infoplease.com/ipa/A0900149.html.
24. James T. Patterson, *Freedom Is Not Enough: The Moynihan Report and America's Struggle Over Black Families from LBJ to Obama* (New York: Basic Books, 2010), cited in Rich Lowry, "The Moynihan Report and Ongoing Family Breakdown," *National Review*, May 11, 2010, http://www.nationalreview.com/articles/229730/moynihan-report-and-ongoing-family-breakdown/rich-lowry.
25. Wynton Hall, "Boomtown 2: Taxpayers Have Spent $15 Trillion on 'War on Poverty,'" April 5, 2013, http://www.breitbart.com/Big-Government/2013/04/05/BOOMTOWN-2-Taxpayers-Have-Spent-15-Trillion-On-The-War-on-Poverty.
26. "US Poverty Rate to Hit Highest Level Since 1965, Economists Say," CNBC News, July 23, 2012, http://m.cnbc.com/us_news/48281252. In 2012, the poverty level was $23,021 a year for a family of four.
27. "The Growing Wealth Gap," CNN Money, November 7, 2011 http://money.cnn.com/galleries/2011/news/economy/1110/gallery.wealth_gap_growing.fortune/.
28. Annie Lowrey, "Wealth Gap among Races Has Widened Since Recession," *New York Times*, April 28, 2013, B1, http://www.nytimes.com/2013/04/29/business/racial-wealth-gap-widened-during-recession.html?.
29. The Urban Institute, "The Moynihan Report Revisited," June 2013, 6, http://www.urban.org/UploadedPDF/412839-The-Moynihan-Report-Revisited.pdf. In 1960, 50 percent of black women were married; today only one-quarter are married. A similar pattern has prevailed among Hispanics and whites. Two-thirds of white and Hispanic women were married in 1960; today, only two-fifths of Hispanic and half of white women are married and living with their husbands.

30. William Julius Wilson, *When Work Disappears: The World of New Urban Poor* (New York: Vintage, 1997) discusses the disappearance of business, banking, and other establishments from parts of urban America. For a different view, see Myron Magnet, *The Dream and the Nightmare: The Sixties' Legacy to the Underclass* (New York: William Morrow, 1993), 60–67.
31. Charles Murray, *Coming Apart: The State of White America, 1960–2010* (New York: Crown Forum, 2012), 154–56, 160–63.
32. Charles Murray, "The New American Divide," *Wall Street Journal*, January 31, 2012, http://online.wsj.com/news/articles/SB10001424052970204301404577170733817181646.
33. Kay Hymowitz, Jason S. Carroll, W. Bradford Wilcox, Kelleen Kaye, "Knot Yet: The Benefits and Costs of Delayed Marriage in America," The National Marriage Project at the University of Virginia, 2013, http://nationalmarriageproject.org/wp-content/uploads/2013/03/KnotYet-FinalForWeb.pdf.
34. Kay Hymowitz, quoted in H. Brevy Cannon, "Delayed Marriage on Rise: Good for College Educated, Tough on Middle America," University of Virginia, March 18, 2013, https://news.virginia.edu/content/delayed-marriage-rise-good-college-educated-tough-middle-america.
35. Arloc Sherman, "The Safety Net: Lifting Millions Out of Poverty," Center on Budget and Policy Priorities, July 30, 2013, http://www.offthechartsblog.org/2013/0.
36. Arthur Brooks, *Road to Freedom: How to Win the Fight for Free Enterprise* (Old Saybrook, CT: Tantor Media, 2012).
37. Pope Francis I, quotation in "Pope's Q and A with Movements," Vatican City, May 21, 2013, http://www.zenit.org/en/articles/pope-s-q-and-a-with-movements.

Chapter 10: Choosing the Chosen People

1. "Vatican Apologizes over Holocaust," BBC News, March 16, 1998, http://news.bbc.co.uk/2/hi/europe/65889.stm.
2. Sean Yoong, "Ahmadinejad: Destroy Israel, End Crisis," *Washington Post*, August 3, 2006, http://www.washingtonpost.com/wp-dyn/content/article/2006/08/03/AR2006080300629.html.
3. Michael Rubin, "Ahmadinejad: Israel a Stinking Corpse," *National Review*, May 8, 2008, http://www.nationalreview.com/corner/162870/ahmadinejad-israel-stinking-corpse/michael-rubin.
4. Jordan Schachtel, "Al-Quds Day Provides Stage for Incendiary Activity," Breitbart, August 6, 2013, http://www.breitbart.com/Big-Peace/2013/08/06/Al-Quds-day-provides-stage-for-incendiary-activity; Damien McElroy, "Iran's Hassan Rouhani: Israel an 'Old Wound That Should be Removed,'" *The Telegraph*, August 2, 2013, http://www.telegraph.co.uk/news/worldnews/middleeast/iran/10218221/Irans-Hassan-Rouhani-Israel-an-old-wound-that-should-be-removed.html.

5. Hassan Rouhani, interview with Ann Curry, NBC News, September 18, 2013, http://www.nbcnews.com/id/53069733/ns/world_news-mideast_n_africa/t/full-transcript-ann-currys-interview-iranian-president-hassan-rouhani/#.Ur2BprR217o.
6. Reuters, "Hamas to Hezbollah: Leave Syria and Focus on Fighting Israel Instead," *Jerusalem Post*, June 17, 2013, http://www.jpost.com/Middle-East/Hamas-to-Hezbollah-Leave-Syria-and-focus-on-fighting-Israel-instead-316821.
7. "Carmen Weinstein, Leader of Egyptian Jews, Dies at 82," *The Jewish Daily Forward*, April 14, 2013, http://forward.com/articles/174821/carmen-weinstein-leader-of-egyptian-jews-dies-at-/.
8. Stephen Farrell, "Baghdad Jews Have Become a Fearful Few," *New York Times*, June 1, 2008, http://www.nytimes.com/2008/06/01/world/middleeast/01babylon.html?pagewanted=all.
9. Ibid.
10. "Chavez's Venezuela: The Jewish Community Under Threat," The Anti-Defamation League, February 2, 2009, http://archive.adl.org/main_anti_semitism_international/chavez_venezuela_under_threat.html#.Ur2DHrR217p.
11. "ADL Letter to the *New York Times*," The Anti-Defamation League, November 21, 2007, http://archive.adl.org/media_watch/newspapers/nytimes_11212007.html#.Ur2MAbR217o.
12. "France Shooting: Toulouse Jewish School Attack Kills Four," BBC News, March 19, 2012.
13. Cnaan Liphshiz, "Poll: 45 Percent of Britons Favor Banning Kosher Slaughter," *Jewish Telegraphic Agency*, March 29, 2013, http://www.jta.org/2013/03/29/news-opinion/world/poll-45-percent-of-britons-favor-banning-kosher-slaughter.
14. "Europe's New Face of Anti-Semitism," *World Net Daily*, December 3, 2002.
15. Stephen Evans, "German Circumcision Ban: Is It a Parent's Right to Choose?" BBC News, July 12, 2012, http://www.bbc.co.uk/news/magazine-18793842.
16. Jennifer Medina, "Efforts to Ban Circumcisions Gain Traction in California," *New York Times*, June 4, 2011, http://www.nytimes.com/2011/06/05/us/05circumcision.html.
17. "California Governor Signs Law Preventing Male Circumcision Ban," CNN, October 2, 2011, http://www.cnn.com/2011/10/02/health/california-circumcision-law/.
18. George Gilder, "Capitalism, Jewish Achievement, and the Israel Test," *The American*, July 27, 2009, http://www.american.com/archive/2009/july/capitalism-jewish-achievement-and-the-israel-test; George Gilder, *The Israel*

Test: Why the World's Most Besieged State is a Beacon of Freedom and Hope for the World Economy (Minneapolis: Richard Vigilante Books, 2009), 4, 11–14.

19. "ADL Audit: U.S. Anti-Semitic Incidents Declined 14 Percent in 2012," ADL press release, July 22, 2013, http://www.adl.org/press-center/press-releases/anti-semitism-usa/adl-audit-us-anti-semitic-incidents-declined-14-percent.html.
20. Paras D. Bhayani, "'Israel Lobby' Authors Return with Book," *Harvard Crimson*, March 21, 2007, http://www.thecrimson.com/article/2007/3/21/israel-lobby-authors-return-with-book/.
21. Amy Gardner, "Moran Upsets Jewish Groups Again," *Washington Post*, September 15, 2007.
22. William M. Welch, "Crossover Vote Helped Tilt Ga. Races," *USA Today*, August 21, 2002, http://usatoday30.usatoday.com/news/nation/2002-08-21-ga-candidates_x.htm.
23. NBC/WSJ poll, cited in *Washington Post*, 2013, http://m.washingtonpost.com/blogs/right-turn/wp/2013/02/27/democrats-israel-problem/.
24. Stanley Kurtz, "Pro-Palestinian-in-Chief," *National Review*, May 26, 2011, http://www.nationalreview.com/articles/268159/pro-palestinian-chief-stanley-kurtz.
25. Rebeccah Heinrichs, "Does the President Really 'Have Israel's Back'?" Visiting Fellow, The Heritage Foundation, in *Daily Caller*, March 8, 2012, http://www.heritage.org/research/commentary/2012/03/does-the-president-really-have-israels-back.
26. "Remarks by the President on a New Beginning," The White House, Office of the Press Secretary, June 4, 2009, http://www.whitehouse.gov/the_press_office/Remarks-by-the-President-at-Cairo-University-6-04-09.
27. Ethan Bronner, "As Biden Visits, Israel Unveils Plans for New Settlements," *New York Times*, March 9, 2010.
28. Matt Vasilogambros, "Obama and Netanyahu: It's Complicated," *National Journal*, March 19, 2013, http://www.nationaljournal.com/whitehouse/obama-and-netanyahu-it-s-complicated-20130319.
29. Jay Solomon and Carol Lee, "Obama's Israel Surprise," *Wall Street Journal*, May 20, 2011.
30. Heinrichs, "Does the President Really 'Have Israel's Back'?"
31. Deroy Murdock, "Hagel's Anti-Semitism," *National Review*, February 22, 2013, http://www.nationalreview.com/articles/341263/hagels-anti-semitism-deroy-murdock.
32. "Washington's Letter to the Hebrew Congregation of New Port, Rhode Island," August 18, 1790, Heritage Foundation, http://www.heritage.org/initiatives/first-principles/primary-sources/washington-s-letter-to-the-hebrew-congregation-.

33. Max Blumenthal, "Birth Pangs of a New Christian Zionism," *Nation*, August 8, 2006, http://www.thenation.com/article/birth-pangs-new-christian-zionism#.
34. Executive Summary, Stand for Israel Survey, prepared by the Tarrance Group, Washington, DC, 9 October 2002, quoted in http://www.ifcj.org/site/DocServer/IFCJEVANGELICALS.pdf?docID=441.

Chapter 11: The War on Christianity

1. "New Book Tells Asia Bibi's Story from Prison," Catholic News Agency, February 27, 2012, http://www.catholicnewsagency.com/news/new-book-tells-asia-bibis-story-from-prison/.
2. Alastair Beach, "Coptic Christians Under Siege as Mob Attacks Cairo Cathedral," *Independent*, April 8, 2013, http://www.independent.co.uk/news/world/africa/coptic-christians-under-siege-as-mob-attacks-cairo-cathedral-8563600.html.
3. Lisa Daftari, "Christian Pastor Nadarkhani Freed from Jail in Iran After Christmas Day Arrest," Fox News, January 7, 2013, http://www.foxnews.com/world/2013/01/07/christian-pastor-nadarkhani-released-form-iranian-prison/.
4. Senator Rand Paul, "Remarks Prepared for Delivery: Sen. Paul Speaks at Faith and Freedom Coalition," press release, June 13, 2013, http://www.paul.senate.gov/?p=press_release&id=853.
5. *Zorach v. Clauson* 343 US 306 (1952).
6. *Lemon v. Kurtsman*, 403 US 602 (1971).
7. David Skeel, "The Supreme Court Revisits a Religious Lemon," *Wall Street Journal*, May 30, 2013, http://online.wsj.com/news/articles/SB10001424127887323728204578513362640616552.
8. *Lee v. Weisman*, 505 U.S. 577 (1992).
9. Russell Kirk, "We Cannot Separate Christian Morals and the Rule of Law," in Ronald Trowbridge, *In the First Place: Twenty Years of the Most Consequential Ideas from Hillsdale College's Monthly Journal Imprimis* (Hillsdale, MI: Hillsdale College Press, 1992), 156.
10. Mollie Ziegler Hemingway, "The Pentagon's Problem with Proselytizing," *Wall Street Journal*, May 9, 2013, http://online.wsj.com/news/articles/SB10001424127887323744604578470903522950138; Bob Smietana, "Troops Inclined to Proselytize May Face Court Martial," *USA Today*, May 2, 2013, http://www.usatoday.com/story/news/nation/2013/05/02/military-ban-proselytizing/2129189/; Todd Starnes, "Pentagon Classifies Evangelical Christians, Catholics as Extremists," Fox News, August 28, 2013, http://radio.foxnews.com/toddstarnes/top-stories/pentagon-classifies-evangelical-christians-catholics-as-extremists.html.

11. Jay Sekulow, "Religious Liberty and Expression Under Attack: Restoring America's First Freedoms," The Heritage Foundation, October 1, 2012, Legal Memorandum #88 on Religion and Civil Society, http://www.heritage.org/research/reports/2012/10/religious-liberty-and-expression-under-attack-restoring-americas-first-freedoms.
12. Todd Starnes, "University Tells Student to Remove Cross Necklace," Fox News Radio, July 2, 2013, http://radio.foxnews.com/toddstarnes/top-stories/university-tells-student-to-remove-cross-necklace.html.
13. Jeff Schapiro, "Professor Who Told Students to Stomp On Jesus' Name Reinstated," *Christian Post*, June 25, 2013, http://www.christianpost.com/news/professor-who-told-students-to-stomp-on-jesus-name-reinstated-98761/.
14. Kate Brumback and Russ Bynum, "Governor Nathan Deal Orders Bibles Back to Georgia State Park Lodging in Church State Battle," *Huffington Post*, May 16, 2013, http://www.huffingtonpost.com/2013/05/16/georgia-governor-engaged-_0_n_3289487.html.
15. Joni B. Hannigan, "Collier County Denies Bible Distribution on Religious Freedom Day," *Florida Baptist Witness*, January 15, 2009, http://fbwitness.serveronline.net/news.asp?ID=9834.
16. *Hall v. Bradshaw*, 630 F. 2d 1018 (4th Cir. 1980).
17. "Bill Maher's History of Anti-Catholicism, 1998-2013," Special Report, Catholic League for Religious and Civil Rights, November 25, 2013, http://www.catholicleague.org/bill-mahers-history-of-anti-catholicism-1998-2013-2/.
18. Rene Lynch, "Djesus Uncrossed: Most Blasphemous Skit in SNL History?" *Los Angeles Times*, February 18, 2013, http://herocomplex.latimes.com/movies/djesus-uncrosse-snl-skit-guilty-of-blasphemy/.
19. Jeffrey H. Anderson, "Obama Misquotes Declaration of Independence, Again," *Weekly Standard*, October 20, 2010, http://www.weeklystandard.com/blogs/obama-misquotes-declaration-independence-again_511412.html.
20. *Hosanna-Tabor Evangelical Lutheran Church and School v. Equal Employment Opportunity Commission*, 565 U.S. ___ (2012) .
21. Philip Ryken and John Garvey, "An Evangelical-Catholic Stand on Liberty," *Wall Street Journal*, July 18, 2012, http://online.wsj.com/news/articles/SB10001424052702303933704577533251292715324.
22. "October 11, 2012 Debate Transcript," Commission on Presidential Debates, October 11, 2012, http://www.debates.org/index.php?page=october-11-2012-the-biden-romney-vice-presidential-debate.
23. James C. Capretta, "The HHS Mandate Fraud Exposed," *National Review* Online, July 3, 2013, http://www.nationalreview.com/article/352627/hhs-mandate-fraud-exposed-james-c-capretta.

24. Mark Hemingway, "IRS's Lerner Had History of Harassment, Inappropriate Religious Inquiries at FEC: Targeted Christian Coalition," *Weekly Standard*, May 20, 2013, http://www.weeklystandard.com/blogs/irss-lerner-had-history-harassment-inappropriate-religious-inquiries-fec_725004.html#.
25. Sarah Palin, *Good Tidings and Great Joy: Protecting the Heart of Christmas* (Northampton, MA: Broadside Books, 2013).

Chapter 12: The Liberal Messiah

1. Brian Friel, Richard Cohen and Kirk Victor, "Obama: Most Liberal Senator in 2007," *National Journal*, January 31, 2008.
2. Marvin Olasky, "Jim Wallis vs. The Truth," *World*, August 18, 2010, http://www.worldmag.com/2010/08/jim_wallis_vs_the_truth.
3. Matt Bai, "The Framing Wars," *New York Times*, July 17, 2005, http://www.nytimes.com/2005/07/17/magazine/17DEMOCRATS.html?pagewanted=all.
4. Ryan Lizza, "Making It: How Chicago Politics Helped Shape Obama," *New Yorker*, July 21, 2008, http://www.newyorker.com/reporting/2008/07/21/080721fa_fact_lizza.
5. Ibid.
6. "Transcript: Obama's 2006 Sojourners/Call to Renewal Address on Faith and Politics," *God's Politics* (blog), *Sojourners*, June 26, 2006, http://sojo.net/blogs/2012/02/21/transcript-obamas-2006-sojournerscall-renewal-address-faith-and-politics.
7. Jerry Markon, "Health, Abortion Issues Split Obama Administration and Catholic Groups," *Washington Post*, October 31, 2011, http://www.washingtonpost.com/politics/health-abortion-issues-split-obama-administration-catholic-groups/2011/10/27/gIQAXV5xZM_story.html.
8. Todd Starnes, "DOJ Defunds At-Risk Youth Programs over 'God' Reference," Townhall, June 25, 2013, http://townhall.com/columnists/toddstarnes/2013/06/25/doj-defunds-atrisk-youth-programs-over-god-reference-n1627526/page/full.
9. Howard Fineman, "Barack Obama Reelection Signals Rise of New America," *Huffington Post*, November 6, 2012, http://www.huffingtonpost.com/2012/11/06/barack-obama-reelection_n_2085819.html.
10. Neil Shah and Ben Casselman, "Revised Data Show Stronger Growth," *Wall Street Journal*, August 30, 2013, A2, http://online.wsj.com/news/articles/SB20001424127887323324904579042620854945130.
11. Bob Woodward, "Obama's Sequester Deal-Changer," *Washington Post*, February 22, 2013, http://www.washingtonpost.com/opinions/bob-woodward-obamas-sequester-deal-changer/2013/02/22/c0b65b5e-7ce1-11e2-9a75-dab0201670da_story.html.

12. Roll Call Vote 97, United States Senate, April 17, 2013, https://www.senate.gov/legislative/LIS/roll_call_lists/roll_call_vote_cfm.cfm?congress=113&session=1&vote=00097.
13. Margot Sanger-Katz, "All Those People Who Were Supposed to Get Insurance Probably Won't," *National Journal*, June 6, 2013, http://www.nationaljournal.com/magazine/all-those-people-who-were-supposed-to-get-insurance-probably-won-t-20130606.
14. Tom Cohen, "5 Things About the Controversy Surrounding AG Eric Holder" CNN, May 30, 2013, http://www.cnn.com/2013/05/29/politics/five-things-holder/.
15. "'Hardball with Chris Matthews' for Wednesday, May 15th, 2013," transcript, MSNBC, May 15, 2013, http://www.nbcnews.com/id/51904895/ns/msnbc-hardball_with_chris_matthews/t/hardball-chris-matthews-wednesday-may-th/#.Ur3dLrR217o.
16. Maureen Dowd, "Bill [Clinton] Schools Barry on Syria," *New York Times*, June 15, 2013, SR11, http://www.nytimes.com/2013/06/16/opinion/sunday/dowd-bill-schools-barry-on-syria.html.
17. Gerald F. Seib, "NSA Flap Shows Obama's Many Paradoxes," *Wall Street Journal*, June 10, 2013, A8, http://online.wsj.com/news/articles/SB10001424127887324904004578537042229951524.
18. "Remarks of Senator Barack Obama to the Chicago Council on Global Affairs," Council on Foreign Relations, April 23, 2007, http://www.cfr.org/elections/remarks-senator-barack-obama-chicago-council-global-affairs/p13172.
19. Ibid.
20. Mark Hemingway, "Obama's Iraq Revolution," The Corner, *National Review*, July 7, 2008, http://www.nationalreview.com/corner/165504/obamas-iraq-evolution/mark-hemingway.
21. "Chicago Council on Global Affairs," Council on Foreign Relations.
22. Reuters, "Iran Says 3,000 Centrifuges Being Built," *New York Times*, March 3, 2013, A10, http://www.nytimes.com/2013/03/04/world/middleeast/iran-says-3000-centrifuges-being-built.html; Associated Press, "IAEA Report: Iran Blocking Access As It Doubles Number of Centrifuges at Fordo, Covers Parchin," CBS News, August 31, 2013, http://www.cbsnews.com/news/iaea-report-iran-blocking-access-as-it-doubles-number-of-centrifuges-at-fordo-covers-parchin/.

Chapter 13: Reenergizing the Party of Lincoln

1. Rich Lowry, *Lincoln Unbound: How an Ambitious Young Railsplitter Saved the American Dream* (New York: Broadside Books, 2013), 56–57.
2. Religious conservatives flowed into the Republican Party in the 1970s and 1980s, encouraging it to embrace a pro-life, pro-family agenda.

More recently, Tea Party activists have backed candidates who support limited government, constitutional conservatism, and reining in federal spending and debt. This involvement has changed the Republican Party in ways that have not pleased some. For a good discussion of the resulting tensions, see Karen Tumulty, "Republicans Reassess After Shutdown Debacle," *Washington Post*, October 17, 2013, http://www.washingtonpost.com/politics/republicans-reassess-after-shutdown-debacle/2013/10/17/e312159e-375d-11e3-80c6-7e6dd8d22d8f_story.html; for the view of social conservatives, see Ryan Anderson, "A House Divided Cannot Stand: On Social and Economic Conservatism," *First Things*, October 25, 2013, http://www.firstthings.com/onthesquare/2013/10/a-house-divided-cannot-stand-on-social-and-economic-conservatism.

3. *Washington Post*-ABC News Poll, December 13–16, 2012, http://www.washingtonpost.com/wp-srv/politics/polls/postabcpoll_20121216.html.
4. "Key Findings: Public Opinion Strategies Election Night Survey," Public Opinion Strategies, November 7, 2012, http://pos.org/documents/2012_post_elect_final.pdf; "2012 Republican Scorecard: Primaries," CNN Election Center, July 26, 2012, http://www.cnn.com/election/2012/primaries/scorecard/statebystate/r.
5. Sean Sullivan, "Republicans Want Their Party to Change—Just Not the Way You Think," *Washington Post*, August 1, 2013, http://www.washingtonpost.com/blogs/the-fix/wp/2013/08/01/republicans-want-their-party-to-change-just-not-the-way-you-think/.
6. Dan Cox, "Young White Evangelicals: Less Republican, Still Conservative," Pew Research Forum, September 28, 2007, http://www.pewresearch.org/2007/09/28/young-white-evangelicals-less-republican-still-conservative/.
7. James Madison, John Jay, Alexander Hamilton, *The Federalist Papers* (Franklin Center, PA: The Franklin Library/Wesleyan University, 1977), Federalist No. 10, 63–70; "George Washington's Farewell Address," September 17, 1796, Archiving Early America, http://www.earlyamerica.com/earlyamerica/milestones/farewell/text.html.
8. Eric Foner, *Free Soil, Free Labor, Free Men: The Ideology of the Republican Party before the Civil War* (London: Oxford University Press, 1970), 9–18.
9. David Kirkpatrick, "The Evangelical Crackup," *New York Times*, October 28, 2007; Ray Harker, "Is America on God's Side?" *Examiner*, July 5, 2013, http://www.examiner.com/article/is-god-on-america-s-side.
10. "The Tea Party and Religion," Pew Research Center, Religion and Public Life Project, February 23, 2011, http://www.pewforum.org/2011/02/23/tea-party-and-religion/.
11. David Brody, *The Teavangelicals: The Inside Story of How the Evangelicals and the Tea Party Are Taking Back America* (Grand Rapids: Zondervan, 2012), 16.

12. Tim Koelkebeck, "Is the Religious Right Taking Over the Tea Party?", *The Blog* (blog), *Huffington Post*, October 27, 2010, http://www.huffington post.com/tim-koelkebeck/post_1153_b_774964.html.
13. Glen Bolger, "Faith and Freedom Coalition National Survey," Public Opinion Strategies, November 3, 2010. For a similar analysis, see Public Religion Research Institute, "American Values Survey: Religion and the Tea Party in the 2010 Elections," October 5, 2010, http://publicreligion.org/research/2010/10/religion-tea-party-2010/; Huma Khan, "Tea Party Closely Linked to Religious Right, Poll Finds," October 5, 2010, http://abcnews.go.com/blogs/politics/2010/10/tea-party-closely-linked-to-religious-right-poll-finds/.
14. Michael James, "Obama Proposes 'Team of Rivals' Cabinet," ABC News, May 22, 2008, http://abcnews.go.com/blogs/politics/2008/05/obama-proposes/.
15. "Hardball with Chris Mathews," Transcript, MSNBC, August 29, 2013, www.nbcnews.com.
16. John Nolte, "'Washington Post' Catches Democrats Rewriting Civil Rights History," Breitbart, September 6, 2012, www.breitbart.com.
17. Avi Zenilman, "Back Issues: The Compassion of Lyndon Johnson," *New Yorker*, July 2, 2009.
18. Kevin Alexander Gray, "Obama Leaves the Black Community Behind," *Progressive*, May 2, 2013, http://progressive.org/obama-leaves-black-community-behind.
19. Ibid.
20. David Catron, "Republicans and Women's Rights: A Brief Reality Check," *The American Spectator*, April 30, 2012, http://spectator.org/articles/35608/republicans-and-womens-rights-brief-reality-check.

Chapter 14: A Bold Pro-Family Plan

1. Sheryl Nance-Nash, "Is the Bible the Ultimate Financial Guide?", *Forbes*, May 24, 2012, http://www.forbes.com/sites/sherylnancenash/2012/05/24/is-the-bible-the-ultimate-financial-guide/.
2. "Expenditures on Children by Families: 2012," U.S. Department of Agriculture Center for Nutrition Policy and Promotion, Publication 1528–2012, August 2013, 20–21, http://www.cnpp.usda.gov/Publications/CRC/crc2012.pdf; Melanie Hicken, "Average Cost to Raise a Kid: $241,080," CNNMoney.com, August 14, 2013. The figure of $241,080 is in constant 2012 dollars; the $301,790 is adjusted for inflation between 2012 and 2030.
3. Stephanie Landsman, "What College Tuition Will Look Like in 18 Years," CNBC, May 25, 2012, http://www.cnbc.com/id/47565202.
4. Catherine Rampell, "Median Household Income Down 7.3% Since Start of Recession," *Economix* (blog), *New York Times*,

March 13, 2013, http://economix.blogs.nytimes.com/2013/03/28/median-household-income-down-7-3-since-start-of-recession/.

5. Stephen Moore, "The Growth of Government in America," Foundation for Economic Education, April 1, 1993, http://www.fee.org/the_freeman/detail/the-growth-of-government-in-america#axzz2ojLnfwqx.
6. "Six Important Facts about Dependents and Exemptions," IRS Tax Tip 2011-07, January 11, 2011, http://www.irs.gov/uac/Six-Important-Facts-about-Dependents-and-Exemptions-1; "Income, Poverty, and Health Insurance Coverage in the United States: 2011," Current Population Reports, United States Census Bureau, September 2012, http://www.census.gov/prod/2012pubs/p60-243.pdf.
7. Patrick Tyrrell, "Government Will Take Almost Half Your Paycheck in 2013," August 13, 2012, *The Foundry*, http://blog.heritage.org/2012/08/13/government-will-take-almost-half-your-paycheck-in-2013/.
8. Veronique de Rugy, "Marginal Tax Rates Must Surge to Fund Entitlement Spending," Mercatus Center, George Mason University, August 19, 2013, http://mercatus.org/publication/marginal-tax-rates-must-nearly-double-fund-entitlement-spending-0.
9. Robert Stein, "Taxes and the Family," *National Affairs*, no. 2 (Winter 2010), 35–48, http://www.nationalaffairs.com/publications/detail/taxes-and-the-family.
10. Ibid.
11. Cathy Payne, "Fertility Forecast: Baby Bust Is Over; Births Will Rise," *USA Today*, August 1, 2013, http://www.usatoday.com/story/news/nation/2013/08/01/usa-total-fertility-rate/2590781/.
12. Tal Kopan, "Newt Gingrich: No GOP Health Care Plan," *Politico*, August 14, 2013, http://www.politico.com/story/2013/08/newt-gingrich-gop-health-care-plan-95540.html.
13. "Are Health Care Reform Cost Estimates Reliable?" U.S. Senate Joint Economic Committee, July 31, 2009, http://www.jec.senate.gov/republicans/public/?a=Files.Serve&File_id=5802c84c-e821-4ab3-baeb-793f3ae2e036.
14. John McCormack, "Obamacare Could Require Private Insurers to Fund Abortion on Demand," *Weekly Standard*, February 13, 2012, https://www.weeklystandard.com/blogs/obamacare-could-require-private-insurers-fund-abortion-demand_626747.html.
15. Stanley K. Henshaw, Theodore J. Joyce, Amanda Dennis, Lawrence B. Finer, and Kelly Blanchard, *Restrictions on Medicaid Funding for Abortions: A Literature Review*, The Guttmacher Institute, June 2009.
16. "Health Insurance Mandates in the States, 2012," Council for Affordable Health Insurance, April 9, 2013, http://www.cahi.org/article.asp?id=1114.

17. Peter Orszag, "To Fix U.S. Budget, Reform Medical Malpractice Law," February 27, 2013, Bloomberg Opinion View, http://www.bloomberg.com/news/2013-02-27/to-fix-u-s-budget-reform-medical-malpractice-law.html.
18. "Medical Liability Reform Now!", American Medical Association, 2013, 4–9, http://www.ama-assn.org/resources/doc/arc/mlr-now.pdf.
19. "Income, Poverty Level, and Health Insurance in the United States: 2011—Highlights," United States Census Bureau, 2011; "Historical Poverty Tables—People, Table 7, Poverty, by Sex," United States Census Bureau, 2011, http://www.census.gov/hhes/www/poverty/data/historical/people.html.
20. Richard Stearns, *The Hole in Our Gospel* (Nashville: Thomas Nelson, 2009), 69.
21. Paul Roderick Gregory, "Government Study Finds Obama Care Leaves Thirty Million Uninsured," *Forbes*, February 22, 2013, http://www.forbes.com/sites/paulroderickgregory/2013/02/22/government-study-finds-obama-care-leaves-thirty-million-uninsured/.
22. "Remarks by the President in State of the Union Address," news release, The White House Office of the Press Secretary, January 27, 2010, http://www.whitehouse.gov/the-press-office/remarks-president-state-union-address.
23. "Evaluation of the DC Opportunity Scholarship Program: Final Report," National Center for Education Evaluation and Regional Assistance, U.S. Department of Education, June 2010, http://ies.ed.gov/ncee/pubs/20104018/pdf/20104032.pdf; Robert Samuels, "Parents Rush to Apply for D.C. Private School Vouchers," *Washington Post*, June 25, 2011, http://www.washingtonpost.com/local/education/parents-rush-to-apply-for-dc-private-school-vouchers/2011/06/25/AG4Ju9kH_story.html; "The D.C. Voucher Example," *Wall Street Journal*, July 12, 2013, A12, http://online.wsj.com/news/articles/SB10001424127887324879504578599792705897724?cb=logged0.4729050522388316.
24. Anne Hendershott, "The Problematic Legacy of Fr. Hesburgh," *Catholic World Report*, July 2, 2013, http://www.catholicworldreport.com/Item/2387/the_problematic_legacy_of_fr_hesburgh.aspx#.Uq-C-vRDsfU.
25. Lydia Saad, "'Pro-Choice' Americans at Record-Low 41%," Gallup Politics, May 23, 2012, http://www.gallup.com/poll/154838/pro-choice-americans-record-low.aspx.
26. CNN/ORC Poll, August 22–23, 2012, http://i2.cdn.turner.com/cnn/2012/images/08/24/rel8a.pdf.
27. Michael J. New, "Why Were So Many Pro-Life Laws Passed in 2011?", *The Corner* (blog), *National Review*, January 6, 2012, http://www.nationalreview.com/corner/287372/why-were-so-many-pro-life-laws-passed-2011-michael-j-new; Sarah Kliff, "2011: The Year of the Abortion Restrictions," *Wonkblog*, *Washington Post*, December 29, 2011, http://www.washingtonpost.com/blogs/wonkblog/post/2011-the-year-of-the-abortion-restrictions/2011/12/29/gIQAbJqjOP_blog.html.

28. Steven Ertelt, "NARAL President Quitting, Cites Lack of Young Abortion Activists," LifeNews.com, December 27, 2012, http://www.lifenews.com/2012/12/27/naral-president-quitting-cites-lack-of-young-abortion-activists/.
29. Sarah Kliff, "NARAL President Nancy Keenan to Step Down," *Wonkblog*, *Washington Post*, May 10, 2012, http://www.washingtonpost.com/blogs/wonkblog/post/exclusive-naral-president-nancy-keenan-to-step-down/2012/05/10/gIQAn85PGU_blog.html.
30. Steven Ertelt, "Pro-Abortion Rape Myth Debunked, 99% of Abortion Clinics Do Ultrasounds," LifeNews.com, February 22, 2012, http://www.lifenews.com/2012/02/22/planned-parenthood-rape-myth-debunked-99-do-ultrasounds/; Alana Goodman, "Planned Parenthood Says It Won't Do Abortions Without Ultrasounds," *Commentary*, February 22, 2012, http://www.commentarymagazine.com/2012/02/22/planned-parenthood-abortions-ultrasounds/.
31. "The Case for Investigating Planned Parenthood," Americans United for Life, July 7, 2011, http://www.aul.org/wp-content/uploads/2011/07/PPReport_FULL.pdf.
32. Nathan Koppel, "Planned Parenthood Settles in Fraud Case," *Wall Street Journal*, August 16, 2013, A3, http://online.wsj.com/news/articles/SB10001424127887323455104579016951262314732.
33. "Planned Parenthood Receives Record Amount of Taxpayer Support," Fox News, January 8, 2013, http://www.foxnews.com/politics/2013/01/08/planned-parenthood-receives-record-amount-taxpayer-support/.
34. "Divorce Rates per 100 Married Women," University of Maryland, October 8, 1999, www.vanneman.umd.edu.
35. Ashley McGuire, "The Feminist, Pro-Father, and Pro-Child Case Against No-Fault Divorce," *Public Discourse*, The Witherspoon Institute, May 7, 2013, http://www.thepublicdiscourse.com/2013/05/10031/.
36. Barbara A. Butrica and Karen E. Smith, "The Retirement Prospects of Divorced Women," *Social Security Bulletin* 72, no. 1 (2012), U.S. Social Security Administration, Office of Retirement and Disability Policy, http://www.ssa.gov/policy/docs/ssb/v72n1/ssb-v72n1.pdf.
37. Ashley McGuire, "The Feminist, Pro-Father, and Pro-Child Case Against No-Fault Divorce."
38. Ibid.
39. Stephanie Chen, "Children of Divorce Vow to Break Cycle, Create Enduring Marriages," CNN, September 22, 2010, http://www.cnn.com/2010/LIVING/09/22/divorced.parents.children.marriage/.

Chapter 15: A Call to Christian Citizenship

1. Suetonius, *The Lives of the Caesars at Lacus Curtius*, trans. Loeb Classical Library (Chicago: University of Chicago, 1914), 355–57.
2. Ibid., 381.
3. Ibid., 347.
4. "Knowing God from Caesar: The Duty of a Christian Citizen," Interview with Archbishop Charles Caput, *Faith & Justice* 5, no. 3 (2012), https://www.alliancedefendingfreedom.org/content/docs/FnJ/FnJ-5.3.pdf.
5. Amy Sullivan, "Q&A: Religious Leader Chuck Colson," *Time*, September 24, 2009, http://content.time.com/time/nation/article/0,8599,1925795,00.html.
6. Jon Zens and Cliff Bjork, "A Better Society Without the Gospel?: The Unbiblical Cultured Expectations of Many Christian Leaders," *Searching Together* 27, 1–3 (Spring–Fall 1999) http://www.searchingtogether.org/articles/bjork/better-society.htm.
7. Gloria Steinem, *Detroit Free Press*, April 15, 1974.
8. Naomi R. Goldenberg, *Changing of the Gods: Feminism and the End of Traditional Religions* (Boston: Beacon Press, 1979), 3.
9. Larry King with Rabbi Irwin Katsof, *Powerful Prayers* (Los Angeles: Renaissance Books, 1998), 181–84.
10. Seth McLaughlin, "GOP Fealty to 'No New Taxes' Pledge Slipping," *Washington Times*, November 26, 2012, http://www.washingtontimes.com/news/2012/nov/26/gop-fealty-to-no-new-taxes-pledge-slipping/?page=all.
11. Eugene Robinson, "The NRA's Insane Idea About More Guns in Schools," *Powerful Prayers* (blog), *Washington Post*, December 21, 2012, http://www.washingtonpost.com/blogs/post-partisan/wp/2012/12/21/the-nras-insane-idea-about-more-guns-in-schools/.
12. "The I.R.S. Does Its Job," *New York Times*, March 7, 2012, A30, http://www.nytimes.com/2012/03/08/opinion/the-irs-does-its-job.html?_r=0.
13. Richard Stengel, "Two Cheers for Good Old, Sloppy Democracy," *Time*, November 10, 2000, http://content.time.com/time/nation/article/0,8599,87613,00.html.

About the Author

Ralph Reed is chairman and CEO of Century Strategies and founder and chairman of the Faith & Freedom Coalition. He was executive director of the Christian Coalition from 1989 to 1997. He served as senior adviser to George W. Bush's presidential campaigns and chaired the Georgia Republican Party. He holds a BA from the University of Georgia and a PhD in American history from Emory University. He lives in Atlanta, Georgia.

WORTHY

PUBLISHING

IF YOU ENJOYED THIS BOOK, WILL YOU CONSIDER SHARING THE MESSAGE WITH OTHERS?

- Mention the book in a Facebook post, Twitter update, Pinterest pin, or blog post.
- Recommend this book to those in your small group, book club, workplace, and classes.
- Head over to facebook.com/worthypublishing, "Like" the page, and post a comment as to what you enjoyed the most.
- Tweet "I recommend reading #Awakening by @ralphreed // @worthypub"
- Pick up a copy for someone you know who would be challenged and encouraged by this message.
- Write a book review online.

You can subscribe to Worthy Publishing's newsletter at worthypublishing.com.

Worthy Publishing Facebook Page

Worthy Publishing Website

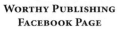